Mourning Religion

STUDIES IN RELIGION AND CULTURE

Frank Burch Brown, Gary L. Ebersole,
and Edith Wyschogrod, *Editors*

Mourning Religion

EDITED BY
WILLIAM B. PARSONS, DIANE JONTE-PACE,
AND SUSAN E. HENKING

UNIVERSITY OF VIRGINIA PRESS
CHARLOTTESVILLE AND LONDON

UNIVERSITY OF VIRGINIA PRESS
© 2008 by the Rector and Visitors of the University of Virginia
All rights reserved
Printed in the United States of America on acid-free paper

First published 2008

1 3 5 7 9 8 6 4 2

Library of Congress Cataloging-in-Publication Data

Mourning religion / edited by William B. Parsons, Diane Jonte-Pace, and
Susan E. Henking.
    p.   cm. — (Studies in religion and culture)
Includes bibliographical references and index.
ISBN 978-0-8139-2745-9 (cloth : alk. paper) — ISBN 978-0-8139-2746-6
(pbk. : alk. paper)
1. Bereavement—Religious aspects. 2. Loss (Psychology)—Religious
aspects. 3. Grief—Religious aspects. 4. Religion. I. Parsons, William B. II.
Jonte-Pace, Diane E. (Diane Elizabeth), 1951– III. Henking, Susan E., 1955–
    BL65.B47M68 2008
    204'.42—dc22

2008021514

*To those we mourn and those
who have taught us to remember and hope*

Contents

CONTENTS

Acknowledgments

WE ARE grateful to many whose enthusiasm, skill, and intellectual vitality nourished the ideas behind this book, helping us bring it to fruition. Cathie Brettschneider, our editor at the University of Virginia Press, showed time and again that she cared, not only about the ideas, but also about helping us negotiate the hurdles of the publishing process. Our anonymous readers made constructive and insightful suggestions. Peter C. Reynolds's editorial skills strengthened our arguments and ensured clarity and consistency of expression. Kristin Love Boscia, at Santa Clara University, as well as Susan Reece and Tina Phillip at Hobart and William Smith, made our work easier. The Center for Religion and Psychotherapy of Chicago and the University of Chicago Divinity School supported us in the form of a related conference organized by Celia Brickman with support from Wendy Doniger, William Schweiker, and Richard Rosengarten. Jonathan Z. Smith bestowed upon us a generous gift: a handwritten copy of his unpublished remarks from a 1989 session at the American Academy of Religion devoted to Peter Homans's *The Ability to Mourn*, from which we drew in our introduction. We would like to extend our thanks to the Martin Marty Center of the University of Chicago Divinity School and to the Divinity School itself for providing critical funding that helped bring the publication of this book to completion. Finally, as scholars, teachers, and editors, we are indebted to Peter Homans, whose influence reaches well beyond the chapter and conversation included here. To these and others, we are deeply thankful.

Mourning Religion

Mourning Religion

AN INTRODUCTION

NEARLY A century ago, reflecting on the cultural crises of his era, Sigmund Freud argued that mourning is the product not only of personal loss but also of cultural and social disorientation, a "reaction to the loss of a loved person or to the loss of some abstraction . . . one's country, liberty, an ideal, and so on."[1] And he speculated, famously, that there are both effective and ineffective ways of confronting loss. He called these "mourning" and "melancholia" in an essay of that title written and published under the sign of war.

Like Freud's efforts to wrestle with loss, the wrestling with loss in this volume occurs against a backdrop of social and religious transformation. In theorizing mourning and loss, we have theorized history, memory, nostalgia, race, gender, and other key concerns of our era. We have exposed the multivalent meanings of both "mourning" and "melancholia," and we have imagined hope.

In moving with and beyond Freud, most theorists of loss, mourning, and melancholia have remained ambivalent about religion. In Freud's work, religion appears and disappears, under the signs of illusion, morality, the oceanic feeling, and taboo. And yet, religion, some have argued, is central to the Freudian mythos. So, too, is contemporary wrestling with loss. Not unlike Freud, we contend with the enigma of religion in individual and cultural experiences of loss—and in our reflections on those losses. Yet paradoxically, religion and religious studies remain relatively invisible in today's theorizing of loss. Religion appears, disappears, and reappears in our reflections, an uncannily real ghost of our times. Freud's oeuvre offers multiple routes through the entanglements of religion and mourning, as does the work of those whose agreements and disagreements with Freudian models constitute the psychoanalyses of our time.

Since the 1917 publication of "Mourning and Melancholia," much has been written about loss. Indeed, one might argue that the twentieth and early twenty-first centuries have been characterized by the centrally contested question of loss, mourning, and melancholia. Exemplary psychoanalytic approaches to cultural loss and cultural change can be found in Alexander and Margarete Mitscherlich's *The Inability to Mourn: Principles of Collective Behavior*, Eric Santner's *Stranded Objects: Mourning, Memory and Film in Post-War Germany*, and Peter Homans's *The Ability to Mourn*. The Mitscherlichs argue that one can point to Western twentieth-century democracies, with their emphasis on individual liberties and freedom of speech, as examples of cultural forms of productive mourning, while other institutional forms grow out of cultural failures to mourn. In the sociopolitical sphere, the National Socialism of the Third Reich, with its focus on intolerance and absolutism, they argue, involves an inability to mourn. Democracy and fascism, they argue, function as bookends of a spectrum of social processes that, in the first half of the twentieth century, either facilitated or hindered the ability to mourn the losses and changes associated with modernity.

Eric Santner extends the Mitscherlichs' thesis, inquiring into the difficulty of integrating the memory of the Holocaust in postwar Germany, the ubiquity of the "discourse of mourning" in postmodernity, and the way German cinema has functioned in the project of "recollecting cultural identity out of stranded objects of a poisoned past."[2]

Peter Homans has argued that the creative discovery of psychoanalysis itself emerged from a successful mourning of the loss of the "common culture" that had shaped Sigmund Freud's early life. David L. Eng and David Kazanjian have produced a substantial edited collection, *Loss: The Politics of Mourning*, that reexamines mourning and melancholia and articulates the inevitability of melancholia for the twenty-first century. Judith Butler has extended this inquiry with *Precarious Life: The Power of Mourning and Violence*.[3]

Behind and beneath these cultural struggles with loss emerged a veritable industry of literature on grief, mourning, and bereavement. As the twentieth century routinized the psychologization of everyday life, our responses to death became similarly psychologized. Elizabeth Kubler-Ross, perhaps the best known of the theorists of death and dying, stands as synechdoche for a substantial clinical and historical literature on grief and its consequences. This literature has significantly redefined what Freud called "the work of mourning" through empirical investigations, case histories, and efforts to situate both mourning and melancholia in history and lives.

Little of this literature, whether clinical or theoretical, takes up religion directly. Yet religion echoes uncannily throughout the

Freudian corpus on loss and the literature that follows. The editors and contributors to this volume are particularly interested in the place of religion and religious studies in this broad frame of cultural loss and scholarly reflection on loss. A few scholars, notably Peter Homans and Jonathan Z. Smith, have begun to theorize the place of religion in this context.

Homans examines the creative reconstructions that can occur in the wake of the loss of religion. Not only the psychoanalysis of Sigmund Freud but also the sociology of Max Weber, he argues, emerges from the struggle to respond to religious loss: "Both Freud and Weber found themselves torn out of their respective communal pasts or religious heritages which had become a torment and a prison for both and others like them, and each struggled creatively to transform that break or rupture, by demarcating a space in the mind in which thought itself, in the form of natural, human curiosity, could move freely and unimprisoned, as it never had before."[4] Out of loss, argues Homans, emerges a project "for the enjoyment of theoretical curiosity about the inner world and especially about its social manifestations."[5] Psychology and sociology thus emerge from religiously inflected loss and grief, resulting in creative ideas and institutions.

Jonathan Z. Smith has extended this analysis, arguing that the thesis by Homans has significant implications for the "analytical space" that became the field of religious studies: this analytic space "offers—for the first time—a genuine *tertium quid.*" He explains: "Religious studies, as we know it today, came into being by rejecting its roots in the religious and proclaiming its new location within the secular university. Over time, in language as dualistic as its subject matter, it offered a galaxy of all but synonymous oppositions and sought to associate itself usually with one or the other, as the shifting (and often political) valances of the times demanded. Religious/Secular. Singular/Plural. Committed/Disinterested. Hot or near/cool or distant. Personal/Impersonal. Or, more recently: embodied/disembodied."[6]

Smith sees religious studies (and psychoanalysis) as residing in a permanent way "in a third, transitional space," lying between or bounded by religion and science, "always participating, and always observing." He continues: "Their structures and processes have had to be forged anew, eschewing both simple imitation of science and simple repetition of religion."[7]

It is our thesis that religious studies embodies mourning and expresses the process of creative meaning making, that "the profession of religious studies, which has evolved in the last forty or fifty years primarily in American universities . . . is the product, in part, of a bit of mourning and a bit of individuation and a bit of creation of meaning."[8] The theorists whose ideas shaped the field of religious studies "individuated out of religious communities." No longer able to lavish their "ultimate concern" upon religion, they experienced loss out of which they created religious studies. "These theories spring from a successful coming to terms with mourning in the social and historical sense."[9] In offering this argument, we, with Homans and Smith, examine the creation of cultural products and intellectual disciplines from the pain associated with mourning.

This analysis renders visible the ambivalence that defines the academic study of religion. Both historically and more recently, tensions between theology and religious studies appear and reappear in ever more particular locations within the academic study of religion, offering insights into the "new" approaches to the academic study of religion associated with the inclusion of women and feminism, lesbian/gay themes, and issues of race and nation. Debates about secularization and the "death of God" (mourned or unmourned) return as debates about globalization and sociocultural transformation.

Framing the Thesis: Mourning Religion in the Academy

The chapters collected here examine an array of cultural productions and losses through the lens of Freud's "Mourning and Melancholia" and the extensive literature responding to that work. Critically engaging this literature, the chapters rethink cultural production and loss with an eye to religion and religious studies. By both enacting and critiquing the ambivalence that is religious studies, these texts approach the paradox of the loss and continuity of religion and the paradox of mourning and melancholia. How, these essays ask, might we deal with loss well? First, perhaps, by recognizing the complex layerings of religion's presence and absence in our lives, by allowing ourselves to mourn what can be mourned in modernity. In addition, several chapters uncover contested assumptions about healthy versus unhealthy responses to loss, the ability versus inability to mourn, and the question of whether melancholia is inevitable (and even adaptive) in modernity: perhaps, these chapters suggest, we cannot complete the grieving process, but rather must continually remember and renegotiate the losses of the past. The essays move from loss and theory formation in religious studies to analyses of religion itself and, finally, to mourning religion in culture and the acknowledgment that grief is never over.[10]

This volume proceeds from the notion that the study of religion in the academy, in both secular and religiously affiliated universities, represents a socially legitimated, institutionalized forum for the mourning of religion (or the melancholic response to the loss of religion) in contemporary culture. The essays in the volume apply psychoanalytic theories of loss to the dramatic changes in traditional religious practices and institutions that have marked modernity, finding the social and psychological work of mourning evident in the study of religion. The volume begins and ends with thinkers foundational in the discipline: psychoanalyst Sigmund Freud and historian of religions Mircea Eliade are the focus of the first chapter, and an interview with philosopher and theologian Paul Ricouer concludes the volume.

The collected essays of part 1, Loss and Theory Formation in Religious Studies, illustrate how the methodologies and theories constituting the field represent the creative product of mourning. The works of central social-scientific and humanistic theorists in the study of religion (e.g., Freud, Durkheim, Weber, Marx, Eliade), as well as contemporary influential theorists (e.g., Kakar, Kristeva), are interpreted as products of successful mourning of traditional cultures and ideas. We believe that mourning provides a more useful theoretical framework than "secularization" in the understanding of the origins of the work of these thinkers: we hold that "secular" is defined always in tandem with religion, and always entangled with mourning.[11]

Part 1 begins with an analysis by Peter Homans of the impact of modernization on thinkers central to the discipline of religious studies. Homans explores the interplay of life and theory, arguing that both Freud and Eliade experienced "symbolic losses" of cherished and socially shared religious values and symbols. Both theorists, in his view, creatively transformed their experience of symbolic loss of "common culture," constructing powerful ideas and practices that led to new institutions and disciplines. The chapter by Homans thus initiates the volume's argument by suggesting that the field of religious studies grows out of the mourning of religion.

Celia Brickman focuses on the slippages in work by Freud surrounding "primitivity" and in work by Homans surrounding the understanding of religion as part of the "past." She urges a discursive shift from modernity to postmodernity; from secularization to globalization; from "common culture" to "dominant discourse"; from primitivity to "vulnerability"; and from mourning to melancholia. In melancholia, she argues, the past stays with us: closure and successful mourning elude us.

William B. Parsons investigates method and mourning with an eye to the complex entanglement of India with the Western imagination. Focusing on the works of Masson, Kakar, and Kripal, theorists who write on Indian religion from a psychoanalytic and cultural perspective, he argues that each writes out of an idealization and disillusionment with religion. As in the chapter by Homans, life and theory coincide, each embodying loss, mourning, and the creative meaning making that produces the discipline of religious studies.

Diane Jonte-Pace explains the increasing significance of French feminist theory in religious studies in terms of its analysis of mourning. She traces Julia Kristeva's psychoanalytic interpretation of how cultures and individuals mourn (or fail to mourn) in modernity, discovering in Kristeva's work a shift from mourning to melancholia and an explicit exploration of the study of biblical and religious texts as a constructive and creative way of engaging with postmodern, post-religious melancholia.

Part 2, Mourning the (Dis)Contents of Religion, focuses less on theory formation and more on the actual work of critical analysis found in religious studies. Religious studies scholars share a common canon composed of not only religions in and of themselves, but also seminal figures who, in their own acts of mourning, have created a body of thought that has also become canonical. Thus every professor, in engaging this work, joins in the intellectual tradition of mourning. We see the fascination in religious studies with timeless universals such as mysticism, morality, and ritual as a "working through" of loss and change and as part of a cultural and intellectual process of mourning. This section, then, is designed to show how theories of mourning shed light on the process and result of critical analytic work in religious studies.

Part 2 begins with a focus on mysticism. William B. Parsons shows how the formation of mystical psychologies in originative psychologists such as Jung, Maslow, and the Transpersonalists was a creative response to the loss of their religious heritage. He links the dissemination of such psychologies with their acceptance as part of an unchurched spirituality and the rise of a new social type, Weber's inner-worldly mystic. Casting this analysis back on classic and ongoing controversies in the academic study of mysticism, he argues that it is this cultural soil, itself the product of mourning, that has produced the classic controversies.

6

Turning to religious ethics, Ernest Wallwork critiques contemporary approaches to religious ethics that suggest a narcissistic decline in morality in the West. Rather than decline, he sees moral change. He recounts three case studies from his own psychoanalytic practice, examining how moral change involves loss, how moral loss is productively mourned, and how a postmodern ethic emerges. This new ethic is emotionally engaged, tolerant of otherness, and characterized by a creative, and self-reflexive moral stance.

Harriet Lutzky examines the essential contribution of the work of mourning to the category of immortality. She compares two types of analysis: the anthropological work of Robert Hertz, who analyzed the symbolism of the double burial ritual, and the work of psychoanalytic thinkers who analyzed the intrapsychic process of mourning. Her comparison brings out the creative aspect of the mourning process, which, viewed from the perspectives of both ritual and psychoanalysis, produces immortality or intrapsychic permanence.

The chapters collected in part 3, Mourning Religion in Culture, apply the concept of mourning to the intersections of religion and culture in the context of significant crises of our era. If religion in the contemporary West can be conceptualized as undergoing rapid change, these chapters, focusing on contemporary cinema, AIDS, and the memory books of the Shoah, explore the vicissitudes of mourning and collective memory in the context of historical and contemporary traumas with powerful spiritual dimensions.

Mary Ellen Ross focuses on the psychoanalytic perspective of Melanie Klein and the cinema of Polish writer and director Krzysztof Kieslowski. Cinema, Ross suggests, gives a post-Christian culture the ability to mourn. In her view, Kieslowski's films create a collective space for the work of grieving. They not only chronicle the way grieving proceeds, but they also offer a screen for individuals to enter a shared community, enabling us to mourn our losses and continue with our lives. Kieslowski's film *Blue,* she argues, traces a shift from the Kleininan "paranoid schizoid" to the "depressive" position in which faith, hope, and love are again possible. Ross reads Kieslowski as a deeply religious filmmaker whose work negotiates the religious and symbolic losses of modernity.

Susan E. Henking reflects on the crisis of HIV/AIDS in relation to mourning, religion, and pedagogy. She focuses on the meanings (and the impossibility of meaning) in the symbol widely used by AIDS activists, "SILENCE = DEATH." She reflects on the paradoxes of silence, testimony, and mourning, and the challenge of teaching about AIDS in the context of what has been called "after-education."

Bertram J. Cohler addresses the fragmentation and disorientation produced by the Holocaust. Nostalgia, he believes, is an adaptive solution to the sense of fragmentation produced by significant loss. The memory books produced during and after the Holocaust represent adaptive forms of nostalgia for their creators and readers. The study of nostalgia in the memory books provides Cohler with a window into the understanding of nostalgia in a broader sense, as a response to the disillusionment produced by modernity.

The conversation between Peter Homans and Paul Ricoeur, included in its entirety, concludes the volume. Conducted shortly before Ricoeur's death, the conversation focuses on Ricoeur's reading of Freud, his understanding of mourning and melancholia, and his speculations on memory and monuments. He suggests that melancholia, an illness typical of our era, emerges from the loss of community. It involves a distortion in remembering, a "repetition" linked to a resistance to memory, a denial of the past, and a continuous repetition of griefs and accusations. Mourning he associates with memory: it bridges presence and absence. Weaving together two of Freud's famous metapsychological essays, he suggests that melancholia is to repetition as mourning is to memory.[12]

Ricoeur also reflects on the impossibility of separating personal from collective memory—all our memories are both individual and dialogic: in language, "authorized" by others, and by a "relational alterity." He notes that monuments can authorize us to remember, to reclaim history as part of ourselves. Ricoeur's elegiac remarks about the past ("it is lost . . . and I mourn it") are fitting as a conclusion to the volume. His sense of the centrality of memory, mourning, and melancholia echoes our sense of the significance of loss in religious studies: it is no accident that Ricoeur, one of the foremost thinkers in religious studies, articulated these concerns as he looked back over his career in religious studies—and over the twentieth century. In the wake of his death shortly after the interview at age ninety-two, we borrow his own words: "and we mourn him."

The contributors to this volume, in utilizing the concept of mourning, start with Freud, build on (and challenge) the multiple conceptualizations of mourning and melancholia in the secondary literature, and apply these ideas to the dynamic process of academic theorizing. Contributors ask how religion is grieved, and how religious studies functions as a site of what Freud called "grief work" for our culture. They raise new questions about academic disciplines as the nexus of nostalgia, memory, history, loss, and theory formation. They engender new discussions of the subtleties of the process of personal and collective mourning and expose contested assumptions about mourning and melancholia, "terminable and interminable."

The contributors offer varied avenues for rethinking the relation between religion, culture, and loss, in the hope of engendering further reflection and debate. We are hopeful that readers inspired by the arguments presented here will, in future works, apply these theories to religious traditions and phenomena—Islam, Buddhism, and fundamentalism, for example, that are not represented in these pages.

Notes

1. Unless otherwise noted, references to the work of Sigmund Freud are from *The Standard Edition of the Complete Psychological Works of Sigmund Freud*, trans. and ed. James Strachey (London: Hogarth Press, 24 vols., 1966–1974). Sigmund Freud, "Mourning and Melancholia," *Standard Edition*, 14: 243–60 (first published 1917).
2. Eric Santner, *Stranded Objects: Mourning, Memory and Film in Postwar Germany* (Ithaca: Cornell University Press, 1990), 151.
3. Alexander and Margarete Mitscherlich, *The Inability to Mourn: Principles of Collective Behavior*, trans. Beverley R. Placzek (New York: Grove Press, 1975; first published 1967); Judith Butler, *Precarious Life: The Powers of Mourning and Violence* (London: Verso, 2004); David L. Eng and David Kazanjian, eds. *Loss: The Politics of Mourning* (Berkeley: University of California Press, 2003).
4. Peter Homans, *The Ability to Mourn: Disillusionment and the Social Origins of Psychoanalysis* (Chicago: University of Chicago Press, 1989), 256–57.
5. Ibid., 312.
6. Jonathan Z. Smith, "Comments on *The Ability to Mourn*," unpublished manuscript, presented at the American Academy of Religion, 1991.
7. Ibid.
8. William B. Parsons, "The Ability to Mourn: Disillusionment and the Social Origins of Psychoanalysis: A Conversation with Peter Homans," *Criterion* 30, no. 1 (Winter 1999): 2–8, 5.
9. Ibid., 5.
10. Jeffrey Weeks, *Invented Moralities: Sexual Values in an Age of Uncertainty* (New York: Columbia University Press, 1995).
11. Jonathan Z. Smith, "Comments on *The Ability to Mourn*."
12. Freud, "Remembering, Repeating, and Working Through," *Standard Edition*, 12: 147–56.

PART I

LOSS AND THEORY
FORMATION IN
RELIGIOUS STUDIES

PETER HOMANS

Symbolic Loss and the Re-creation of Meaning

FREUD AND ELIADE AS CULTURE MAKERS

Personal Experience, Theory Construction, and Culture Making

THIS ESSAY asks how the personal experiences of creative people shape their theoretical constructions and views of the world. In other words, it asks about the interplay between life-course development and work. This question is a modern version of a much older one: what is the relation between "path" or "way," on one hand, and "method" or hermeneutical style or work, on the other?

My examples are the life and work of Sigmund Freud and Mircea Eliade. Each of these remarkable men founded a new discipline consisting of ideas that have inspired and informed the lives and minds of many. I call both of them "culture makers." Although both men and their respective followers are utterly alien to each other, both underwent a similar life-course experience: the loss of cherished and socially shared historical ideals and symbols, followed by a struggle to replace them with a new form of thinking. I call this the experience of symbolic loss. I draw upon the human sciences, upon the recent surge in historical writing on collective memory and collective loss, and upon psychodynamic studies of experiences of loss in individual lives. Of necessity, symbolic loss is at once individual and sociohistorical.

I claim that both Freud and Eliade confronted the experience of the loss of symbols of their past. Whereas Freud recognized the passing of these and then came to terms with his loss of them, Eliade instead chose not to relinquish the loss, although like Freud he too recognized it. Instead, Eliade rediscovered these symbols in new forms and devised new ways to appropriate them. Both developed theories that gave rise to significant institutions—the psychoanalytic move-ment and the academic discipline of the history of religions.

In both cases, fascism and the primitive played a central role. Freud saw fascism as the enemy of decency and dignity, of all progress and advance, whereas Eliade saw it as a handmaiden of his new religious vision, as a kind of secret tunnel into the past that opened out into the splendors of the archaic. Yet Freud's search for the archaic roots of traditions and cultures was similar to Eliade's: both sought "the primitive" and used the same term. Exploring the issue of symbolic loss in these two men shows that the similarities and differences between them are even more profound than has been realized.

In this essay I first note briefly the way other times and places have understood the interplay between personal experience and theory construction and the consequent activity of culture making. Second, I explain in more detail how the sociohistorical process of modern-ization has always and still continues to bring about symbolic loss and psychological stress, damage, or trauma. Third, I outline a series of stages in each theorist's life and work. Fourth, I describe the cul-ture maker as a type of modern figure. I am neither a Freudian nor a religious studies scholar: I am not an "advocate" for Freud or for Eliade. Rather, I have great admiration for both theorists and for the cultures—psychoanalysis and the history of religions—that they created.

Path and Method: Traditional, Modern, and Contemporary Perspectives

Traditionally, religions have been the primary means of understand-ing the world. This was certainly the case in the earliest civiliza-tions, for example, in the Near East, India, and China. And it was also so for the early Middle Ages of the West, although that civiliza-tion emerged later than the others. While religious elites in these societies may have made distinctions between path and method, the societies they shaped were on the whole informed by a single, uni-fied worldview. That unity was the sine qua non of the civilization's identity and cohesion. To be born was, in effect, to know the world. Path and method were one and the same, and consequently culture makers in every generation refashioned what had already been made by the preceding generation, creating a shared sense of cultural and biological continuity and sameness century after century.

The gradual emergence of modernity in the West, first in the form of physical science in the seventeenth century and later in the form of the so-called social sciences in the eighteenth and nineteenth centuries, gradually split up this ancient sense of continuity. As a scientific point of view began to co-exist alongside the traditional religious one, path gradually split off more and more from method. The advent of psychology, and especially the depth psychologies, in the twentieth century, framed this split as a conflict or tension between "the developmental" and the "existential" dimensions of life, between the personal experiences of the life course and the values and beliefs of one's society as a whole. Now, rather than refashioning what had already been fashioned, the modern culture maker broke up what tradition and the past had already made. More and more, modern culture makers have become "culture breakers" first and only then "culture makers."

Many have observed that the first half of the twentieth century was a time of great emphasis—in study and research as well as in everyday life—upon the subjective dimensions of self-understanding, accompanied by a suspicion of most forms—traditional or modern—of sociality. This emphasis brought a new and much needed dignity to the inner life and uniqueness of the single person, not really appreciated in earlier times. In the 1950s and 1960s the sociologist Philip Rieff referred to this sea change as the rise of "psychological man."[1]

This new psychological approach in effect dignified the inner life and its chief form, fantasy processes, while attempting to introduce a dimension of emotion into the understanding of social structures and history. However, the new understanding also distracted attention from the realization that although historical and political social structures distorted and sometimes even destroyed consciousness and self-understanding, they were also essential and life-giving elements in the organization of consciousness. Such structures were, in other words, also "part of the equation" of personal, psychological development and self-understanding. Emblematic of recent attempts to call attention to the limits of psychological understanding is Richard Sennett's *The Decline of Public Man.*[2]

In the last twenty or so years, however, historical writing has begun to speak of "memory" rather than "history" in referring to social or collective phenomena, past and present; and in depth psychology, the older ego psychologies such as that of Hartmann have been replaced by the emergence of object-relations theory in England and self-psychology in the United States.[3] An identifying mark of object-relations psychology is the presence of loss as a central, developmental issue. In self-psychology the emphasis is on pre-oedipal issues, especially on massive distortions of the mother-infant relation;

15

and implicitly (and sometimes quite explicitly) loss emerges as the central developmental issue. Understandably, many have seen in these two revisionist schools a shared concern for issues of separation and loss.

However, neither the psychological nor the historical discussions recognize that it is mourning that puts loss and history together. Mourning is a part of both loss and memory. In fact, loss, mourning, and memory are inseparable from each other. Furthermore, this continuity makes it possible to explore the dark side of modernization: its failure to recognize that a dimension of loss—at times personal, at other times collective and historical—always accompanies progress.

Modernization as the Loss of a Whole Way of Life

The concept of modernization is widely used in the human sciences and public life as massive and rapid social-structural change (sociology), as cultural disintegration (anthropology), as secularization (theology), and as historical development (as in "developing" nations). However, none of these disciplines has chosen to think of modernization specifically in terms of loss. Even when that is on occasion done, it is thought of largely in cognitive or intellectual rather than emotional terms: one "loses" one's beliefs.

Recently, however, two accomplished, widely known, and admired historians with very different points of view have discussed modernization in terms that accommodate inquiry into the way modernization has affected persons emotionally, as an experience of loss. Interestingly, both write world history, which can also be called the history of civilizations. J. M. Roberts has made it clear that loss is a fundamental and ever-present dimension of modernization in his recently published study, *The History of Europe*.[4] According to Roberts, the central dynamic of European history is the progressive disintegration and loss of integrative symbolic structures. It has been a sweeping "civilizational" process, begun in the early modern period, achieving maximum intensity in the nineteenth century, and then leading to virtually total cultural disintegration in the wars and other losses of the twentieth century. So understood, modernization is the loss of "the unifying influence of great indigenous civilizations." In Robert's view, religions were the symbolic structures that performed this unification. Civilizations and their religious traditions once accomplished this task of unification, he says, by bringing together "different languages, stocks and customs." Roberts also makes it clear that the loss of a "unifying influence"—what I am calling symbolic loss—is a central feature of (European) modernization.

Similarly, William H. McNeill has described with sociological precision the historical consequence of modernization. He speaks of the disruption of the primacy of biological and cultural continuities that pre-industrial, agricultural societies and their village cultures established over many centuries. He thinks of these structures as virtually universal "since Neolithic times."[5] Even more important, he thinks that for most people in the world the breaking up of the autonomy or absoluteness of these continuities began only in the twentieth century, and he describes the consequences as "cultural disintegration." There is every reason to think early twentieth-century Romania and late nineteenth-century Austria were organized in this way, allowing Eliade and Freud to experience early in their lives the autonomy and absoluteness of village life as well as the onset of cultural disintegration.

Others have written about the psychological aspects of the disruption of "biological and cultural continuities." A great many civilizations and the cultures and subcultures they contain underwent this process, for all of them began as "premodern." The crucial issue is time. If modernization occurs over a period of many generations, then assimilation and adaptation become possible, in some cases customary, welcomed, and sought after. But when modernization "descends" like a tidal wave upon a community within a single generation, then its effects are experienced subjectively by individuals as wholly unimaginable and therefore intolerable. One is forced to give up a whole way of life in a span of one generation.

"A whole way of life" includes not only one's beliefs and values but also one's ways of loving and hating, as well as the objects of one's love and hate, as these have been confirmed and certified within one's family and one's culture and one's past. Therefore, the best analogy for the subjective, psychological dimension of modernization—indeed, this analogy may be as homologous as it is analogous—is the modern experience of neurosis. At the outset of such an illness, healing is cognitively wished for but affectively unimaginable, and is therefore in fact intolerable. A neurosis is a "whole way of life," that is, one's whole emotional-psychological way of life. The only other analogy that respects the integrity of the person is the religious one. To undergo modernization in less than one generation is similar to being forced to undergo a conversion experience. But if one is already religious—as were/are all traditional village communities—why should one undergo the inner degradation of self that a forced conversion inflicts?

What Symbolic Loss Looks Like

We may theorize these reflections by saying that symbolic loss is a cluster of closely intertwined experiences that often occur in sequential form: attachment, loss, mourning, the revising of memory, and the re-creation of meaning. Attachment is primary: people do not internalize cultural symbols, as psychoanalysts claimed for many years, nor do people simply believe in cultural symbols, as priests have often said. Rather, people form attachments to their symbols in the same way they form attachments to other people. In much the same way, groups and nations form attachments to symbols. Such symbolic attachments produce a sense of social identity based upon a sense of connectedness or belonging to the social structures and ideals they stand for or represent. In other words, symbols create and represent cultural integration by grounding persons in a shared understanding of an entire way of life. However, the process of modernization repeatedly disconfirms the authority of these symbols, thereby breaking up attachments to them and to the past they represent. When these symbols "die," experiences of loss ensue and cultural disintegration begins.

Symbolic loss is experienced subjectively as a gradual relinquishing of the past, of a once unifying and vivifying symbol and the social identity it conferred. Some creative persons are capable of recognizing this loss for what it is and of letting go of it. Such an experience can in turn generate the discovery of something as yet unseen in the new and emerging situation. In the case of the culture maker, this creative work is the construction of what will later become the work.

Once this work of mourning is over and the new understanding of the past is made and formulated, the culture maker attempts to become the leader of a movement composed of like-minded followers and organized around the culture maker's new discovery or vision. The goal of such movements is legitimation, usually in the form of institutionalization. When and if legitimation is achieved, it can be said that movement has become method, that is, what was once only one person's path has become "reality" for society as a whole. And when that happens, then the culture maker's path becomes an exemplary model for understanding the new method. The writing of an autobiography can be a culture maker's effort to expedite this final step.

18

Freud and Eliade both looked long and hard at modernization and saw in it the collapse of the past. They shared the same starting point. But from that point on each took a different path. Freud recognized the irreversibility of modernization and enumerated its consequences: the famous "three blows" to man's narcissism—first Copernicus, then Darwin, and then himself. Eliade also looked at modernization—but he refused to give up the past. Instead, he created a powerful new vision of its persistence, describing how ordinary people, who were not religious nor wanted to be, could become religious without being religious in a traditional, institutional way.

In some crucial sense, fascism was the central issue for both, not only as a modern political movement but also as a theory of the past in contemporary self-understanding. Given the presence of this powerful and sensitive issue in the life and thought of both men, the way one approaches it becomes as important as what one says about its place in their lives.

In writing as he did about anti-Semitism, prejudice, and authoritarianism in groups and cultures, Freud addressed fascism in a number of different ways. He also initiated a probe, late in life, into "the past," understood as the ways civilizations take shape and what holds them together, creating "a people." The idea of a "deep past" is useful here, for it conveys an approach that distinguishes between the past as history and the past as something "underneath" history. Freud's favorite words for this kind of past were "tradition" and "the unconscious," and his most direct statement of it is *Moses and Monotheism*, which he wrote as fascism descended—as fascism "drove" him to write it.[6] In it, he searched for the archaic mental circumstances and conditions that evolve into prejudice. Freud's deep past is similar to Eliade's search for the archaic and the primordial as they are "camouflaged" by history.

In my understanding of Eliade's life and thought, I have been greatly helped by Steven M. Wassserstrom's historical discussions of fascism.[7] In particular, I take it for granted that as early as 1928, the year of his formative trip to India, Eliade knew important European and Romanian fascist writers, such as Julius Evola, a leading Italian fascist, and of course his mentor and teacher, Nae Ionescu, a well-known and respected professor at the University of Bucharest. In 1928 Evola advised Eliade to seek out and experience personally the practices of yoga while in India, as part of their shared program for the recovery of ancient religious traditions and their incorporation of these traditions into the emerging fascist ideology. The two met again in Bucharest in 1937, and Eliade cited the works of Evola over a period of many years, up to 1960.

The Culture Maker as a Type of Modern Figure

The term "culture maker," exemplified here by Freud and Eliade, is a type of modern figure first explored in the work of Erik H. Erikson.[8] As a type of person especially prominent in the modern world, culture makers have many features in common: a critical alienation from the modernizing world, a persistent attachment to aspects of tradition, a distinctive social setting in which an experience of symbolic loss takes place, and the actual generation of something new. This re-creation of meaning is usually followed by a movement founded by the culture maker, in turn leading to the institutionalization of the culture maker's work.[9]

Symbolic Loss in Freud's Life and Thought

Freud's life and thought is especially suited to the study of the culture maker hypothesis. He is one of the most studied among the architects of modernity; his life was filled with many losses, both personal and symbolic; and his theory of mourning has been used by many in both the humanities and the helping professions, in a variety of different contexts.[10]

Scholars generally agree that Freud's leading ideas took shape in the period 1896–1901, and that these ideas were first published in *The Interpretation of Dreams* in 1899.[11] It is also agreed that this was a time of great inner struggle on Freud's part, during which he resolved, at least to his own satisfaction, three critical issues: his own personal identity, his creative discovery of psychoanalysis, and a practical technique (psychoanalytic treatment) for understanding and resolving the first two. These became the ground plan of his life and work, the relation between his path and his method. However, life and thought were decisively modified on two subsequent occasions, each also characterized by profound loss, followed by creative work: the leadership of the psychoanalytic movement, roughly from 1902 to 1920, and subsequent to that, the late-in-life struggle to reconcile his science (psychoanalysis) and his "Jewish" identity.

Loss and Freud's "Discovery" of Psychoanalysis

In 1896, when Freud was forty years of age, married with a family, and a struggling neurologist living in the city of Vienna, he began to explore what was to become the theory of the unconscious. The impetus for this inquiry was his largely epistolary friendship with the Berlin physician Wilhelm Fliess, while the principal life-course event, which precipitated this articulation of the theory, was the death of his father. As Freud wrote to Fliess: "I find it so difficult to write just now that I have put off for a long time thanking you for the moving words in your letter. By one of those dark pathways be-hind the official consciousness the old man's death has affected me deeply. . . . In [my] inner self the whole past has been reawakened by this event. I now feel quite uprooted."[12] Freud himself only realized the deepest meaning of this experience of loss eight years later. As the preface to the second edition of *The Interpretation of Dreams* (1908) explains: "For this book has a further subjective significance for me personally—a significance which I only grasped after I had completed it. It was, I found, a portion of my own self-analysis, my reaction to my father's death—that is to say, to the most important event, the most poignant loss, of a man's life."[13]

Three motifs are prominent here: loss (death of his father), cre-ativity (the writing of *The Interpretation of Dreams*), and the realiza-tion that the deepest significance of a creative event is sometimes discovered only years after it has occurred.

But this was not the only loss to occur at this time. Up until the start of the psychoanalytic movement, Freud's life and world were predominantly Jewish. When he was only four, his family moved to Vienna and settled into the largest of several ghettos. He himself spoke of his "childhood engrossment in the Bible stories."[14] As an adolescent and young adult, he had come to take for granted the liberalization of the laws and customs that had restricted Jews in the past from participating fully in the civil life of the city. And as a young man making his way in a new profession, he had been befriended by several older, well-established and highly respected Jewish men, the most notable of whom was probably Josef Breuer, with whom he collaborated in writing *Studies on Hysteria*.[15]

All this gradually changed. The climate of tolerance, which the Jews of Vienna had come to take for granted, became increasingly anti-Semitic. In 1897 Carl Luger, who had campaigned on a platform of anti-Semitism, was elected mayor of Vienna. Freud was passion-ately committed to political liberalism and its practice of tolerance and was emotionally attached to the social ideals and values of his society. Luger's election meant that the liberals had abandoned the Jews.

The effect of Vienna's advancing racism illustrates the way in which symbolic loss, the loss of a loved and cherished symbol in contrast to the loss of a loved person, takes place. The historian William McGrath, who has written extensively about this period in Freud's life, refers to these events as "disillusionments."[16] The experience of disillusionment stripped Freud of the only hopes and ideals he had ever known, thereby weakening his previous attachments to Viennese society. In response, he was driven inward into an introspective crisis and began to reflect upon the way in which fantasy processes drive political and religious thinking. In this way political disillusionment gradually became a form of psychological discovery and inquiry, and his ability to reckon with the loss without distortion (e.g., rage, or apathy, or denial) linked the two. This symbolic loss added stress to the loss of his father. Freud spent the rest of his life attempting to de-code the apparatus of anti-Semitism. At the time, however, he had yet to undergo another very different experience of loss, one wholly unexpected.

Loss and the Formation of the Psychoanalytic Movement

With the publication of *The Interpretation of Dreams*, Freud became "the first psychoanalyst." He was excited by his new ideas. Profoundly convinced that he had made a contribution to medicine and to society, he wanted others to know about his work. This meant forming and leading a movement. I want to describe the formation of the psychoanalytic movement and then explain how the departure of Jung from the movement was an occasion of a second loss, one both personal and symbolic.

Only a year after Freud completed his self-analysis and finished writing "the dream book," he sent postcards to four men who had expressed an interest in the new book, inviting them to meet in his home to discuss his work. The number of visitors rapidly increased, and they began to call themselves the Wednesday Psychological Society. From the beginning, Freud took the role of teacher, and all the others assumed the role of student. Freud thought of these meetings as a recruitment and training device. He was looking for talent and loyalty, and he had a movement on his mind. His goal was the social legitimatization of psychoanalysis in the form of an organization that would lead to institutionalization.

New people continued to come. What Ernest Jones called Freud's "circle" quickly became "the psychoanalytic movement." In 1906 Freud began to correspond with a young Swiss psychiatrist, Carl G. Jung, and in 1908 Jung joined the circle. Shortly after that, Freud named Jung his successor as leader of the movement. Their friendship deepened, and a remarkable correspondence ensued, deeply emotional, personal, and affectionate, but also intellectually complex and innovative, each man professing loyalty and commitment to the other, while at the same time testing his new ideas out on the other.[17] It consisted of over three hundred letters. For both, it was "ideal": Freud had the ideas and the vision but was personally and professionally isolated. He knew no one outside his Jewish-Viennese world, and his new ideas—for example, on sexuality and on childhood—were objectionable to most in the worlds of European psychiatry. Jung was nineteen years Freud's junior, just beginning his career as a psychiatrist at the internationally prestigious and largely gentile mental hospital and clinic in Zurich, the Burgholzi. He had no original ideas, but he was gifted and ambitious. In Freud he found a mentor with a brilliant new approach to mental disorder who was also a born leader in need of followers.

The movement expanded, and psychoanalysis became more and more complex. Freud wanted power and loyalty; Jung wanted intimacy and a mentor. Each began to feel more and more frustrated and compromised by the other, and their relationship disintegrated into bitterness and accusations of betrayal. By 1912–1913, both agreed to permanently break off all personal and professional contact. Freud became disconsolate and depressed, and the movement became unstable.

To understand why Jung's departure was a major loss for Freud, one must view it from within Freud's mental world. First, Freud knew himself to be brilliant, creative, and powerfully charismatic. But he was also realistic, understanding that the future of psychoanalysis depended upon conquering the gentile world—and that this world was increasingly anti-Semitic.

Second, like most brilliant, creative persons, his emotional investment in the future success of his discoveries was total. An observation by Ernest Jones captures the quality and strength of this emotional investment.[18] Jones pointed out that Freud's relationship to psychoanalysis was very like a mother's relation to her baby: psychoanalysis was part of him, even part of his body. Jung was the key to the gentile world, so his departure severely jeopardized the success of psychoanalysis, in Freud's mind. The break with Jung was for Freud tantamount to the "death" of psychoanalysis. The loss of this attachment was both personal and symbolic.

We also know that Freud went through a process of recovery from the loss at this time, which led to a creative flowering second only to that which accompanied the self-analysis. In the two or three years following the break with Jung, Freud completely revised his theory of the mind, the metapsychology, by introducing and then making central the psychological process of narcissism, from which followed many other new concepts.[19] He also wrote one of his most famous and widely known studies, "Mourning and Melancholia," and a short essay illustrating symbolic loss, "On Transience."[20]

After he recovered from the sadness that Jung's departure created, Freud intensified his until-then casual relationship with a loyal follower, Karl Abraham. He described to Abraham his fears and hopes, feelings and fantasies, as he went about writing "On Narcissism," very much as he had talked about writing the book on dreams with Wilhelm Fliess. Abraham's replies empathically mirrored his master's distress, and then the flurry of letters between them gradually subsided.

Freud turned to Abraham for the same reason he turned away from Jung, and he knew exactly why. Abraham was, he explained, Jewish, and that made them compatible. But Jung was a gentile, the son of a pastor, and Freud had found it difficult to feel at ease with him. Freud slipped easily into and out of emotionally deep and intimate relationships with other Jews but found intimacy with non-Jews difficult, if not impossible.[21]

During the interwar years, the future of psychoanalysis became secure (even without Jung), and Freud was on his way to fame. As the events of those years unfolded, he became more and more preoccupied—both as a man and as a Jew—with his "Jewishness" and the relation between that and psychoanalysis. For a long time it seemed as though he would have to give up one or the other, for one was a religion and the other was a science.

Loss and Freud's Jewish Identity

For many years, biographers of Freud have simply pointed out that he was a self-declared atheist—in Dennis Klein's words, "Godless and ethical"—and moved on to what they thought was most important to him and his colleagues, his new scientific discoveries.[22] Recently, however, the study of Freud's life and work has made the study of his Jewish identity a major topic, and—albeit from a very different perspective—the epistemological and scientific status of psychoanalysis. These discussions reflect a third loss in Freud's life, his attachment to the Jewish past.

In the final period of his life, Freud turned away from the clinical and theoretical aspects of psychoanalysis and explored their implications for history and culture. He became especially interested in how traditions shape present-day attitudes and, in particular, the escalating intolerance of his own social surroundings. Prominent among these were the long history of anti-Semitism in the Christian traditions, especially in the Catholic churches. In addition, there was also a growing hatred of psychoanalysis itself, partly because of the Jews in its midst, but also because of its forthright and tolerant discussions of sexuality and childhood. This hatred caused Freud to reflect more deeply than ever upon his own Jewish heritage and the claims to the science of psychoanalysis. In his mind, psychoanalysis was a science, and in no way a religion, and, furthermore, psycho-analysis could be used as an impartial tool for the understanding of prejudice. In his book *Moses and Monotheism* Freud attempted to clarify these distinctions.

His solution was a kind of ruthless psychological truth telling made up of three closely linked assertions. First, he said that the Jewish people have always considered themselves more distinguished, of higher standing, and superior to others, while at the same time holding themselves apart from all others. Such Jewish convictions are rooted in a peculiar confidence in life that derived from the belief that God chose them for their superior qualities. In this way, they acquired a share of God's grandeur, which in turn fueled their high sense of pride and self-esteem. This conviction was given to the Jews by Moses. In his book Freud used such words as "pride" and "esteem" to describe the Jews.

Second, he then inflicted a disillusionment or disenchantment upon them by carrying out a historical-psychological explanation grounded in psychoanalysis. He discredited the biblical account of Moses (asserting Moses was an Egyptian and not a Hebrew) and then asserted that Jews suffer from the illusions of collective narcissism. Freud in effect expressed the psychodynamic infrastructure of the Jewish faith. And third, it is as if Freud said to the anti-Semitic world, "See, through psychoanalysis we Jews can give up our national pride, that is, our shared sense of narcissism, which has given us our sense of superiority over you, so why cannot you 'others,' you Catholics and gentiles, give up—also through psychoanalysis—your pride and its religious embodiments which gives you your sense of superiority over us?" This was, in a sense, a reiteration of the theory of the three blows to the narcissism of all men, which Freud had set forth in an earlier essay.[23]

In a basic and general sense, Freud is here simply re-affirming what he had always thought and said. Psychoanalysis was a science and as such it explained and discredited religion. Furthermore, Freud's strong and insistent sense of his own Jewish identity was well known. Where then is the loss? The loss is in the risk Freud took in writing this book. He risked offending fellow Jews whose Jewish identity had a strong grounding in belief, and he risked being criticized by them for his merely social attachment to the Jewish historic community. On the other hand, he also risked rejection by the scientific and nonreligious community, which might find in his minimally naturalistic faith some sort of crypto-religious commitment.

Most of the scholars who have assessed Freud's influence on the twentieth century would agree, either in whole or in part, with the historian D. M. Roberts, who states: "more than any other person, [Freud] changed the way educated people thought of themselves. He provided a new cultural mythology, a way of understanding and an idiom in which to express it. . . . His influence quickly spread into literature, personal relations, education, and politics."[24] In Roberts's assessment, Freud was a culture maker.

Symbolic Loss in Eliade's Life and Thought

At first glance, the many differences between the life and thought of Freud and Eliade would appear to make any kind of comparison impossible, but Eliade's life and thought can be organized along lines similar to those found in Freud's: loss of life-orienting symbols, creative response, the formation of a movement, and institutionalization of the new ideas.

Eliade's autobiography presents his life story as a trajectory divided into three parts: everything before India, India, and everything after India. Later, a second division takes shape: childhood and adolescence in Romania (1907–1928), India (1928–1931), return to Romania (1931–1940), emigration to England (very briefly), Lisbon (1940–1945), Paris (1945–1957), and Chicago (1957–1986). Each period or time frame contributes some significant sociohistorical and sociopsychological information about the overarching process of loss and gain. Historically, it tells us when and where symbols disintegrate; psychologically, it tells us how and why Eliade responded reparatively to this disintegration as he did.

In the following I lift out major life-course events and experiences, then comment upon them psychologically, suggesting emotional significances in Eliade's life as a whole. I trace three central psychological issues: Eliade's ego-centricity, empathy/intimacy, and attachment. The entire autobiography—almost every sentence—reflects a primary self-regard, assessing events, persons and so forth in terms of their usefulness to his central ambition as a maker and remaker of culture. Empathy and intimacy, which I treat together as a single issue, are strongest in his childhood and adolescence and then weaken progressively, beginning with his emigration from Romania to Western Europe. Third, I trace the quality and extent of attachments or social bonds, especially the extent to which Eliade formed weak or strong social attachments. These three themes frame my discussion of loss in Eliade's life and work.

The theme of loss is particularly visible in the way Eliade has patterned some events in his life course. Many passages consist of episodes with a similar structure. That structure forms a sequence: (1) the events and feelings of ordinary everyday life are flowing without incident; (2) one such event becomes disturbing and confusing, for it makes no sense—a rupture in the flow of everyday experience has occurred, taking the form of a loss of some sort; (3) distress and an inner struggle to understand the meaning of the disrupting event follow but are unsuccessful; (4) Eliade realizes that the rupture or loss is of import for his identity and future, but he does not know what that future holds; (5) Eliade realizes the meaning of the disturbing event, and the flow of everyday consciousness becomes once again benign. The theme of this pattern appears to be loss and recovery. It appears mostly in the early parts of his narrative but does not occur after the departure to Western Europe.

Loss and Eliade's Romanian Identity

Eliade opens the story of his life with memories of events from early childhood. For example, he remembers seeing a little girl while on a walk down a street with his grandfather. The pattern is clearly visible here:

> I think that I was four or five years old and was clinging to my grandfather's hand . . . when I noticed a girl about my own age . . . we gazed deeply into each other's eyes . . . for several seconds we stared at each other . . . I didn't know what happened to me; I felt only that something extraordinary and decisive had occurred. For years the image of the girl on Strada Mare was a kind of secret talisman for me. . . . Never have I forgotten the face of that girl . . . I searched for that girl on every street that I walked with my grandfather, but in vain. I never saw her again.[25]

This memory is highly ego-centric and contains all four elements of Eliade's narrative pattern, showing that loss was prominent even

27

in Eliade's early years. Loss appears in the narrative line ("I searched
...."). The episode also evokes a sense of mystery and awe and gives a
hint of destiny. In Eliade's work, many everyday events are regularly
experienced as containing deep (but hidden) meanings, messages,
and guidances, suggesting that he understood his life very much as
a folktale. A faint aura of the superstitious is also present. At the
age of five, he recalls, his family took daily mud baths because his
father thought they had "a miraculous quality," and his mother told
him that following a minor accident he had "believed in a miracle"
without knowing it.[26]

Some time between childhood and adolescence Eliade developed
an important and well-known trait, one that remained throughout
his life and in fact intensified as he matured. He was seized by the
conviction that no matter how much he knew or learned in school,
his understanding was insufficient and inadequate and that he needed
more time. This dread or anxiety threw into motion an intense and
relentless will to learn more, chiefly through reading and writing.
Only words such as "drive" and "compulsion" can describe this desire
because its satisfaction required all-encompassing and exhaustive
knowledge of the entire world—a grandiose and impossible goal.[27]

The passages below describe the experience of symbolic loss
during Eliade's adolescence. In these passages Eliade forthrightly
identifies himself with the traditional and ancient culture of his
homeland, which he typifies as peasant life, making it clear that
the appeal of this life for him lay in the simplicity and constancy of
its agricultural and biological rhythms and continuities over generations of time.[28] This loss of the past was the breaking up or rupture
of a highly charged emotional attachment, recognized as irreversible
and therefore accompanied by feelings of helplessness and despair.
Such feelings were common to many culture makers in historical
situations similar to Eliade's. These feelings drove them to transform their helplessness, with a minimum of denial, into a new, more
adaptive, vision.

We can sympathize with these feelings more easily once we recognize their sociohistorical context. At the time of the passage cited
below, Eliade was between fifteen and twenty years of age in the
Romania of the 1920s. Romania did not even begin to emerge from
its centuries-old, traditional, agricultural, and peasant-centered
economy until after World War II (1945). The most vibrant cultural
symbols available to Eliade were those associated with peasant
life and traditional folk culture. These were the kinds of symbols
that made Romanians feel that there was "enough time," and they

anticipate Eliade's preoccupation with time and transience. The following segment from the autobiography announces and describes in considerable detail the shape, presence, and salience of symbolic loss as the single most important theme in Eliade's emotional life:

> There was only that terrible . . . feeling that I had lost something essential and irreplaceable. . . . I was trying desperately to identify what it was that I had "lost." . . . Soon, however, I discovered that my inexplicable sadness sprang from numerous other, unsuspected sources: for instance, the feeling of "the past," that simple fact that there have been things that are no more, that have "passed," such as my childhood or my father's youth. . . . Sometimes I regretted that I had not been reared in the country, that I did not know as a child the village life that seemed to me to be the only true kind, and that now I was severed irrevocably from that idyllic world.[29]

The source of these troubling feelings was the disappearance of a stable common culture to which he had belonged—that is to say, to which he had been strongly attached. This disappearance had taken place, quite literally, before his very eyes, for his was a transitional generation. He had been socialized into the Old World, which was beginning to disintegrate, but he had no firsthand—that is, experiential—knowledge of the new world, nor did he have access to any leaders experienced in the ways of the new. As the taken-for-granted sense of the past became less and less memorable, accessible, and representable, he became more despairing.

In the late 1920s, at roughly the age of twenty, Eliade began to seek a way of looking at the world that would relieve his despair. He found himself at a fork in the road: one led to India and the other to fascism. As he would have us understand it, he was aware only of the first, the road leading to India, an ancient civilization drenched in repetitions and returns, one rich in symbolic gain. He hopes to find there the kind of deeply shared sociality and its systems of representation that he had recently lost at home. Thanks to the research of Wasserstrom and others, we know that there was a second road, this one also leading back into the past, to the mentalities of Balkan folk religion, via Italian fascism.

India, Recovery from Loss, and the Discovery of Culture Making

As Eliade tells it, his plan to go to India occurred unexpectedly and dramatically and was accompanied by a powerful sense of totality and certitude. In the spring of 1928, at the age of twenty-one, he visited Rome and its libraries for several months. There he stumbled upon a well-known history of Indian philosophy by an eminent historian (Surendranath Dasgupta), which included the author's acknowledgment of a patron and the gift of a grant. In a flash, Eliade decided to apply for—and later received—the same grant, and with it an invitation to study with the great Dasgupta himself.

The opportunity to study in India convinced him that "destiny," to use his word, had arranged a specific identity for him, and a plan by which he should acquire it. He became elated and zealous:

> India fascinated me, it drew me like a mystery through which I seemed to foresee my destiny. It was necessary that I tear myself away from everything and everyone, at any cost . . . and if I did not do it now . . . that mystery of which I knew nothing except that it was there for me to decipher and that in deciphering it I would at the same time reveal to myself the mystery of my own existence; I would discover at last who I was and why I wanted to be what I wanted to be, why all the things that had happened to me had happened to me.[30]

Some time after he arrived in India, his mentor/teacher/guide, the eminent Dasgupta, invited him to join his household. The great scholar would teach, and he would assist by translating, editing, and writing. But this invitation meant something very special to Eliade, far beyond what it in fact promised. His belief was that it would allow him to fulfill his deepest wish of all and thereby to consolidate his "destiny": his wish to become a part of Indian culture, to abandon middle-European culture and become an Indian instead, that is, to inwardly own and attach himself, in his inner, subjective world, to the myriad spiritual riches of India by way of its symbols of the past.

However, Dasgupta had a daughter, and the two fell in love and became physically intimate. When Dasgupta realized this, he ordered Eliade out of his house and broke off all relationships with him. The two men never saw each other again. Eliade was disconsolate: "Never would I be able to attain an Indian identity." He fled and isolated himself for the next six months. The life of a hermit, he said, made it possible to sort things out. It also made it possible to prepare himself to return, and to create something new.

By Christmastime, he said, "I was a 'changed' man," but then added cryptically, "I shall not try to repeat here the steps of that inner transformation."[31] The following declarations summarize these changes, stating, in a nutshell, the central ideas that resolved, for him at least, his years of gloom and loss. These ideas are, in effect, the culture Eliade made:

> If "historical" India were forbidden to me, the road now was opened to "eternal" India. I realized also that I had to know passion, drama, and suffering before renouncing the "historical" dimension of my existence and making my way toward a trans-historical, a-temporal, paradigmatic dimension in which tensions and conflicts would disappear of themselves. Later I understood that my drama itself followed a traditional model . . .
>
> What I had tried to do—renounce my Western culture and seek a 'home' or a 'world' in an exotic spiritual universe—was equivalent in a sense to a premature renunciation of all my creative potentialities. I could not have been creative except by remaining in my world—which in the first place was the world of Romanian language and culture . . . my vocation was culture, not sainthood.[32]

At this time, Eliade was able to identify in a very specific way the topics and issues that should occupy that creativity for the rest of his life:

> It seemed to me that we Romanians could fulfill a definite role in the coming dialogue between the two or three worlds: the West, Asia and cultures of the archaic folk type. . . . The common elements of Indian, Balkan, and Mediterranean folk culture proved to me that it is here that organic universalism exists, that it is the result of a common history (the history of peasant cultures) and not an abstract construct. We, the people of Eastern Europe, would be able to serve as a bridge between the West and Asia.[33]

That is how—many years later—Eliade had come to make sense of his trip to India—that is to say, how Eliade would have us understand and remember him.

Let us summarize. As Eliade came of age in the late 1920s, introspectively and intellectually gifted, ambitious, and searching, he realized his country's traditional ways were disintegrating and that it could no longer ignore the new, advancing trends from Europe. Still further, he realized that he no longer knew who he was. Impelled to find out, he decided that he would do for his country what he could not do for himself: he took upon himself the role of national culture maker—strictly speaking, a national culture remaker. From this point on, there was no difference in his mind between his own sense of personal identity and his social identity as a world-historical figure.

To realize this aim, he immersed himself in the religious ways of India, to acquire there what he had lost at home. At the same time and for the same reason, we know from contemporary scholarship that he associated himself with leaders of Italian and Romanian fascist movements then developing. These efforts were by and large successful. He had indeed formed a new vision for his country. And we may assume that his account of his thinking upon return from India is more or less accurate, even though written many years later. What is important at this point, however, is not only what Eliade said but what he left out.

Loss and the Search for a Movement

Eliade's trajectory exemplifies a broader pattern. After a decisive experience of loss, culture makers often shift from self-discovery to movement. There they struggle to legitimate and eventually institutionalize their newfound convictions, as can be seen in the next phase of Eliade's narrative.

Eliade's narrative undergoes a major emotional shift at the time of his turn to fascism. From his earliest efforts up to the return from India, the author represents himself as introspective, capable of spontaneous emotion and interested in his immediate social world. Personal and social identity were each firm and sufficient and interconnected. But after the return from India the text becomes emotionally impoverished: his ego-centricity intensifies; descriptions of social relations are bereft of intimacy, warmth, and reciprocity; friendships are instrumental only; and the social world is generally viewed with suspicion. By the time of his emigration to Western Europe (1940), and especially beginning with the Paris period (1945–1954), Eliade's inner landscape became increasingly barren and reduced in emotionality.

Eliade's creative recovery from his experience of loss of symbols was not complete. He needed more time, and this was not given to him. History had asked that he give up a whole way of life in the span of only a few years, less than even one generation. As long as he remained in Romania, he felt inwardly comfortable and was outwardly confident. But, his renunciation dynamically incomplete, he needed a social ethos grounded in a symbolically powerful past and the support of a structure of social authority that would ask little in the way of intimacy.

Authoritarian groups typically demand total obedience to their leaders and total loyalty among all members, but at no point do these groups demand—or even tolerate—demonstrations of intimacy, empathy, or affection. In the light of these considerations, fascism seems particularly apt as the ideology and sociality of choice in Eliade's case. The period described below was in fact the time when Eliade was most in touch with—socially and intellectually—fascist movements.

During the last years he spent in Bucharest, Eliade worked simultaneously in three well-established fields—journalism, creative writing, and university teaching. Each was a potential source of movement. He began with journalism by writing short pieces for a semipopular journal edited by his mentor, Nae Ionescu, and giving radio talks. He also began to develop himself as a public speaker, lecturing about his experiences and travels in India. From the start he was a successful raconteur, sometimes speaking from notes but often without any. He was soon invited to join the editorial board of the same journal and later became a regular contributor. His "attic" (the name he gave to his bedroom/study on the top floor of his parents' house) became an occasional salon. He joined a small group of students, and together they thought of themselves as the Romanian avant-garde.

Eliade also received his doctorate from the University of Bucharest. As one of Ionescu's prize students, it was easy for him to offer classes on topics he considered most important and to develop new contacts of his own, thereby further legitimating his own ideas.

Even before his trip to India, Eliade had begun to write, first as a journalist, then producing feuilletons and what we would call "op-ed" pieces and short essays. By this time he had already begun to write as a novelist. In 1923–1924, he completed an early version of a biographical novel. As the 1930s progressed, Eliade successfully established himself in three separate areas of movement, thereby achieving considerable recognition, at least within his homeland.

However, as the 1930s advanced, it also became increasingly clear that war was approaching, that Romania would eventually be occupied, and that it was prudent for him to leave. By this time he had married. He and his wife lived briefly in London and then sat out World War II in Lisbon, Portugal, as a Romanian secretary of cultural affairs. During that period (1940–1945), he could do little to legitimate further either his ideas or his career, for obvious reasons. But he was employed for the first time in his life, and the post he held gave him time to think and write. The autobiography says little that is intellectual or personal about this period, and this kind of omission only increased in the years that followed.

As soon as the war ended, the Eliades moved to Paris, where they remained until the final move to the United States in 1956. During this time he consolidated his intellectual oeuvre, and his emotional life took on its final shape. Eliade was totally committed to culture making and to Romania. But he could not return. The Paris years were his first substantial exposure to European international intellectualism. It was, of course, the opportunity he needed, but it was also a taxing and formidable struggle. He was unknown and without friends, apart from a small group of like-minded Romanian scholars. Through enormous energy, persistence, and skill he was able to advance himself further than he ever could have in Romania by building and nurturing a relatively stable network of "weak ties"—that is, weak personal relationships in a cluster of like-minded men. These men shared with Eliade similar views about the dangers of modernity and the need to offset it by means of a historically conservative and religiously grounded view of the world. It was understood by this group that such a religious grounding should derive from the mythic, symbolic, and mystical features of both the great religions and folk traditions while eschewing traditional dogma and institutions.

This group included men of sufficient accomplishment and position on whom Eliade could prevail for favors without having to reciprocate. In this way he acquired a considerable number of introductions to publishers, invitations to lecture at prestigious universities, and contacts with which to replenish his network. Eliade wrote in French and published in France the major books that would bring him fame for the rest of his life.

The closest he came to belonging to an organized and more socially stable element or structure of movement was his participation in the Eranos conferences in Ascona, Switzerland.[34] Eranos was itself something of a movement, and its better-known features appealed greatly to Eliade. The conferences occurred regularly, the speakers often had international reputations, and the participants were like-minded, preferring ancient or traditional forms of thought and experience over modern ones. An aura of historical urgency and mission to bring this knowledge to "save" modernity from itself prevailed. The papers were published in an annual or yearbook, and—last but not least—the amenities were elegant and the staff deferential.

But if we are guided by the affective tone of the autobiography, in other significant respects Eliade was not successful during his Paris years, and he did not like being there. He failed to acquire what he wanted most of all, a university teaching position in Europe and preferably in Paris, which would support him financially, give him more time to study and write, and provide a flow of fresh contacts. These were not forthcoming. There is little evidence of his former capacity for introspection, empathy, or intimacy with another person. He tells us less and less about his feelings and impressions of events and people, and more and more about external, behavioral details—who he had lunch with, the name of the scholar who arranged that he give an important lecture, or the name of another who responded positively or negatively to this or that paper, and so forth.

The pages of the Paris years also contain a number of short, negative statements interjected without context or discussion. Some of these refer to American or British activities during or after the war. These remarks express increasing resentment and scorn toward the emerging modern world to which he was being forced to submit, especially toward its commitments to democracy, liberalism, science, and the social sciences.[35]

One of the most mystifying paragraphs of the autobiography is Eliade's account of the death of his first wife, Nina, from cancer, in 1944. Nina had begged her doctors and friends not to tell her husband that she was dying, lest "it cause me to suffer, to worry, to be unable to work. To the amazement of everyone, the secret was kept. I did not learn the true nature of her illness until a few days before it killed her."[36] However, Nina had been ill for some time, and Eliade had ample opportunity to learn the truth. Instead, he interprets her silence and her ensuing death as an act of fate, implying that perhaps he himself was its hapless victim.

In this account, we see that the ego-centricity of Eliade's earlier years has noticeably increased. No mention is made of feelings of grief or thoughts that might indicate processes of mourning. Eliade did not mourn Nina's death, for she was not a link to his national past, and so he did not miss her that much. Later, while still in Paris, Eliade learned of the death of his father, and his response was telling:

> For days afterward I lived in another world, a world long forgotten, consoled only by sorrow. I sensed that I had lost another part—the largest part—of my past. Alone, I walked the streets around Sacre Coeur, remembering scenes from childhood, adolescence, and early youth. In recent years I had succeeded in controlling my longing for the homeland; it came upon me only in sleep, in certain dreams. Now it overwhelmed me again. If I had been free to do so, I would have begun to write my memories from childhood.[37]

Eliade did not mourn the death of his father, but he did mourn, albeit incompletely, what his father symbolized: the homeland.

Eliade as Culture Maker

Eliade often referred to his work as "making culture," and I have spoken of him as a culture maker. The culture Eliade made was, simply, his theory of the sacred—what it was, how it could be known or experienced, and why it was at the root of all religions.

As such, Eliade's work has appealed to our society at two levels, one highly academic, the other social. The first has been explained clearly and succinctly by Steven Wasserstrom. "Eliade," Wasserstrom says, "virtually created the field now known as the history of religions in the United States; he is, by nearly unanimous consent, the most influential student of religion in the world today; he remains among the most widely-read historians of religion around the world, and his global influence on the history of religions remains dynamic."[38]

Eliade also contributed decisively to the social shape of postmodern religion in America. He created a system of religious thinking that legitimizes an experience of religion as highly individualistic, non-institutional, and psychological. Much of what is referred to as the return of the sacred, or the re-sacralization of religion, reflects this aspect of Eliade's work. Today, many people are finding it possible to be religious without belonging to churches or denominations. In this sense, the following short summary of Eliade's thought captures the core ideas that have influenced academe and the social sciences.

Eliade thought in terms of oppositions, and his oeuvre is composed of an intersecting series of oppositions. Most basic is the passage of time and the experience of transience, which he frequently referred to simply as "history." But, "history" referred to some periods more than others. It was virtually synonymous with modern and secular, such that history and social change were virtually identical. For this reason, Eliade also spoke of "the terror of history." Social change led to the abandonment of the past and eventually to death itself. Therefore, Eliade juxtaposed history to an assortment of redemptive or remedial contexts within which to locate and annul the passage of time, such as transcendence, the eternal, the sacred, and, more simply, the archaic or beginnings or the center.

These historical oppositions were paralleled by another set referring to method or to how time and transience were annulled, as he liked to put it. The finality of time and historical change was only apparent, a mask or camouflage hiding its own ontological oppo-site. For, a religious reality contained—in the sense of "tamed" or "domesticated"—the tensions of history. The reality of the sacred was "there," so to speak, all the time, concealed in history, but only interpretation could cut beneath the camouflage of history and reveal the sacred.

A third opposition further clarifies these two. Eliade grounded his temporal oppositions in a social one. He spoke of the annulment of time as a kind of sociality, a particular form of community or com-mon culture. Its prototype or model was the folk society, that is, cultures of the archaic folk type.[39] Unlike history, this was a time and a condition wherein men and women lived together fully in the present and at one with one another.

The above oppositions constitute "the culture that Eliade made." However, these ideas, like any other set of ideas, can exist only within a social context. In the past, religious ideas have for the most part ex-isted in the context of religious institutions, such as sects, churches, denominations, and the like. However, the culture that Eliade made achieved its primary reality in the context of a quite different kind of institution, that of the university and the academic study of religion within the university, as well as a more diffuse secondary reality in contemporary American, postmodern, non-institutional religiosity.

The Institutionalization of the Culture That Eliade Made

Eliade's effort to achieve institutionalization for his life's work suc-ceeded only in the last period of his life, in the United States. There, he occupied a prestigious position in a prestigious university, as works written and published earlier in France were easily translated into English for American consumption. Impressive as these achieve-ments were, genuine institutionalization came only when his ideas, his "oeuvre," gradually infused a recently established institution, the American Academy of Religion (AAR), and departments of reli-gious studies in colleges and universities.

At first, in the 1950s, the AAR was an incompletely formed move-ment in search of leaders, members, and audiences. Its organizing idea was that the study of religion no longer had to be conducted only in a theological school or seminary, controlled by a church or sect for the purpose of training its personnel and propagating its be-liefs. Rather, religion could be studied and understood by persons not associated with or even committed to ecclesiastical institutions. Instead, religion could be, and perhaps should be, taught and studied in a university, alongside other forms of historical and cultural phenomena and expressions.

Teachers and graduate students interested in and aspiring to the study of religion became members of the AAR and advanced the goals of their own institutions. Many were women and men who had grown up in some sort of traditional religious culture or subculture, then had become disillusioned with their traditional forms of religiosity but nonetheless had also retained significant residues of traditional commitment and, beyond that, curiosity as well. The AAR was seen by many as an institution where one could work out such conflicts and pursue such interests, transposing them into an intellectual challenge, an epistemic negotiation, and in the course of this also learning more about their own past.

In sum, AAR personnel needed theories of religion that were non-institutional, universal (that is, inclusive of all religious groupings, ancient and modern), and preferably highly experiential or psychological—indeed, the more psychological a theory was, the less institutional it needed to be. Eliade's thought fit hand in glove into these evolving needs and interests of the AAR leadership and membership.

Interpretive and Integrative Summary: Modernization as Historical and Psychological Change

We can now link Eliade's life course and thought to the sociohistorical and emotional dimensions of modernization. This is best done by interpreting the life course portrayed in the autobiography and in Eliade's fascism in the context of modernization and symbolic loss understood as the intolerably rapid loss of a whole way of life.

At the time of Eliade's birth in 1907 in Bucharest, Romania was torn by an irreconcilable conflict. On one hand, he was born into and grew up in a society still organized by ancient customs, morals, and ways of thinking and feeling about self and others. As we noted, Romania did not even begin to modernize its centuries-old traditional, agricultural, and social structures until after World War II. At that time Eliade was already thirty-eight years old. On the other hand, at the same time, Romania was exposed to patterns of advanced modernization as these were mediated by an emerging mass media, as well as by a highly vocal and visible European intellectualism and by the technologies supported by both.

Brilliant and precocious, Eliade was drawn early on into a small cohort of talented young intellectuals responsive to these essentially extra-Romanian trends. These trends were, of course, the result of shared experiences of the reform of traditional ways—in particular, of politics (leading to democracy), of science (leading to technological advances and industrialization), and of psychology (leading to social and personal autonomy from traditional moral restraints). Most important of all, these trends had taken shape in Western European countries over a period of many generations—in many cases over a period of several centuries—and not just within one generation.

Eliade recognized this irreconcilable conflict and knew that it was the paramount emotional and cognitive issue in his life. This realization appears most poignantly in his early adolescent nostalgia and yearning for the customs and habits of the past in a homeland he clearly loved, and also accounts for the emotional tone of helplessness in the face of something lost and still desired, but nonetheless unobtainable, as we saw earlier.

Eliade gradually transformed his loss of the past into his theory of religion. His word for his attachments to his Romanian past was "culture," and especially "making culture." He would replace his lost Romanian past with new symbols that he had made. The irreversibility of modernization gradually became "time" and "history," and his fear that modernization might triumph over the ancient folkways became "terror"—hence, "the terror of history." Once forgotten, the original loss could re-appear in the search for—and the finding of—living proof that the cosmos did indeed support a transcendent, timeless dimension and the techniques by which one could gain (or regain) access to it.

Most important, Eliade's inability to tolerate the clash between modernity and tradition in Romania appears in his attachments to fascism. In order to understand how and why this happened, it is necessary to turn away from the historical circumstances that modernization created and consider instead Eliade's psychological responses to those circumstances. At this point, Erik Erikson's understanding of adolescence is especially valuable. Although Erikson addressed societies undergoing rapid modernization, his theories apply as well as to societies overwhelmed by early modernization, for the realities of symbolic loss are implicit in both.[40]

Adolescence is a specific period in the life course when a person turns emotionally away from parents and family and toward society to integrate the inner mental world of personal self-definition (identity) and the outer social world of morals and creeds (ideology). Adolescence in traditional societies involves no dramatic change in the cultural and biological rhythms and cycles that organize life. Little more was asked of growing children than that they acquire the parents' values and outlooks. These had been everywhere, "in the air" so to speak, since infancy.

However, modernization creates social conditions that differ from those that confronted the adolescent's parents. Each emerging generation faces new social conditions. This in effect depotentiates and thereby strips away the symbolic structures that earlier generations created and that are no longer workable. When the creation of new forms of thought and adaptation lag behind the changes that demand them, symbolic loss occurs. This was especially so in Eliade's Romania, shortly before he went to India.

At that time and in that place, history offered Eliade three options: monarchy, communism, and fascism. The first promised to retain the ancient ways, the whole way of life to which he was already strongly attached, and that probably would have suited him best. But the monarchy was crumbling, and it had no coherent understanding of how and why the present situation was different. Communism, in demanding a total break with the past, only terrified him even more. In fact, communism was the real "terror of history," the quintessence of modernity.

On the other hand, fascism offered him a theory that anchored the deepest realities of life in the past, preserved national boundaries, permitted religious symbols, and provided the kind of ideology that in turn created the kind of sociality into which his unique identity needs could fit. That was because identity and ideology are always in constant interplay. The two must fit or match each other. Ideology must be so shaped that it supports and stabilizes the adolescent's inner psychological organization, and in turn the growing adolescent will adapt his or her identity to the most fitting ideology. The social ethos of fascism—and of other kinds of authoritarian organizations and movements as well—offered powerful bonds of attachment to its leaders and asked strong bonds of loyalty among members. However, both leaders and those led could rest assured that there was no place in such a social structure for relationships of intimacy or affection.

Conclusion

In this essay I have studied culture making in the lives and works of Sigmund Freud and Mircea Eliade. Current scholarship on each of these figures finds little in common between them and, by implication, little in common between their theories of psychoanalysis and religious thought. Freud dismissed religion, and especially mysticism, as a form of developmental failure, and Eliade dismissed psychoanalysis as reductionistic.

I have not compared systems of ideas, beliefs, or theories. Rather, I have centered upon the historical and developmental contexts of the two men and have concluded that both were exposed to highly similar circumstances—emerging, modernizing societies demanding new forms of understanding—and that both responded by creating new cultural symbols that subsequently appealed to many people in the societies they inhabited. Freud recognized these circumstances for what they were, and gradually accepted the loss of the past and all that it entailed. On the other hand, Eliade, faced with a similar mandate, created a new past, stitching together Romanian, Indian, and fascist elements. Yet both created rich intellectual and institutional trajectories that continue to flourish today.

The interpretive terms I have used to discuss psychoanalysis and the history of religions are not primarily those of their respective founders. Rather, my terms are "memory," "meaning," "culture," and "symbol." I have understood the interplay between these in terms of the human experience of loss, at times individual, at times collective, at times historical, and at other times experiential.

Furthermore, I have attempted to shed more light on the disciplines these two men created. In the case of psychoanalysis, other figures in its movement were also culture makers shaped by loss. Loss was central to Melanie Klein's life, in the form of her gradual relinquishing of her Jewish heritage. And loss and mourning are central to her theory of the life course. Loss and mourning were also widely shared in England during the time in which Klein formulated her ideas in London: World War I, the interwar period, and the 1940s. Loss was also the principal issue for major figures in the school of object relations—for example, the work of John Bowlby.[41]

The historical study of religion is equally suggestive of loss, although this has not been widely discussed by historians. Nineteenth-century liberalism and fundamentalism were two different responses to the same experience—the waning or loss of traditional religion in the wake of rapid modernization—and the history of these losses and their effects on religion are only now being written. Significantly, the intellectual and emotional structures of Western religions also reflect loss and mourning in their core narratives and practices. The Christian mass is built around the loss, memory, and memorialization of Jesus Christ, and the history of Judaism and Islam are both histories of losses and survivals.

Notes

1. Philip Rieff, *Triumph of the Therapeutic* (New York: Harper, 1968).
2. Richard Sennett, *The Decline of Public Man* (New York: Norton, 1992).
3. Heinz Hartmann, *Ego Psychology and the Problem of Adaptation*, trans. David Rapaport (New York: International Universities Press, 1958).
4. J. M. Roberts, *The History of Europe* (London: Penguin, 1996).
5. William H. McNeill, "Eclipsed at Last?" *Times Literary Supplement*, 22 Oct. 1999, 14–15.
6. Unless otherwise noted, references to the work of Sigmund Freud are from *The Standard Edition of the Complete Psychological Works of Sigmund Freud*, trans. and ed. James Strachey (London: Hogarth Press, 24 vols., 1966–1974). Freud, "Moses and Monotheism," *Standard Edition*, vol. 23 (first published 1939).
7. Steven M. Wassserstrom, *Religion after Religion: Gershom Scholem, Mircea Eliade, and Henry Corbin at Eranos* (Princeton: Princeton University Press, 1999).
8. Erik H. Erikson, *Young Man Luther: A Study in Psychoanalysis and History* (New York: Norton, 1958) and *Insight and Responsibility: Lectures on the Ethical Implications of Psychoanalysic Insight* (New York: Norton, 1964).
9. The concept of type used here is less complex that Max Weber's "ideal type," as discussed in *The Sociology of Religion*, trans. Ephraim Fiscoff (Boston: Beacon Press, 1963). I use type as "a simple description of the commonly found features of a modern, real-world phenomenon" (*Oxford Dictionary of Sociology*, 231–32).
10. The best-known discussion of loss in psychoanalytic theory is Fred Weinstein, *History and Theory after the Fall: An Essay on Interpretation* (Chicago: University of Chicago Press, 1990); see also his *Freud, Psychoanalysis, Social Theory: The Unfulfilled Promise* (Albany: SUNY Press, 2001).
11. Freud, "Interpretation of Dreams," *Standard Edition*, vols. 4 and 5 (first published 1900).
12. Masson, 2, November 1896. In *The Complete Letters of Sigmund Freud to Wilhelm Fliess, 1887–1904*, ed. Jeffrey Masson, (Cambridge, MA: Belknap Press of Harvard University Press, 1985).
13. Freud, "Interpretation of Dreams," 4: xxvi.
14. Freud, "An Autobiographical Study," *Standard Edition*, vol. 20 (first published 1925).
15. Sigmund Freud and Josef Breuer, *Studies on Hysteria*, *Standard Edition*, vol. 2 (first published 1895).
16. William McGrath, *Freud's Discovery of Psychoanalysis: The Politics of Hysteria* (Ithaca, NY: Cornell University Press, 1986).
17. William McGuire, ed. *The Freud-Jung Letters*, trans. Ralph Manheim and R. F. C. Hull (Princeton, NJ: Princeton University Press, 1974).
18. Ernest Jones, *The Life and Work of Sigmund Freud* (New York: Perseus, 1981).
19. Freud, "On Narcissism," *Standard Edition*, vol. 14 (first published 1914).
20. Freud, "On Transience," *Standard Edition*, vol. 14 (first published 1916). In his essay "Mourning and Melancholia," first published in 1917, Freud said: "Mourning is regularly the reaction to the loss of a loved person, or to the loss of some abstraction which has taken the place of one, such as one's country, liberty, an ideal, and so on" (*Standard Edition*, 14: 243). However, he did not refer again to the second (the loss of some abstraction, etc.), and it is this portion of his thought I am attempting to develop further in this essay.
21. Hilda C. Abraham and Ernst L. Freud, eds. *A Psycho-analytic Dialogue: The Letters of Sigmund Freud and Karl Abraham, 1907–1926* (New York: Basic Books, 1965), 9, 34.

22. Dennis Klein, *Jewish Origins of the Psychoanalytic Movement* (New York: Praeger, 1981).
23. Freud, "A Difficulty in the Path of Psychoanalysis," *Standard Edition*, vol. 17 (first published 1917).
24. Roberts, *History of Europe*, 534.
25. Mircea Eliade, *Autobiography*, vol. 1 (New York: Harper and Row, 1981), 4–5.
26. This episode also illustrates another feature of the typical experience: the repeated use of clichés and stereotypy. Two of the more frequently used are "I shall always remember" and "I will never forget."
27. Eliade, *Autobiography*, 1: 63–64.
28. McNeill, "Eclipsed at Last."
29. Eliade, *Autobiography*, 1: 72–74. For further evidence of Eliade's attachment to a traditionalist, agricultural past see *Autobiography*, 1: 16, 217.
30. Ibid., 1: 153. At this point in his life Eliade became what could be called a "free-floating absolutist" or "totalizer"—a person convinced that an absolutely omniscient authority exists and that one could eventually come to know the will of this authority for oneself. Toward the end of the three-year visit to India, Eliade tells us, the answer to his many questions was disclosed to him, and he was able to return home, having discovered his true self and his true calling, as well as "the truth," in the sense of a commanding and trustworthy absolute.
31. Ibid., 1: 190.
32. Ibid., 1: 199–200.
33. Ibid., 1: 204.
34. Wassserstrom, *Religion after Religion*.
35. See Eliade, *Autobiography*, 1: 96; vol. 2 (Chicago: University of Chicago Press, 1998), 103, 107, 117–18, 145. For example: "The whole world was in the process of being transformed. . . . I had foreseen it and announced it in many writings between 1933 and 1940." *Autobiography*, 2: 107.
36. Eliade, *Autobiography*, 1: 276.
37. Ibid., 2: 156–57.
38. Wassserstrom, *Religion after Religion*.
39. Eliade, *Autobiography*, 1: 204.
40. Erik H. Erikson, *Identity and the Life Cycle* (New York: Norton, 1980).
41. John Bowlby, *Loss: Sadness and Depression* (New York: Basic Books, 1982).

CELIA BRICKMAN

The Persistence of the Past

FRAMING SYMBOLIC LOSS AND RELIGIOUS STUDIES IN THE CONTEXT OF RACE

THE LOSS of great historical cultural formations, as with the personal loss of loved ones, produces grief in those who have held them dear, a grief that must be mourned. In certain gifted individuals, the psychological work involved in mourning eventuates in creative activity that leads to new cultural inventions. This theory of symbolic loss, first elaborated in the work of Peter Homans on the origins of the psychoanalytic movement, links the creation of psychoanalysis to the social and cultural processes of secularization, especially to the loss of religious belief.[1] Freud's genius lay, in part, in his negotiation of that mourning through a creative exploration of the contours of the psyche, leading to the insights of psychoanalysis. The further extension by Homans of his theory of mourning and symbolic loss to the life and work of the pioneering sociologist Max Weber suggests that a connection between the loss of religious faith and intellectual creativity is at work in other modern academic disciplines as well: not only in psychoanalysis and sociology, but in the academic study of religion.

The application of the psychoanalytically based theory of symbolic loss to the study of religion has the potential to highlight the subjective dynamics of those who study religion in the academy. However, it may also reproduce concepts embedded within classical psychoanalytic theory that could usefully be reconfigured. This essay teases out the racial meanings implicit in the "primitivity" that is said to characterize the psychological and social location of the religion that is lost with the coming of modernity. After a brief consideration of some of the ways that symbolic loss can be seen to have been at work in the academic study of religion, this essay addresses four themes that preside over the underlying structure of the theory of symbolic loss. I suggest that as we consider the psychodynamics of the study of religion, past and present, we move from a framework of *secularization* to *globalization*, from a context of *common culture* to one of *dominant discourse*, from the psychoanalytic category of *primitivity* to one of *vulnerability*, and from the psychoanalytic trope of *mourning* to that of *melancholia*.

The Work of Mourning and the Question of Primitivity

In applying the psychoanalytic trope of mourning—elaborated upon by Freud as a dynamic of individual psychology—to social phenomena such as the origins of the psychoanalytic movement or of *verstehen* sociology, Homans follows in the footsteps of the landmark mid-twentieth-century work of Alexander and Margarete Mitscherlich, *The Inability to Mourn*.[2] This influential work, published in German in 1967 and in English in 1975, helped place "mourning" as the quintessential psychological challenge facing members of Western nations in the latter part of the twentieth century, as they attempted (or not) to understand how the enormous crimes of the Holocaust had emerged out of the heart of European civilization.[3]

Freud had presciently analyzed the psychic economy described by the Mitscherlichs in his *Group Psychology and the Analysis of the Ego* approximately fifty years earlier, in 1921.[4] In this text, he defined group psychology as a condition in which members of a community lack, or temporarily lose, the function of the superego, the internal seat of conscience. Instead, they are in thrall to an external leader who occupies the psychological space where the superego would otherwise be. Group psychology, for Freud, corresponded to the psychology of barbarians or primitive peoples. On the analogy of *Totem and Taboo*, group psychology could be likened to members of the primal horde *before* the primal crime: group psychology was like the psychology of the brothers who had not yet gone through the progression of rebellion, murder, and remorse—object cathexis followed by object loss that would lead to the internalization of paternal prohibition and hence the development of the superego. Instead, the group leader would be retained as an idealized, *external* object, to function in the place of what, under other conditions, might become the internal superego. Thus the great power of the leader or demagogue: his or her charisma exerts such force as to usurp the psychic agency through which the individual might exercise moral independence. Members of such a community or group lack the hallmark

of individuality but enjoy what the Mitscherlichs call "the pleasure of submission," not unrelated to what Durkheim had called
the "effervescence" produced by immersion within the religious
crowd.[5]

The foresight of this formulation can be seen in the uncanny
echoes it finds not only in the Mitscherlichs' description of the group
psychology of Germany under Hitler but also in Hannah Arendt's
postwar analysis of totalitarianism.[6] Arendt describes the travesty of
totalitarianism not only in terms of the political havoc it wreaks and
the violence on which it depends to perpetrate itself but also in the
way it enlists its members *from within themselves* to participate in
a form of governance that is destructive to them as members of the
social polity it is meant to serve. Freud's description of the hypnoid-
like enthrallment of the group member with the leader is the equivalent of Arendt's description of the "total, unrestricted, conspicuous,
unconditional and unalterable loyalty of the individual" required by
totalitarian movements, which have "discovered a means of domi-
nating and terrorizing human beings from within."[7]

However, as I have discussed elsewhere, Freud had inscribed his
analysis of group psychology within a racially indexed evolutionary
framework: group psychology was the "primitive" psychology out of
which the modern mind, with its moral independence, had evolved.[8]
Writing in the second decade of the twentieth century, Freud had
all too easily absorbed the social evolutionism that still pervaded
much of the social sciences. In his cultural texts, he set his metapsychological theories within a historical framework that was meant
to explain the origins of the modern structures of the mind. The
historical framework he made use of was taken from the evolutionary anthropology of the first generation of Anglo-American anthropologists, with their central construct of the "primitive" who was
considered to be both Europe's racial other and the representative of
Europe's past. For Freud as for the anthropologists from whom he
borrowed, such as Sir James Frazer, E. B. Tylor, John McLennan, and
others, this "primitive" (or "savage" or "barbarian") was understood
both as the evolutionary ancestor of humankind and as the dark-
skinned, culturally different, and evolutionarily inferior other of the
Western imaginary.[9]

Freud's essay on group psychology, like much of the rest of his
work, exhibits a constant slippage between two senses of "primitivity": in the first sense, it comprises the earliest stages of a universally conceived, ontogenetic psychological development; in the

second, it is the psychological and cultural condition of Europe's racial/cultural other. This slippage allows his essay to be read in two different ways: both as a description of the psychology that ensues when, through political oppression or manipulation, a group of people is held in thrall to tyrannical leadership; and as a description of the innate psychology of the (racially indexed) "primitive" communities out of which the modern subjectivity has evolved. One reading sees the primitivity of group psychology as politically and socially constructed; the other sees it as an anthropological, evolutionary, and racially marked designation.

The slippage between these two forms of primitivity can be related to the inextricability of the contradictory yet co-constructed opposition of primitivity and civilization, as we find in Freud; of "bare life" and sovereignty, as theorized by Giorgio Agamben; or of captivity and emancipation, as described by Rey Chow.[10] In each case, the introduction of the conditions that make possible the social and political realm creates a distinction between those very conditions and the presumed form of life that precedes them. A distinction between the human and the citizen/civilized is introduced, and the merely human becomes the debased, inferior term that is included in all forms of subjectivity at the same time as it functions as the exclusion necessary to the construction of the social/political civilized citizen. As Agamben writes, "Man is the living being who, in language, separates and opposes himself to his own bare life and, at the same time, maintains himself in relation to that bare life in an inclusive exclusion."[11]

The introduction of the idea of civilization creates the category of primitivity as that which preceded it and is inferior to it. This "preceding" form of "bare" life is conflated with all those who for one reason or another are seen to remain outside or beyond national, civic boundaries, constituting in this way ethnic and racialized others as possessing merely physical life but lacking political rights (refugees and prisoners of war are current, prime examples). Rey Chow, recognizing the temporal dimension in which this co-constructed reality tends to get played out, describes "a (modernist) process of rationalization in which humanity must first be imagined in some form of captivity (some kind of imprisonment within a condition of barbarism) in order for its putative progress toward a non-oppressive, civilized state to become credible."[12] I return to these questions of primitivity and race in relation to the topic of loss and mourning further on in this essay.

Mourning and the Origins of Psychoanalysis

In his book *The Ability to Mourn: Disillusionment and the Origins of the Psychoanalytic Movement,* Peter Homans has given us one of the richest and most nuanced psychological accounts of the complex historical relationship between psychoanalysis and religion, and in so doing, he has provided a model of the interconnections among the personal losses resulting from historical change, the mourning that accompanies these losses, and the creation of new cultural (as well as psychological) structures. Choosing his title with direct reference to the Mitscherlichs, Homans has used the criterion of the ability/inability to mourn as the fulcrum of his study on the origins of the psychoanalytic movement. Psychoanalysis, according to Homans, was born out of the loss of religious belief that had resulted from the far-reaching social structural changes of industrialization, urbanization, and modernization, and from the accompanying intellectual and scientific changes to which they gave rise. Homans demonstrates how cultural values and ideals are as much libidinal "objects" in the psychoanalytic sense—representations that can be strongly cathected, loved, lost, and identified with—as are the parental and other personal figures usually associated with the term. Historical and social change, therefore, involves supra-personal losses that can be conceptualized as the "lost objects" Freud had in mind when he wrote "the character of the ego is a precipitate of abandoned object-cathexes."[13] The structure of the modern psyche is built on the sedimentation not only of the lost loves of the personal sphere but on the cherished values and ideals that have been lost with modernization. Unlike the Germans of the Mitscherlichs' account, Freud and other members of the first generation of psychoanalysts were able to mourn the historic and cultural losses with which they were faced, to withstand the personal disintegration this mourning entailed, and, through introspection, to re-assemble disaggregated psychological fragments into new patterns of psychological structure and insight.

In creating psychoanalysis, Freud codified his introspection into these processes, which had resulted from his disillusion with or alienation from the Jewish faith of his forebears. Thus, psychoanalysis and the associated psychologies of its time (Jungian analytical psychology, Adlerian psychology) can be seen as the outgrowth of the creative negotiation of the loss of religious faith on the part of these foundational figures. For Freud and psychoanalysis, the answer to the loss of religious faith was to understand religion as a part of the primitive past that the modern subject had or would overcome.

Homans sees Freud and his associates as having progressed only partway along the path of mourning and individuation that they inaugurated. Like the Germans to whom the Mitscherlichs refer, Freud and his colleagues were faced with a task of mourning that was potentially psychologically debilitating and socially isolating. Unlike the Germans, however, they were able to mourn their loss and to renounce its ideal of religious salvation or redemption. However, according to Homans, the early psychoanalysts were able to go only so far in their process of mourning, and as a result, they created the metapsychology (the emplotment of the psyche according to the structures of ego, superego, and id) as a *defense against* a further mourning that might have or should have taken place. As Homans writes, "a particular conception of science can itself become a defense against deeper layers of unconscious subjectivity, in this case largely narcissistic processes, by rationalizing them with excessive rapidity and then encasing them in mechanical models."[14]

Freud and his associates mourned their lost religious pasts by creating innovative psychological systems, but they de-idealized their religious pasts with "too great rapidity," halting their mourning partway, and protecting themselves from further mourning by the defense mechanism of a rigid systematization. This rigid systematization took the form of an oedipal topography that was not able to come to terms with the pre-oedipal registers of experience (variously described as maternal, primitive, or narcissistic). The result was a psychoanalytic "break with the past": that is, a past that was reactivated in neurosis and in psychoanalytic treatment but a past that *needed to be repudiated or overcome*. Religion itself—the cultural symbolic on whose loss or "past"-ness psychoanalysis was predicated—became for Freud the primary topos of the lost past, the very archetype of primitivity.

For Homans, the possibility of individuation begins with an alienation from one's traditional, religious "common culture." This alienation places one on the social margins, where mourning takes place and from which "analytic access"—an altered, critical relationship to the common, mainstream culture—can emerge. The arc of individuation moves from mourning the loss of a religious common culture toward "curiosity about the inner psychological world and . . . its social surround."[15] The work of mourning whose psychological effects were enshrined by Freud in classical psychoanalytic theory led to an even greater curiosity about "the inner psychological world and . . . its social surround" in the generations after Freud. In this regard, Homans points primarily to the British school of object relations that, under the influence of the losses resulting from both world wars, was further able to theorize the pre-oedipal, relational (i.e., social) processes of dependence and attachment.

Mourning and the Academic Study of Religion

Homans has traced a psychological trajectory similar to Freud's in the life and work of Max Weber, who, prior to embarking on the sociological writings for which he is now known, suffered a nervous breakdown. Weber, too, struggled with the loss of the (Protestant) faith that his mother had endeavored to instill in him. Homans sees Weber's recovery from this breakdown as linked to his increased capacity to differentiate himself from his mother and his concomitant writing of *The Protestant Ethic and the Spirit of Capitalism* as a reflection on the social and psychological structures of religious subjectivity that became evident to him through this differentiation.[16] This comparison between two intellectual titans, Freud and Weber, both founders of new disciplines during the same historical era, suggests that similar processes of religious loss and mourning may have been at play in the origins of two other closely intertwined disciplines that emerged around the same time, anthropology and the history of religions.

According to historians of nineteenth-century social thought, the struggle over the loss of religious faith was central for the founding generation of these two disciplines, among whom were such scholars as E. B. Tylor (appointed Oxford's first reader in anthropology in 1884) and Sir James Frazer (author of the monumental *Golden Bough*), both of whom were largely preoccupied with understanding the variety of religious customs and beliefs around the world, made available to European scholars thanks to Europe's colonizing adventures of the previous few centuries.[17] The historian of anthropology George W. Stocking Jr. writes that these late nineteenth-century theorists "grew up in religious homes" but felt the pressure of secularizing thought very strongly. "Belief was . . . critically problematic in their own lives, since they were losing it, along with the emotional security it had once provided."[18] The social changes of incipient industrialization and urbanization at home and imperialism abroad brought in their wake ever growing challenges to their religious beliefs. They too responded to these challenges and to their resulting disillusionment by creating new systems of thought with which to understand religion.

In particular, they applied the "comparative method," found in the works of French and Scottish intellectuals of the eighteenth century, to their understanding of religious and cultural variation. Their comparative method attempted to reconstruct the cultural history of humankind by ordering the vast array of information concerning the myths and religions of the world along an evolutionary scale. Placed within this evolutionary framework, cultural beliefs and practices such as myths and religions were indexed to biological inheritance, which in turn was ordered evolutionarily according to race, largely defined by skin color. The comparative method seemed to shore up the moral superiority of European civilization by placing Western civilization at its apex, as the culmination of the ethical and social progress toward which the evolutionary scale purportedly tended, while containing dark-skinned "primitive peoples" and the religious outlook that supposedly characterized them, at the bottom of the scale, safely in "the past."

The cultural evolutionism propounded by this early generation "offered intellectual balm for minds sorely anguished by philosophical and religious doubt."[19] Their theory building can be seen as analogous to the characterization of Freud's metapsychology by Homans: a precipitous break from a religious background, or in other words, a rapid de-idealization of religious values, resulting in the creation of a rigid theory in which religion was consigned to the primitive past.

Looking ahead, the changes wrought in the academic study of religion by subsequent midcentury generations of academic religionists can be seen as comparable to the characterization of certain key developments in the second and third generations of psychoanalysts by Homans. These analysts (predominantly in Britain) who moved away from the more scientific-sounding oedipal metapsychology and toward a more experiential approach to relationality and dependence were able to countenance religion, primitivity, and narcissism as elements from the past to be recuperated and valued rather than repudiated.

A similar trajectory can be seen in the study of religion by the scholars who initiated the annual Eranos seminars after World War II, inspired in no small degree by the psychology of C. G. Jung.[20] In the words of their chronicler, Steven Wasserstrom, the theoretical works of such scholars as Mircea Eliade, Henri Corbin, and Gershom Scholem comprised a "religion after religion." These scholars, all having rejected the specific religious cultures into which they had been born, promulgated a "history" or "phenomenology" of religions. In this approach, religions were to be understood as timeless, rather than part of a past that had been overcome, and thus still intelligible and pertinent for the contemporary modern age. For both sets of theorists, psychoanalytic and religionist, each writing in the mid-twentieth century, religion was no longer consigned to the past, although it remained in most cases "primitive": a romantic primitivism replacing evolutionism *tout court.*

The relationship between religion, secularization, and psychoanalysis drawn by Homans remains a compelling one, explaining why psychoanalysis is found almost exclusively in the urban metropolises of the West, and only to a small extent elsewhere, and then only in the elite, Westernized elements of the urban centers of certain non-Western countries. It illuminates the work of Freud and Weber and can be extended to theoretical treatments of religion as well. But recent developments, both social and theoretical, suggest a reconsideration of four of the key concepts in the theory of symbolic loss: secularization, common culture, primitivity, and mourning.

From Secularization to Globalization

It has become increasingly difficult to see secularization as an inevitable consequence of industrialization and modernization. Even in the United States, arguably the most industrialized of nations, religious activity has never waned as thoroughly as was predicted by theories of modernization: in the latter half of the twentieth century, religion played a leading role in the civil rights movement, has re-appeared in the form of mega-churches and televangelists, has diversified with the help of immigrant and diasporic communities, attempts to challenge scientific authority in the form of creationism, and has been effective politically to the point of making serious inroads into the separation of church and state.

If we shift the horizon of our concern from the processes of secularization in Europe to a consideration of the global scene, we bring into focus non-Western forms of religions that have not succumbed to secularization even as their host nations have modernized. By the predictions of secularization theory, modernizing nations should be well along in the process of religious decline; but, instead, we find a wide array of old and new forms of religious life: religious revivals as resistance to modernity; politicized religion allied with various forms of nationalism, sometimes violent; and religious revivals aimed at the enlivening of the virtuous life, both personal and communal.[21]

Significantly, the theory of modernization/secularization omits an entire class of social relations that helped to make all the other transformations to modernity possible. These social processes include the European colonization and economic exploitation of non-Western countries, the maltreatment and eradication of the Native peoples of the Americas, and the Atlantic slave trade. These "non-Western" upheavals were intimately related to Western developments, and they are antecedent to the economic arrangements that underlie the processes of globalization today.[22] The rise of industrialism and its concomitant forms of capitalism were assisted to a significant degree by resources and labor made available through the racialized processes of colonization and slavery.

To the degree that secularization is tied to the industrialization of the European West, it can be seen as an intellectual accompaniment to the social and economic changes underwritten by colonialism and slavery. The peoples conquered, colonized, or enslaved became the emblems of "primitivity," with their religious beliefs and practices often taken as the very essence of their primitivity, forming the contradistinction against which Euro-American society was able to define itself as modern and increasingly secular.[23]

This colonial dimension of the concept of primitivity generally goes unrecognized in most psychoanalytic theorizing, where primitivity is held to be a purely psychological state, synonymous with the infantile, immature, or narcissistic. But as was pointed out earlier, Freud's writings, as exemplified by his essay on group psychology, exhibit a constant slippage between "primitivity" as the earliest stage of a universally conceived psychological development and "primitivity" as a colonialist and essentialist term for the Euro-American racial/cultural other. The possibility that this slippage, so deeply embedded in Freud's thought, might continue on in contemporary psychoanalytic usage, even if largely unnoticed, suggests that we revisit the related categories of "primitivity" and "common culture" that are woven through the Homans model.

From Common Culture to Dominant Discourse

Homans contrasts contemporary, (post)modern society with "primitive and traditional" common cultures in which "society as a whole dominates the inner world of the individual."[24] His "common cultures" organize and coordinate social identities according to their religious "overarching symbolic[s]." Common cultures are primitive both on account of the psychology of their members and on account of their more homogenous social structures. But left out of this discussion of common cultures and their psychological and sociological primitivity is any reference to the racial coding and political valence of the construct of "primitivity," which a globalized framework brings to the fore.

Common cultures are those cultures where "the individual predominately defines himself and is defined by the rules and social representations of society which . . . have been imprinted upon him."[25] In this concept of common culture Homans brings together Freud's understanding of group psychology ("the rules . . . of society which . . . have been imprinted upon him"); Durkheim's conception of social solidarity (the social structure that obtained prior to the division of labor); and Lévi-Strauss's analysis of the "savage mind" (steeped in the synchrony of myth and impervious to the workings of history).

Common cultures are primitive, says Homans, in the double sense we find in Freud: their members have a "primitive" or rudimentary psychology or mentality, while the cultures are seen as historically (as in premodern Europe) or developmentally (as in the Third World) prior to the modern West. Moreover, these cultures are narcissistic because narcissism, in psychoanalysis, refers to the earliest processes of psychological functioning, which are presumed to characterize both the earliest stages of childhood development in the West and the psychological processes of adults in "primitive" or traditional cultures. In a manner analogous to Freud's conception of the emergence of the modern individual mind out of the primitivity of group psychology, the narrative of secularization and mourning by Homans traces a temporal sequence whereby the primitive synchrony of the shared mentality of common culture was replaced by the modern, historical diachrony of the secular, individualizing, psychologizing mind.

Importantly, Freud extended the anthropological view of his time by attributing primitivity to Westerners and non-Westerners alike; and Homans pleads for a "more generous" conception of primitivity. But this may not go far enough. If we read contemporary postcolonialist theorists, it is hard not to conclude that the psychoanalytic term "primitive" has been irreparably damaged by its intimate association with its social evolutionist twin, whose meaning cannot be disentangled from its colonial past, even in contexts that intend no such association.

Even if we were to excise the "non-Western" from our conception of the primitive, leaving only the pre-industrial West as the primitive precursor to modernity, a theory of mourning and creativity predicated on the loss of a common culture comes uncomfortably close to what has been called by Raymond Williams a "pastoral narrative": a narrative pattern that poses an idealized landscape of the past, or an age of rural harmony, unhappily superseded by the developments, economic and social, of a harsher urban life.[26] In psychoanalytic theory, the pastoral corresponds to the pre-oedipal stage, temporally prior to the development of our current, adult, historically minded lives. Within psychoanalytic theory, such a site of primitive/maternal origins has always been—problematically—correlated with certain populations who function as the abjected exemplars of those origins: namely, "primitives," "lower races," and women.

We are left, then, to find a way to describe a set of historical changes and to delineate their psychological ramifications without falling prey to interpretations that primitivize and thus, perhaps inadvertently, racialize the past. To make use of the theory of mourning and creativity by Homans in order to think about contemporary religious studies in the academy, we have to reconsider the temporal nature of the relationship between common culture, secularization, and mourning. How might we re-think these terms and still account psychoanalytically for the ways that historical changes take place and disrupt our lives, causing losses that are mourned, and provoking creative responses to those losses?

Homans has indicated the direction I would suggest by placing common cultures in relation to those people on the margins of society who have a critical relation to mainstream culture. This relation of center to margin replaces the temporal relationship between religion and secularization with a spatial one that suggests the possibility of the contemporaneousness of the two at any particular historical moment. From a spatialized perspective, "common culture" is equivalent to what can be called the "dominant discourse." In the sense introduced by Foucault, the term "discourse" refers to the networks and technologies of knowledge and power that organize the sociocultural field.[27] And "dominant discourse" refers to the networks of knowledge and power that provide the most prevalent and commonly available understanding of self and society, propagated by those in power and by the mainstream media, and uncritically accepted by a majority of the population.

The structures of discourse, like the prohibitions of civilization of which Freud wrote, precede us and determine the shape of our thoughts and feelings by providing us with the means with which we can represent them: they constitute us as speaking subjects. The normative subject is, in Foucault's terms, an effect of discourse or, as Homans has described the member of a common culture, someone who is "defined by the rules and social representations of society which . . . have been imprinted upon him." Thus "dominant discourse" retains the notion of a culture whose social representations fully define the subject, while removing such a concept from a temporal location exclusively in the past.

In addition, the term "discourse" alerts us to the political dimension of a common culture. Homans writes of analytic access as arising from the margins of the common culture, but the relationship between the margins and the center is not only spatial but also political. The center—or common culture or dominant discourse—is constituted as such by an active displacement to the margins of all those whose difference from it might disrupt its perceived homogeneity, harmony, or wholeness, and thus its legitimacy. Discourses are constituted within, and reconstitute in their subjects, these relations of power. Thus the term "dominant discourse" returns us to the political register embedded in the Mitscherlichs' account of the inability to mourn, and indeed, in Freud's account of the group psychology of the army and of the church.

For Freud, as for the Mitscherlichs and Hannah Arendt, the psychology ascribed to the group is a form of subjectivity that is an effect of the imposition of power. Although the shared nature of a common culture or group psychology may seem to be one of harmonious accord (as the Mitscherlichs describe the relationship between Hitler and his subjects), this accord is bought at the price of the acceptance of the imposition of an ongoing pre-oedipal, hypnoid-like relationship to the powers that be, with the concomitant repression of difference or its assignment to the margins of the culture. The paradox is that a common culture or dominant discourse requires difference in order to define itself.

Thus the idea put forth by Homans of "analytic access" generated in the margins corresponds to Foucault's "subjugated knowledges": forms of knowledge circulating and practiced by those who stand at a distance from, and in a subjugated relation to, mainstream culture—people thought to not "accede to the sphere of human possibility" or not to "count as human."[28] Those on the margins appropriate, analyze, and criticize the dominant discourse rather than seamlessly reproduce it, giving rise to trenchant critiques that often wind up creating new patterns within the dominant culture itself (as with Freud and psychoanalysis).

Although Homans perceives common cultures as primitive, it is those on the subjugated margins who have generally been constructed as primitive by dominant discourses: those who exemplify racial difference and non-normative practices of gender and sexuality. The Jewish culture of which Freud was a part was, for instance, construed as "primitive" in the German scientific and medical discourse of his time.[29] For his part, Freud saw the "perversions"—that is, the sexually non-normative—as narcissistic and primitive.[30] Thus, those identifying with the dominant discourse of modernism imagine those on the margins to be primitive. For those who believe they have acceded to "the present" or become "modern," as did Freud, the primitivity of the margins is necessarily placed "in the past."

From Primitivity to Vulnerability

From a psychological perspective, primitivity is held to represent those states prior to the ability to know oneself as a human being and to express oneself reflectively as such. But perhaps the critical psychological and nonracial dimensions of the term can be best captured by the notion of *vulnerability* as developed recently by Judith Butler.[31] Butler cuts the Gordian knot (as she has done in many other instances before[32]) between francophone psychoanalysis, which emphasizes the constitutive role of lack or loss in subjectivity, and anglophone psychoanalysis, which emphasizes the constitutive role of relationality. As Butler argues, since relatedness implies vulnerability to the possibility of loss, vulnerability is a fundamental component of all subjectivity. We can become emotionally "undone" in love by those for whom we care the most, and physically "undone" in violence by those who have the power to act on their hatred: "we are not only constituted by our relations but also dispossessed by them as well." Becoming "undone" is a radical possibility at any moment, "a point of identification with suffering itself."[33] Our vulnerability to harm, loss, and grief is fundamental to subjectivity itself, in an ongoing manner not restricted to the past. Tellingly, Butler here writes in the first person plural, from within the position she describes rather than from outside of it.

Asserting our vulnerability to both love and terror captures an omnipresent aspect of human relationships. Like primitivity, vulnerability marks the earliest stages of our physical and psychic life, and like primitivity, it can be brought to the fore by terror and violence. But unlike primitivity, vulnerability cannot be limited to specific stages of development nor to specific groups of people characterized by their skin color, sexual preference, or religious beliefs. Rather, "primitivity" is a vulnerability over which victory has been proclaimed, while vulnerability is primitivity seen from its own vantage point. We are always "vulnerab[le] to a sudden address from elsewhere that we cannot preempt."[34]

If vulnerability cannot be placed safely in the past nor overcome once and for all, then its passing cannot be "successfully" mourned. Moreover, if there is no "primitive" common culture that has been lost and subsequently mourned, but only a dominant discourse in tension with subjugated discourses of the vulnerable and the marginalized, then how does the Mitscherlich-Homans model apply to the academic study of religion?

From Mourning to Melancholia

I suggest that the shift of perspective from primitivity to vulnerability is marked by a shift from mourning to melancholia. If vulnerability to loss cannot be overcome, then the grief occasioned by loss is never fully resolved; this produces the condition that Freud referred to as melancholia.[35] In his famous essay of 1915, Freud paired mourning and melancholy, making the distinction between mourning as a response to grief in which the bonds of attachment to lost objects eventually fade so that new bonds may be forged; and melancholy as an unfinished, incomplete response to grief, without ending or resolution. Mourning eventuates in the withdrawal of libido from the lost object and its transmutation into new psychic structure; it presumes both a loss and an overcoming of that loss. Melancholia, on the other hand, is an unending grief that preserves rather than transmutes the object of loss. Mourning and melancholia presume two different temporal structures: with successful mourning, the lost object is securely in the past; with melancholia, the object continues to haunt the psyche: "the past remains steadfastly alive in the present."[36]

Although Freud posited melancholia as a form of failed mourning, recent discussions of loss have taken up melancholia as a more encompassing recognition of the ways in which the past stays with us, suggesting that "closure" and "successful" mourning by and large elude us. As Butler has written, "The presumptions that the future follows the past, that mourning might follow melancholia, that mourning might be completed are all poignantly called into question."[37] Theorists such as Anne Cheng and David Eng have written of the melancholia of race, whereby unattainable ideals of whiteness held by American mainstream culture are never fully overcome but continue to haunt both white and nonwhite American subjects.[38] "On the one side, white American identity and its authority is secured through the melancholic introjection of racial others that it can neither fully relinquish nor accommodate. . . . On the other side, the racial other['s] . . . identity is imaginatively reinforced through the introjection of a lost, never-possible perfection, an inarticulable loss that comes to inform the individual's sense of his or her own subjectivity."[39]

In the same way, religions represent various idealized representations of the possibility of humanity's relationship to divinity. As Homans points out, even Freud indicated, in his final and posthumously published *Moses and Monotheism,* that a "total break" with the religious past was not entirely possible. Academic theorists and theories of religion have not superseded the religious traditions they explicate; they do their work on the margins of the dominant religious discourses, existing at the same time as the religious traditions they examine.

Over and above the anthropological and sociological evidence that testifies to the enduring nature of religious activity, we also find a "turn to religion" in the heart of the academy, a process exemplified in the continental philosophies of Derrida and Levinas, two writers who continue to wield considerable influence in the American humanities; among certain psychoanalytic feminists such as Luce Irigaray who, in their attempts to fashion a nonpatriarchal psychoanalysis, have improvised feminist figurations of the sacred; and in the work of psychoanalytically influenced writers such as Eric Santner, who recuperates a theological impulse at the heart of Freudian psychoanalysis, a theory that has long been thought to be structurally founded on a critique and even disdain for religion.[40]

In his discussion of these recent developments within the discipline of philosophy, Hent de Vries suggests that what we find here is not a "return" or a "remaining" in the past but rather a recovery of "an irreducible 'interconnectedness' of 'religious belief' and the 'sacrosanct,' on the one hand, and 'knowledge,' 'technoscience,' and 'calculation' on the other." Such an interconnectedness was, of course, established by Max Weber in his famous work on Protestant-ism and capitalism; it is attested to in a somewhat different vein by the work of Homans as well.

As de Vries points out, the "adieu" to religion that has charac-terized Western rational thought ever since the Enlightenment is a fundamentally ambiguous gesture.[41] "Adieu" means "goodbye," but it also means "to God," (à Dieu), wishing the departed a renewed encompassment within the divine, as does the English "God be with you" of which "Goodbye" is a contraction. The gesture of saying goodbye to the sacred simultaneously commends us to its care. It is not surprising that Derrida's deconstruction, which has all along been bent on demonstrating the inadequacy of the antimonies that undergird Western thought, should apply its force to the antimony of religion/critique and sacred/profane, on which the critical social sciences, and psychoanalysis in particular, have built. This retrieval of the religious within the language of its critique is not simply a retrieval of an unambiguously positive theological moment, how-ever, but simultaneously a recognition of religion's "always possible relationship to evil and the worst violence."[42]

Like its "primitive" twin, race, religion haunts the very identities that are built upon its purported loss. If we think it primitive, we believe we have overcome and mourned it, and that our theories rep-resent our mastery over it. But if religion is a way of expressing a vul-nerable relationship to something that exceeds the human capacity to represent or figure it, then we as scholars of religion, irrespective of our personal beliefs, can still recognize our melancholic relation-ship with the subjects of our study.

Notes

I would like to thank the Martin Marty Center of the Divinity School of the University of Chicago for helping to support the writing of this essay, and I also thank Susan S. Gooding, Susan E. Henking, Maureen N. McLane, and Winnifred Fallers Sullivan for their readings and suggestions.

1. Peter Homans, *The Ability to Mourn: Disillusionment and the Social Origins of Psychoanalysis* (Chicago: University of Chicago Press, 1989); Homans, in-troduction to and "Loss and Mourning in the Life and Thought of Max Weber: Toward a Theory of Symbolic Loss," in *Symbolic Loss: The Ambiguity of Mourning and Memory at Century's End*, ed. Peter Homans (Charlottesville: University Press of Virginia, 2000).

2. Alexander and Margarete Mitscherlich, *The Inability to Mourn: Principles of Collective Behavior*, trans. Beverley R. Placzek (New York: Grove Press, 1975/1967).

3. While the Mitscherlichs address themselves strictly to the German postwar sit-uation, Robert Jay Lifton's preface to the 1975 English-language edition draws

parallels to the Vietnam War and the American post-Vietnam period. Within Western academic discourse, the theoretical turn to postmodernism has been saturated with what Eric Santner has called the "rhetoric of mourning," an emphasis on loss aimed at addressing what are seen, in effect, as the effects of a narcissism central to the Western philosophic tradition as a whole, of which the Holocaust is taken to have been a culmination. See Eric Santner, *Stranded Objects: Mourning, Memory and Film in Postwar Germany* (Ithaca, NY: Cornell University Press, 1990), esp. ch. 1, "Postwar/Post-Holocaust/Postmodern: Some Reflections on the Discourses of Mourning," 1–30.

4. Unless otherwise noted, references to the work of Sigmund Freud are from *The Standard Edition of the Complete Psychological Works of Sigmund Freud*, trans. and ed. James Strachey (London: Hogarth Press, 24 vols., 1966–1974). Freud, "Group Psychology and the Analysis of the Ego," *Standard Edition*, 18: 69–143 (first published 1921).

5. Mitscherlich and Mitscherlich, *Inability to Mourn*, 22; Emile Durkheim, *The Elementary Forms of the Religious Life*, trans. by Joseph Ward Stain (New York: Free Press, 1965), e.g., 250, 258, 269.

6. Hannah Arendt, *The Origins of Totalitarianism* (San Diego, CA: Harcourt Brace, 1979/1948).

7. Ibid., 322, 325.

8. Celia Brickman, *Aboriginal Populations in the Mind: Race and Primitivity in Psychoanalysis* (New York: Columbia University Press, 2003), esp. ch. 3.

9. See George W. Stocking Jr., "The Dark-Skinned Savage: The Image of Primitive Man in Evolutionary Anthropology (1968)," reprinted in Stocking, *Race, Culture and Evolution: Essays in the History of Anthropology* (Chicago: University of Chicago Press, 1982), 110–33.

10. Giorgio Agamben, *Homo Sacer: Sovereign Power and Bare Life*, trans. Daniel Heller-Roazen (Stanford, CA: Stanford University Press, 1998); Rey Chow, *The Protestant Ethnic and the Spirit of Capitalism* (New York: Columbia University Press, 2002). See also Seyla Benhabib, *The Rights of Others: Aliens, Residents and Citizens* (Cambridge: Cambridge University Press, 2004).

11. Agamben, *Bare Life*, 8.

12. Chow, *Protestant Ethnic*, 39.

13. Freud, "The Ego and the Id," *Standard Edition*, 20: 29, 48 (first published 1923).

14. Homans, *Ability to Mourn*, 113, 185.

15. Ibid., 314.

16. This is a very simplified rendering of a complex argument that can be found in Homans, *Ability to Mourn*, 231–50, and "Loss and Mourning," 225–38.

17. George W. Stocking Jr., *Victorian Anthropology* (New York: Free Press, 1987), esp. 144–237; J. W. Burrow, *Evolution and Society: A Study in Victorian Social Theory* (London: Cambridge University Press, 1966), 93–98; Robert Ackerman, *J. G. Frazer: His Life and Work* (Cambridge: Cambridge University Press, 1987), 33.

18. Stocking, *Victorian Anthropology*, 190, 196.

19. Ibid., 187.

20. Steven M. Wasserstrom, *Religion after Religion: Gershom Scholem, Mircea Eliade, and Henry Corbin at Eranos* (Princeton, NJ: Princeton University Press, 1999).

21. The contemporary anthropological and sociological evidence can still be explained within a certain expanded version of secularization theory, one that posits that only those who are not the beneficiaries of the fruits of modernization/development console or avenge themselves for this lack through renewed religious activity.

22. For the centrality of the slave trade to the development of the American economy, see David Brion Davis, *Inhuman Bondage: The Rise and Fall of Slavery*

in the New World (New York: Oxford University Press, 2006); and for the contribution made by the profits of slavery to the rise of English industrialization, see Robin Blackburn, *The Making of New World Slavery: From the Baroque to the Modern, 1492–1800* (London: Verso, 1997).

23. On primitivity see, for instance, E. B. Tylor, *Primitive Culture: Researches into the Development of Mythology, Philosophy, Religion, Art, and Custom,* 2 vols. (London: J. Murray, 1871). For an excellent introduction to the role of epistemological violence in the distortion of human possibility, subjectivity, and governance in Africa, see Achille Mbembé, "On *Commandement*" in his *On the Postcolony* (Berkeley: University of California Press, 2001; first published as *Notes provisoires sur la postcolonie*), 28.

24. Homans, *Ability to Mourn,* 5.

25. Ibid.

26. In his *Stranded Objects,* Eric Santner brings together Raymond Williams's analysis of the pastoral in *The Country and the City* (New York: Oxford University Press, 1973) with James Clifford's critique of anthropology's "salvage paradigm" in his "Of Other Peoples: Beyond the 'Salvage' Paradigm," in *Discussions in Contemporary Culture,* ed. Hal Foster (Seattle: Bay Press, 1987), 87. See *Stranded Objects,* 85–86, 180.

27. Michel Foucault, "The Unities of Discourse," in *The Archaeology of Knowledge and the Discourse on Language,* trans. A. M. Sheridan Smith (New York: Barnes and Noble, 1993), 21–30.

28. Mbembé, *On the Postcolony,* 28; Judith Butler, *Precarious Life: The Powers of Mourning and Violence* (London: Verso, 2004), 20.

29. See, for example, Sander L. Gilman, *The Case of Sigmund Freud: Medicine and Identity at the Fin de Siècle* (Baltimore: Johns Hopkins University Press, 1993).

30. Sigmund Freud, "Three Essays on the Theory of Sexuality," *Standard Edition,* 7: 135–43, 146 (first published 1905).

31. Butler, *Precarious Life.*

32. Butler's work has been notable for, among other things, forging new paths amid theorists or theories otherwise at odds with each other. For example, she has rethought questions of sexuality and gender using both psychoanalysis and Michel Foucault, whose *History of Sexuality* presents a trenchant critique of "the repressive hypothesis" on which psychoanalysis is built; and her theory of performative iteration provided a way out of the contentious but unproductive quarrel between essentialism and constructivism in the question of gender identity.

33. Butler, *Precarious Life,* 23–24, 28, 30.

34. Ibid., 29.

35. See, e.g., David L. Eng and David Kazanjian, eds., *Loss: The Politics of Mourning* (Berkeley; University of California Press, 2003); Anne Anlin Cheng, *The Melancholy of Race: Psychoanalysis, Assimilation and Hidden Grief* (Oxford: Oxford University Press, 2001).

36. David L. Eng and David Kazanjian, "Introduction: Mourning Remains," in Eng and Kazanjian, *Loss,* 3.

37. Judith Butler, afterword in Eng and Kazanjian, *Loss,* 467.

38. Cheng, *Melancholy of Race;* David L. Eng, *Racial Castration: Managing Masculinity in Asian America* (Durham, NC: Duke University Press, 2001).

39. Cheng, *Melancholy of Race,* xi.

40. Eric Santner, *On the Psychotheology of Everyday Life: Reflections on Freud and Rosenzweig* (Chicago: University of Chicago Press, 2001).

41. Hent de Vries, *Philosophy and the Turn to Religion* (Baltimore: Johns Hopkins University Press, 1999), x, 24, 26, 435.

42. Ibid., 19.

WILLIAM B. PARSONS

Mourning and Method in Psychoanalytic Studies of Indian Religions

IN THE preface to his psychobiography of Ramakrishna, Narasingha Sil turns Freud's analytic attitude back on himself in relating how it is that his own methodological preferences evolved biographically.[1] We learn that he was socialized into the rituals and narratives of Hinduism as a child, that the tales of the saints captured his adolescent imagination, and that the illusions of hagiography were more important and meaningful than historical fact. However, the transition from adolescence to adulthood was marked, he tells us, "by a growing detachment—worse, disenchantment—with prophets and Godmen" (6). This disillusionment was fueled by his academic training, which led him "to discount the realm of the magic, miracle, and anagogic" (5). He came to appreciate the value of sober, objective analysis and, specifically with respect to unearthing the secrets of Ramakrishna, became a convert to psychoanalytic method. Sil understands that his project "will not be taken kindly" by believers (5). In speaking to those who may find what is clearly a reductive project offensive, Sil calls on Freud, who, in his psychobiographical study of da Vinci, noted that his aim was not to "drag the sublime into the dust," but rather to show how even great men are subject to the psychoanalytic laws that govern the mind (6). It is imperative, Sil continues, to speak honestly, freely, and fearlessly. Indeed, in recalling his adolescence and tendencies toward "jejune fascination," Sil bluntly chastises those still fixated: "I find a naïve enchantment with the exotic Eastern mystics . . . as frankly obscene" (6).

Sil's example is instructive in a number of ways. Psychoanalytically speaking, his early allegiance to Hinduism engaged the narcissistic sector of his personality, there to help fashion an emerging sense of identity. These early idealizations and identifications were then de-idealized, leading to a change in his relationship to Hinduism. Such a change can take numerous forms, depending on the individual and the nature and degree of de-idealization, including a complete abandonment of faith or a more sophisticated appreciation of it, as is so well captured by Ricoeur's term "second naiveté." In Sil's case the change was closer to the former, and it was fueled through the auspices of the university. Indeed, one can speak of the university, and by definition a Department of Religious Studies, as institutionalized places of mourning. To a discernable degree this social space, as Sil found, encourages the gradual detachment from the Tillichian object of ultimate concern. As Peter Homans observes, religious intellectuals are committed to an objective, critical study of religious phenomena (*Religionwissenschaft*). This requires a bracketing of one's religious convictions. To be deprived of this "lavishing" is "to undergo an experience of loss, and this in turn generates an injunction to mourn."[2] In this regard it is relevant to note that Sil quotes with approval Trevelyan's claim, made in 1923, that "no Hindu who has received an English education ever remains sincerely attached to his religion."[3]

Sil's disillusionment was similarly fueled by the clinic. This is so because an analysand, once inside the "double-doors" of the psychoanalytic session, enters into a liminal space. Through free association and related techniques, the analysand becomes detached from the repressive power of the cultural super-ego, there enjoined to mourn valued personal and cultural objects. Applied psychoanalysis, derived from clinical insight, is a theory about mourning and its psychological mechanisms. By adopting psychoanalysis as a preferred method, then selecting those models within the broad expanse of metapsychological theory that seemed appropriate to the task at hand, Sil was both expressing and working through his disillusionment with and mourning of his native Hindu tradition. This is so because applied psychoanalysis asks that one become what Kohut calls "experience-distant" with respect to the identifications and idealizations that bond one to the ideals and values of one's personal and cultural past. Psychoanalysis was a tool, so to speak, that Sil utilized to facilitate his ongoing process of disillusionment and attempt to creatively respond to the loss of his religious past.[4]

Sil's example is instructive in yet another way. While early psychoanalytic studies of Eastern religions were few and far between, the last two decades have seen an explosion of interest in this area. More importantly, the link between mourning and method apparent in Sil is equally visible in many of these theorists. To demonstrate this, and to add further nuance to the pattern we see emerging in Sil, we look at three influential scholars who have used psychoanalysis to analyze Eastern religious figures and ideation. In each we endeavor to establish the existence of mourning and how that process engaged religion and the turn to psychoanalytic method. These theorists, while not "originative" theorists such as Freud or Jung, nevertheless creatively responded to their loss by expanding psychoanalytic theory. We will, then, be alert to how individual vicissitudes in the process of mourning can be linked to these diverse applications of method.

The Guru and the Apostate

Jeffrey Masson is undoubtedly best known for his ascendancy to the esteemed position of director of the Freud Archives, the controversy that ensued over his comments concerning Freud's seduction theory, and his eventual excommunication from the ranks of the psychoanalytic elite.[5] This biographical narrative, however, has obscured previous incarnations: his early tutelage under the "guru" Paul Brunton, a Harvard doctorate centered around the study of Sanskrit and Indian religions, and a long bibliography of published works on psychoanalysis and religion. Moreover, in the case of Masson, an application of the mourning thesis is hardly a matter of guesswork. He all but tells us directly in an autobiographical text aptly entitled *My Father's Guru: A Journey through Spirituality and Disillusion.* In that autobiographical reflection one finds all the elements of mourning: the psychological mechanisms of idealization and identification and the formation of narcissistic structures through merger with the Other and specific ideals/values, followed by loss, disappointment, disillusionment, feelings of abandonment, and narcissistic rage. It is further to our benefit that Masson makes clear how the mourning process led him directly to psychoanalysis and a creative response to his feelings of loss.

Though Masson was born into a Jewish family, his upbringing was nevertheless deeply influenced by Eastern religions. As a boy he frequented the local Hindu temple presided over by Swami Prabhavananda, took solace in the protective power of Sanskrit mantras, and became fully conversant in the relevant nomenclature: "We talked about reincarnation and past lives the way other families discuss Super Bowl Sunday."[6] This climate was due principally to his father, Jacques Victor Masson, an earnest spiritual seeker taken with the East, gurus, and the occult. Jeffrey's world was forever changed when Jacques invited Paul Brunton to be their residential guru. A short, frail Englishman, Brunton had been a disciple of Sri Ramana Maharshi, was the author of many popular books on mysticism and spirituality, and was hailed by the Masson family as a "living master" (x).

Brunton behaved much like the stereotypical guru. He claimed to have paranormal powers and knowledge of past lives, and he demanded allegiance and attention to practices (celibacy, meditation, purification). He also held a set of other, more idiosyncratic views: that he came from another planet, that apes were descended from humans, and that the Holocaust was a divine punishment (112).[7] Most important for our consideration is how Brunton, by sharing knowledge of their past lives together and details of life on other planets, elicited Jeffrey's idealization and fueled his adolescent narcissistic fantasies. By the age of thirteen, Masson relates that Brunton's books were his "constant companions," providing "fantasies of far-off places and mysterious mystic powers" (xi). Masson became convinced that Brunton was a "General" in a spiritual army and that he was "his young but valiant aide-de-camp" (xi). Brunton told Jacques that Jeffrey was destined to become a spiritual leader. In turn, his parents began to think of him as "a kind of Jiddhu Krishnamurti destined to play a leading role in the spiritual life of mankind" (106). Indeed, Brunton made the entire family feel "special, unique, and extremely privileged" (11).

Like Sil, then, Masson's early conception of self was inexorably intertwined with values and concepts linked to Eastern religious worldviews. He idealized them, identified with them, and was nourished by them through Brunton and a supportive family environment. Slowly but surely, however, these early idealizations began to wane. The precipitating event in this regard was Brunton's prediction, relayed to Jaques as early as 1956, that a third world war would take place in the near future. At a critical juncture he advised the Masson family to move to South America to avoid the brunt of nuclear fallout. Taking his advice, the Massons moved to Uruguay in 1959 (Jeffrey being eighteen) with the expectation that Brunton would eventually join them. He never did. Instead, he moved to New Zealand, the rationale (revealed only many years later by his son) being that his allotted spiritual task, which consisted in influencing Mao and the communists through meditation, would be enabled by being in closer geographical proximity to China. As Masson notes, in the absence of war and a deserved explanation for his no-show, Brunton's disciples felt "abandoned" and "even tricked": it was "a permanent and transformative disappointment. Nothing would ever be quite the same" (142–43). As for Jeffrey, although his "illusions were falling fast," he still held out for the wisdom of India: "Even if P.B. was not the right guru for me, gurus as such, and . . . Indian Philosophy—were my life. I wanted to study Sanskrit" (150). And so he did—at Harvard.

In a chapter entitled "Harvard and Disillusion," Masson related the impact his studies had on his previous conception of Indian religions. His understanding of Sanskrit, as mediated by Brunton and those with whom he "sent" Masson to study (notably Judith Tyberg, a "professor" of Sanskrit and Eastern religions at Theosophical University in Point Loma, California), was that it was essentially spiritual, that it consisted entirely of mantras, and that it was not to be read or spoken but chanted. At Harvard he was surprised to learn that it was an inflected language complete with cases (genitive, dative, etc.) and that it could be studied without the guidance of a spiritual guru. Similarly, through reading the works of scholars such as the Indologist Louis Renou and Buddologist Etienne Lamotte, he began to understand the true complexity and nuances that characterized Indian religions. As Masson relates, "I was beginning to know something. And I was beginning to recognize when somebody else did not" (157). And among those "somebodies" stood Paul Brunton: "The more I learned about India, the more I realized how little P.B. actually knew. This began to enrage me. I felt that I had been taken in, duped . . . he was just a hodgepodge of misread and misunderstood ideas . . . he was a phony, a charlatan, a mounteback, an imposter, a quack. I couldn't find enough words to describe my disappointment" (160).

A third phase of Masson's path of disillusionment was ushered in when he discovered psychoanalysis. In a "personal note" in the preface of his book *The Oceanic Feeling*, Masson confirms how his studies at Harvard demystified his early socialization to Indian philosophy. He then goes on to relate how, after writing several scholarly works on Indian texts, he was still troubled by the sheer amount of bizarre material found therein. It was reading psychoanalysts such as Freud, Glover, Fenichel, and others that led him to undergo a full clinical training (including a personal analysis), which, in returning to Indian texts, gave him the ammunition to decipher the tales of Eastern religions he found so troubling. "I now returned to Indian studies," he writes, "my enthusiasm rekindled by a new perspective."[8]

This new perspective certainly aided Masson in coming to grips with his bankrupt relationship with Brunton. He speaks throughout

My Father's Guru of his "transference" to Brunton, how the belief in life on other planets is but a version of the "family romance," of the "fixation" that developed with regard to sexuality and secrecy. But it was also utilized in several books and articles to decipher the true psychological meaning of the religious ideation that had so captured his imagination as an adolescent seeker. What is particularly curious is the precise nature of the hermeneutic Masson chooses to employ. Even a cursory glance at his work reveals that it is indebted to the tradition of the most pejorative of psychoanalytic works on religion. Like Sil, Masson can be branded as a classic reductionist. Masson follows in the footsteps of psychoanalytic predecessors such as Freud, Roheim, and Jones in proclaiming a psychoanalytic universalism that eschews the kind of meaningful dialogue with other social sciences that would allow space for culture to play a definitive role in the hermeneutical enterprise. Masson has no need for ethnographic meditation or thick description. What constitutes a wink, much less a perversion, is readily ascertained. It would never occur to Masson to see Freud as a psychologically gifted ethnographer or psychoanalytic metapsychology as an ethnoscience that, when applied cross-culturally, harbors a form of Orientalism that reflects the norms and values of Western society. This reductionistic universalism, then, holds that no religion harbors ontological truths. Indeed, only those truths perceived by the rational intellect and empirical method are allowable. The primarily mystical assumptions of Eastern religions are a priori negated, being traceable to the vicissitudes of development and conflict between the structural elements of the psyche, there to be diagnosed as pathological.

Thus it is that Masson can confidently state that Vedanta philosophy, with its emphasis on the world as illusion, can only signify derealization, depersonalization, and aggressive annihilation fantasies. The Tantric emphasis on celibacy, watching one's breath, and quieting the mind betrays an inability to work through the dangerous possibilities inherent in sexual excitement. The ascetic diet can be explained with recourse to anorexia nervosa. The narrative of Krishna's encounter with the hunchback indicates oedipal issues and castration anxiety. An analysis of Buddha's four noble truths reveal that he was deeply depressed. Abandoned by loved ones as a child and engaged in introspective meditative activity to find the root of suffering, the Buddha proclaimed the cure of nirvana—a cure that indicates a manic defense against the emergence of severe trauma. Ramakrishna was a pervert whose *sadhanas* reflect gender confusion, infantilism, and autoeroticism. Indeed for Masson,

Ramakrishna is a "happy" pervert only because the pathology inherent in his religio-cultural surround countenanced, if not encouraged, his bizarre behavior.[9]

For Masson, then, it is not simply the case that there is a direct link between mourning and method. What is of further interest is the "type" of psychoanalysis he chooses to employ. Despite the fact that in the past century the psychoanalytic study of religion has developed interpretative models sympathetic to religion, Masson chooses to ignore all of them. Masson's psychoanalytic hermeneutic seeks to diagnose all Indian religions as indicative of personal and cultural pathology. Set in biographical context, this is not surprising; it indicates that Masson's de-idealization of Eastern religions (and gurus) was massive and total and ignited narcissistic rage.

In a fitting afterword to *My Father's Guru*, Masson, reflecting as a mature man of fifty-one years of age on his relationship with P.B., speaks of a degree of "nostalgia, even melancholy. The world was never again to seem so charged, so filled with mystery. . . . I wish it were all true. I wish P.B. had been the person we all thought he was."[10] At the same time, keeping in mind how Brunton held his family in emotional bondage, Masson insists that one important underlying reason for writing the book is to drive home the point that one should never live life "in subjugation to the will of any other human being."[11] It is with a certain psychoanalytic irony, then, that Masson admits he now lives in New Zealand—"just minutes away" from where P.B. lived after he exiled the Masson family to Uruguay.

Indian Second Naïveté

Like Masson, Sudhir Kakar is a trained psychoanalyst who has written multiple books and essays on Indian culture and religion. However, while Masson gives the impression of having had quite enough of things Indian, Kakar defends India and its culture in a way Masson never would (or has). Kakar does not offer us a formal spiritual autobiography on a par with *My Father's Guru*. Nevertheless, his works are littered with autobiographical reflections that, seen in the context of his psychoanalytic innovations, imply a direct link between mourning and method.

Kakar's fondness for India and Hinduism is readily evident. He speaks of how Ayurvedic medicine is behind his use of a tongue scraper, of his superstition that the twig from the neem tree "does infinitely more than just clean the teeth," and of a "passionate extolling" and "deep and persistent undercurrent of nostalgia, almost sensual in character, for the insights, smells, tastes, sounds" of India.[12] We also know that he did his academic and clinical training in Europe and America (which he refers to as a "self-chosen exile"), where he learned to critically distance himself (what he calls a "violent rejection") from his Indian past. It is the internalization in Kakar of two cultures, the "modern" West and "traditional" India, that gave rise to what he calls a personal "battleground," one in which he tried to bring together "the Indian 'background' and the Western 'foreground' onto a single canvas."[13]

The process of mourning evident in the above is a persistent mood that marks Kakar's work. As Homans has rightly observed, Kakar's books "display unmistakable tones of genuine sadness and disappointment. In places they are noticeably and deliberately elegiac."[14] In his first "breakthrough" work, *The Inner World*, Kakar confesses that his is not simply a professional work but "is also related to personal needs . . . a return to and into a personal past, a reconnaissance of my own origins" (12). The insights gleaned during the course of research had "a therapeutic effect insofar as they have clarified and engaged the deeply Indian parts of myself" (13). What is of further interest is how Kakar frames this process of mourning. As noted above, Kakar allies himself with the agenda of the academy and the clinic. But going one step further, Kakar locates himself in the tradition of the "Indian intellectual," characterized as "an intellectual tradition more than a hundred years old, starting with Ram Mohan Roy (1774–1833), a tradition devoted to the vicissitudes of Indian identity in modern times" (13). Kakar shares with us his deep identification with Nehru, another member of this tradition, who made it part of his life task to capture not simply the geographical, physical, and diverse cultural strands of India, but that "peculiar spirit" and "identity" that mark India as unique (13).

Kakar's membership in Western academia, the clinic, and the "tradition" of the modern Indian intellectual reveals the source of his nostalgia for ("passionate extolling") and his repudiation ("violent rejection") of Indian culture. The mourning ("battleground") engendered in his inner world by academia and the clinic led him to adopt an intermediate position, that of the Indian intellectual who strives, using the terminology and methodology created in the West, to not simply repudiate, analyze, and dissect but also to assimilate and resurrect the unique wisdom of India and its culture. Given this, it is both relevant and understandable that the pervading postmodern theme of his works lies in denying the (culturally mandated) discovery of an absolute truth, walking the fine line between psychological universalism and cultural relativism, and respecting different (and equal) visions of reality, mental health, gender identity, and selfhood.

One finds this "intermediate position" reflected in Kakar's creative expansion and application of a culturally sensitive psychoanalytic metapsychology. Contra Masson, Kakar is particularly fond of ego-psychology and object-relations theory as found in Erikson, Kohut, and Winnicott, all of whom rejected Freud's myopic, pejorative evaluation of religion. Indeed, while Freud had at best an ambivalent relationship to his Jewish past, Erikson was a committed Episcopalian, Winnicott a "mystic" of psychoanalysis (as Kakar refers to him[15]), and Kohut an advocate of an unchurched mysticism, evident in his idealized portrait of Dag Hammarskjold, former secretary-general of the United Nations, as an "instance" of a heroic man "of constructive political action" who had achieved "a transformation" of archaic structures of narcissism into "a contentless, inspiring personal religion."[16]

Kakar is also aware of the tendency of cross-cultural applied psychoanalysis to be marred by unarticulated value judgments and hidden developmental norms. Kakar rejects psychoanalytic theorists who have analyzed Eastern cultures, such as Roheim and Devereux, on just such grounds. "Cultural judgments," writes Kakar "about psychological maturity, the nature of reality, 'positive' and 'negative' resolutions of conflicts and complexes often appear in the garb of psychoanalytic universals."[17] Kakar insists that all attempts at cross-cultural analysis must be qualified by taking into account new information gleaned through specifically Indian case history material and relevant ethnographic observations (e.g., the conceptual import of Geertz's "thick description" and Marriott's notion of the "-dividual"). Kakar, then, not only champions the use of "adaptive" psychoanalytic theories of religion; he literally extends their cross-cultural applicability by creating, through his case histories and inclusion of relevant ethnographic detail, a new form of culturally sensitive metapsychology.

It is not surprising, then, that Kakar chastises Masson for utilizing reductive psychoanalytic models and practicing a form of psychological Orientalism. For Kakar, Masson's work "must be of special interest to an Indian psychoanalyst . . . [for it] can only lend credence to the position of an increasing number of third-world intellectuals who maintain that the western sciences of man, including psychoanalysis, are in fact culture-bound ethnosciences whose claim to universality is both based upon and is an aspect of the global political and economic domination by the West."[18]

Indeed, the analysis and evaluation of the diverse aspects of Indian religious phenomena found in Kakar's work differ in every respect from that of Masson. For example, Vedanta philosophy, far from indicating pathology and regressive states, often reveals a transformation of narcissistic structures approximating Kohut's psycho-religious goal of "cosmic narcissism" and Winnicott's goal of a subjectivity imbued with the delight of creative apperception.[19] Buddha's proclamation of *dukkha* does not mean he is "depressed but in perfect attunement with the reality principle."[20] While a cursory overview of Ramakrishna may exhibit the behavior and symptoms of homosexuality and psychopathology, Kakar insists that when seen in cultural context, Ramakrishna's visionary activity is, like that of the artist, a transitional form of experience that engages the "unknowable ground of creativeness as such"; his sexuality and seeming gender confusion are part and parcel of a *bhakti* path to God that develops the "pure female element" and advocates "being" and "receptive absorption" over "doing" and "active opposition."[21] Likewise, the immobilization of seminal fluid found in Tantra, far from indicating fears about sexuality and death, is expressive of a part of a lifestyle whose aim is to realize a culturally specific adaptation to reality that includes androgyny and "focused receptivity," defined as a permanent form of psychological transformation centered around a receptive, empathic attunement with the flow of everyday events.[22] In other words, the methodological variations apparent in Kakar and Masson are everything one would expect given how the vicissitudes of the mourning process led one to become a disillusioned apostate, the other an Indian intellectual.

Visions, Dreams, Method

In 1995 there appeared a psychobiography bearing the title *Kali's Child: The Mystical and the Erotic in the Life and Teachings of Ramakrishna*. The author, Jeffrey J. Kripal, subsequently became the focus of both lavish praise (the book won a prestigious national award) and considerable controversy (the book was considered a scandal by believers; the Indian government debated banning it). The cause of this discord was the book's central thesis: that Ramakrishna was a Tantric practitioner whose visions were fueled by unconscious homoerotic desire. Kripal found evidence for his thesis everywhere: in biographical texts, in Ramakrishna's practices, in his relationships with his boy disciples, and in the mystical imagery and symbolism of his teachings. The central thesis gave way to the central problem of the book: how to expose the homoerotic dimension of Ramakrishna's religiosity while simultaneously legitimating the ontological ground of his mystical visions. It was this seeming paradox, of bringing together sexuality and mysticism, that was for Kripal both a scholarly knot and a deeply personal crisis. Appropriately, the solution came in the form of a series of methodological formulations produced through the process of mourning.[23]

Turning first to methodological formulation, Kripal's initial task consists in restoring the "text." Whereas most interpreters portray Ramakrishna as championing a neo-Advaitan form of spirituality, Kripal sees in him the eroticism of Tantra. So Kripal unearths what he refers to as Ramakrishna's "secret talk": highly erotic accounts of mystical practices and visions found in the original Bengali texts but absent from bowdlerized translations. Along the way, Kripal inserts his central comparativist claim: Ramakrishna rejected the nondualism of Advaita Vedanta in favor of a Tantric worldview. The text reinstated, Kripal articulates the relation between sexuality, mysticism, and significant others in Ramakrishna's life and thought. Building on reductive psychoanalytic theorists, including Masson, Kripal interprets some aspects of Ramakrishna's visions and practices, as well as his homoeroticism, misogyny, and asceticism, as reflecting developmental trauma and intrapsychic conflict. At the same time, in explicitly rejecting Masson's "dogmatic, universalizing rhetoric" and the "ontological reductionism it implies," Kripal insists that Ramakrishna's mystical visions were at times revelatory.[24] Here Kripal promotes a reading of Ramakrishna's mysticism that would account for "a homoerotic infatuation harnessed and 'winged' for ecstatic flight" (24). His aim is to relate mystical experience to both "the physical and emotional experience of sexuality and . . . the deepest ontological levels of religious experience" (23). In so doing, Kripal builds a dialogue that includes a new cross-cultural category he calls "the erotic," Lacan and the "mystics" of psychoanalysis, and the philosophical and anthropological takes on Freud found in Paul Ricoeur and Gananath Obeyesekere.

The best example of Kripal's method at work can be found in his analysis of Ramakrishna's famous initial vision of Kali. Sifting through the multiple versions of this pivotal vision, Kripal isolates two significant psycho-social facts: (1) the tradition-based drama where Kali's sword demands one's severed head in return for mystic vision and (2) Ramakrishna's homoerotic "vocabulary of desire" ("anxious longing," "enkindling," "attraction," "strange sensation," and "wrung like a wet towel"). Exegeting the former with respect to Hindu iconography and rooting the latter in Ramakrishna's developmental past and later homoerotic longing for his boy disciples, Kripal concludes it was the shame Ramakrishna felt over illicit homoerotic desires that ignited his first vision of Kali. Left here, Kripal would be directly following in the footsteps of Masson. However, by locating the meaning of Ramakrishna's mystico-erotic energies in a Tantric worldview and by utilizing Obeyesekere, Ricoeur, and Lacan, Kripal goes further than Masson in arguing that Ramakrishna's visions engaged both sexual conflict and divine ground.

Noting Lacan's commentary on Bernini's statue, "Teresa in Ecstasy," Kripal unpacks Lacan's question concerning where her *jouissance* is coming from. Kripal observes that Lacan rejects the reduction of mysticism to sexuality, insisting that it points to an ontological ground. Then, drawing a parallel between Teresa and Ramakrishna "coming" in samadhi, Kripal goes on to state: "I have respected the religious world of Tantra and have chosen to interpret Ramakrishna's mystico-erotic experiences within that universe. I would argue, then, that the saint's experiences were 'coming from' the ontological ground of his Tantric world. . . . I would insist, moreover, that such a realization be understood on its own terms, as a genuine religious experience" (326).

In bridging psychoanalytic and Tantric notions of sexuality and vision, Kripal sees in the symbols and acts of Ramakrishna's homoerotic mysticism a progressive (cultural-mystical) as well as regressive (psychoanalytic) meaning. It is Obeyesekere's anthropological take on Ricoeur's dialectic between arche and telos that paves the way for providing a relation between the two:

> Sometimes, in exceptional cases, we find genuine two-way "symbols" that function *both* as symptoms, hearkening back to the original crisis, *and* as numinous symbols, pointing to a resolution of the crisis, greater meaning, and what Obeyesekere calls a "radical transformation of one's being." Obeyesekere identifies Ramakrishna as one of those "exceptional cases." . . . Here, then, is where I would locate the meaning of Ramakrishna's eros—*both* in his obvious infatuation with his boy disciples, an infatuation somehow connected with the archaic "regressive" motivations of his own personal history . . . *and* in a "progressive," essentially mystical, order of rapture and vision. (323–24)

74

This progressive movement, however, cannot be accounted for by simple sublimation. It requires an alchemical transformation of bodily energies and a move to a specifically Tantric worldview, one in which libido receives its definition in relation to the erotic-mystical energy known as *shakti*: hence the new category of *realization* as opposed to sublimation, that is, the realization that the ground of the sexual already and always was the mystical. So too must one note the very different view of development inherent in such a worldview. It is the opening of those psycho-physiological structures known as *cakras* and the mystical understanding they bequeath that become the markers of development. From this perspective, libido-based notions of development are relativized and turned on their head. As Kripal points out, from the standpoint of the successful Tantric: "Freud only got to the third Cakra" (43).

The both/and solution to the problem of how to conjoin (heretical) sexuality with divine vision was not simply born of intellectual curiosity. For Kripal both the problem and solution were manifestations of the disenchantment with and mourning for his native Catholicism. In several of his writings he affirms the same structured biographical narrative. He was born into a Roman Catholic family and attended a Catholic seminary with the desire to explore the possibility of a monastic vocation. At the latter he became interested in the relation of sexuality and mysticism. Confronted with the reality of celibacy and the language of bridal mysticism, he became troubled. The excising of sexuality and the language of bridal mysticism blocked his commitment to a monastic vocation: "I could not appropriate the bridal mystical tradition because its homoerotic structure was in conflict with my own heterosexuality."[25] Additionally, in taking seriously the mystical injunction toward things ascetic, Kripal lost over one hundred pounds and gained a diagnosis of anorexia. These conflicts led him into therapy with a professionally trained priest at the seminary. Through therapy he understood the dynamics of a rather pronounced Oedipus conflict and learned how fasting and sexuality were equated in his unconscious. "Freud," admitted Kripal, "literally saved my life."[26]

Therapy bore fruit in other, more significant ways. As an adolescent, Kripal had been tormented by a fantasy "very much as Jung's fantasy of God shitting on a Cathedral used to torment him" (90). The content of Kripal's fantasy consisted of "a naked ithyphallic Jesus on the cross with myself and the Virgin Mary standing beneath him" (90–91). This fantasy was similarly understood to be structured around oedipal themes (the phallus "raised" in the Virgin Mother's presence) and related to his later asceticism: "I was about to "crucify" my sexuality for its unresolved Oedipal dimensions" (91). However, the imagery of other dreams, myths, and visions that erupted during and after the course of analysis made Kripal pause to reconsider the adequacy of a purely psychoanalytic hermeneutic. "Something more" was needed:

> This "something more" soon crystallized itself, not surprisingly, in another dream. . . . The dream involved three presences: myself, a young, attractive maiden dressed in the manner of a Greek or Roman woman, and a winged unicorn whose literally burning body appeared like brilliant black lightning. The maiden said nothing but simply smiled and led me to the edge of what looked like a very deep, very turbulent black sea. Just below the waters burned the fires of a terrifying beautiful winged horse with a single horn coming out of its head. Neither the horn nor the wings were fully grown. The Fire fascinated me—dangerous, dark, and yet filled with light. I instinctively knew that it was my task to get this mysterious being out of the water, and so I entered the waves and tried to pull him up, but to no avail. The scene then shifted and I saw myself as a youth riding naked on the now fully winged and fully horned being into the sky. (92–93)

Kripal thought the above could be conceived of in oedipal terms (93). But he concluded that this "myth-dream" or "dream-vision" (which he later called the "vajrasva vision") was far too numinous and mythological to be wholly subsumed under Freudian categories. So it is that Kripal, in typical Jungian fashion, searched books in the history of art and religious myths to find similar structural content. He came to realize that the dream was "structured around a profound *coincidentia oppositorium* that would engage me for years to come, that between the mystical and the sexual, or what I would later call the erotic . . . if this was sex, it was God's sex" (93).

The problem presented to him by this vision, alongside his heterosexual orientation and "an ontological crisis," eventually barred him from seeking religious fulfillment in the Catholic Church. As Kripal puts it, this quandary "exploded my Catholic world" (94–95). Still wedded to the analytic dynamic promoted by academia and the depth hermeneutic of psychoanalysis (the latter functioning as "a modern or post-modern mystical path" [97]) and following the advice of his monastic therapist to become his own spiritual director,

Kripal enrolled as a doctoral student at the University of Chicago. It was there that he found, in the texts of Hinduism, legends and myths that bore "an almost uncanny resemblance to the truths of my myth-dream" as well as a mystical path "in which a heterosexual male could approach the divine in an explicitly erotic fashion" (96).

Embarking upon a study of Ramakrishna (later to become *Kali's Child*), Kripal was disappointed to find that here too was a mystic whose spiritual path was homoerotic in nature. At first he was inclined to interpret Ramakrishna along the lines of Masson and classical psychoanalysis: "I would have been quite happy with such reductionisms and would have painted the saint as hopelessly neurotic" (202). But then, once again, a vision intervened. In Calcutta, in the midst of research for his dissertation, Kripal entered into a waking dream state "much like the mystico-erotic states I was then uncovering in the Bengali texts" (201). It was this experience, so reminiscent of the experiences of Ramakrishna, that changed his hermeneutical strategy. It made him "very wary of methods that would reduce Ramakrishna's own mystico-erotic experiences to the 'nothing-buts' and clinical jargon of classical psychoanalysis" (202). Alongside textual analysis, psychoanalysis, and the methodologies found in comparative mysticism, the experience became part of his hermeneutical strategy. One could say that he recapitulated his experience with Catholicism. This time, however, detached from a faith commitment to a religious tradition, he utilized the tools of academia to extend psychoanalytic metapsychology with recourse to Lacan, Obeyesekere, Ricoeur, and the formulation of "the erotic" to arrive at a satisfying intellectual and personal solution.

Kripal's case is interesting because unlike Masson (who repudiates religion altogether) or Kakar (who tends to bracket the ontological veracity of religion), he embraces a religious dimension sui generis. Among psychologists this brings him closest to Jung. To be sure, Kripal does not use Jung, preferring a history of religions approach that brings Lacan, a "mystic" of psychoanalysis, into dialogical relation with multiple methodologies. Yet both Jung and Kripal repudiated their native religious faith due to ritualistic and ideological conflict (in the case of Jung, his experience with communion and his cathedral fantasy). In the throes of disillusionment both turned inward, there to be subject to visions transcending the conceptual capacity of classic Freudian psychoanalysis to explain. Again, both used their private visionary experiences as raw data for the creation of a new hermeneutical model for religion.[27] Private visionary experience became public theory. Finally, and most significantly, both affirmed a religious, mystical dimension to the human personality.

Mourning Styles

The case histories offered by Masson, Kakar, and Kripal buttress the thesis that a strong link exists between mourning and method and that, with respect to individual instances, the vicissitudes of mourning can be correlated with fluctuations in method. The implicit suggestion found in this essay—namely, that this thesis can be expanded beyond psychoanalytic studies of Hinduism to include other creative work within the university—must await further scholarly documentation. However, to continue in the suggestive spirit of this now expanded thesis, one could initially turn to the originative psychologists of religion. Certainly Freud's lifelong engagement with Moses, Erikson's with Luther, and Jung's with a variety of religious texts and figures East and West are but the most obvious examples. This pattern could then be widened out to include other significant figures in religious studies. Prominent formulations, such as Ricoeur's "second naiveté," Tillich's "method of correlation," and Eliade's promotion of a "metapsychoanalysis" all indicate a process of mourning insofar as they incorporate psychological theory as well as a rejection of certain elements of the religious past and an acceptance and reconstitution of others. Finally, to take this idea to its furthest extreme, one could speak of the creative work of the "average" professor as exhibiting the hallmarks of mourning. As Homans observes, every creative work in departments of religious studies reveals "a bit of mourning and a bit of individuation . . . new theories of religion . . . are therefore the creation of meaning, the result of a special instance of mourning and individuation."[28] This observation is commensurate with those who see the creative output of university-based departments of religion as constituting a new, if nontraditional, even subversive religious form.[29] The collective body of work found not only in the world's religious traditions but also in originative theorists and prominent secondary commentators has become part of every religious intellectual's shared, standard corpus. In learning, then engaging and creatively responding to this corpus, as well as to the religious past, every religious intellectual participates in a process of mourning that creatively contributes a unique "living" text to a "special" and ongoing religious intellectual tradition. In this way, the notion of mourning becomes indispensable in describing "what we do" as religious intellectuals.

Notes

1. Narasingha Sil, *Ramakrishna Paramahamsa: A Psychological Profile* (New York: Brill, 1991), xi; hereafter cited in text.
2. William Parsons, "The Ability to Mourn: Disillusionment and the Social Origins of Psychoanalysis: A Conversation with Peter Homans," *Criterion* 30, no. 1 (1999): 5.
3. Sil, *Ramkrishna,* 10.
4. See Peter Homans, *The Ability to Mourn: Disillusionment and the Social Origins of Psychoanalysis* (Chicago: University of Chicago Press, 1989).
5. See Janet Malcolm, *In the Freud Archives* (New York: New York Review of Books, 2002).
6. Jeffrey J. Masson, *My Father's Guru: A Journey through Spirituality and Disillusion* (New York: Ballantine, 2003), 68; see also 34, 45–46; hereafter cited in text.
7. See also 18, 20, 29–34, 69, 80, 90, 164–65.
8. Jeffrey Masson, *The Oceanic Feeling: The Origin of the Religious Sentiment in Ancient India* (Dordrecht, Netherlands: D. Reidel, 1980), ix.
9. See Jeffrey Masson, *Oceanic Feeling;* Masson, "Indian Psychotherapy?" *Journal of Indian Philosophy* 7 (1979): 327–32; Masson, "The Psychology of the Ascetic," *Journal of Asian Studies* 35 (1976): 611–25.
10. Masson, *My Father's Guru,* 172.
11. Ibid., 176.
12. Sudhir Kakar, *Shamans, Mystics, Doctors* (New York: A. Knopf, 1982), 220; Kakar, *The Inner World* (Delhi: Oxford University Press, 1981), 13.
13. Kakar, *Inner World,* 12–13.
14. Peter Homans, "Once Again, Psychoanalysis East and West: A Psychoanalytic Essay on Religion, Mourning, and Healing," *History of Religions* 24, no. 2 (1984): 146.
15. See Sudhir Kakar, *The Analyst and the Mystic* (Chicago; University of Chicago Press, 1991), 5.
16. Heinz Kohut, "On Leadership," in *Self Psychology and the Humanities,* ed. Charles Strozier (New York: W. W. Norton, 1985), 70–71.
17. Sudhir Kakar, "Clinical Work and Cultural Imagination," *Psychoanalytic Quarterly* 64, no. 2 (1995): 281.
18. Sudhir Kakar, "Reflections on Psychoanalysis, Indian Culture and Mysticism," *Journal of Indian Philosophy* 10 (1982): 289, 292.
19. See, for example, Kakar, *Inner World,* ch. 2; and Kakar, *Analyst and the Mystic,* ch. 1.
20. Kakar, *Analyst and the Mystic,* 30.
21. Ibid., 34.
22. Kakar, *Shamans, Mystics, Doctors,* ch. 6.
23. I am well aware of the now sizable literature and debates over a broad expanse of issues (the nature of colonialist and postcolonialist analyses, the problem of saintly eroticism, charges of reductionism, faulty translations, etc.) that have arisen as a result of Kripal's work. This essay is not designed to address these issues directly, as it attempts to make a specific point about mourning and method. However, this essay does give rise to one inevitable conclusion that impacts these debates, namely, that Kripal's work is not reductionistic. While

Kripal does state that Ramakrishna was possessed by unconscious homoerotic desire, its is also clear that his use of Lacan, Obeyesekere, and Ricoeur, along with the articulation of the cross-cultural category of Eros and personal confessions of mystical experiences of a Tantric nature, puts Kripal well beyond the reach of the charge of classic Freudian reductionism.

24. Jeffrey J. Kripal, *Kali's Child: The Mystical and the Erotic in the Life and Teachings of Ramakrishna* (Chicago: University of Chicago Press, 1995), 358 n. 71; hereafter cited in text.

25. Jeffrey J. Kripal, "A Garland of Talking Heads for the Goddess: Some Autobiographical and Psychoanalytic Reflections on the Western Kali," in *Is the Goddess a Feminist? The Politics of South Asian Goddesses*, ed. A. Hiltebeitel and K. M. Ernall (Sheffield, UK: Sheffield Academic Press, 2000), 244–45.

26. Jeffrey J. Kripal, *Roads of Excess, Palaces of Wisdom: Eroticism and Reflexivity in the Study of Mysticism* (Chicago: University of Chicago Press, 2001), 92; hereafter cited in text.

27. The importance of personal experience for theory building is, of course Jung's major point in ch. 6 of his *Memories, Dreams, Reflections* (New York: Vintage, 1961) and is the leitmotif of Kripal's *Roads of Excess*. Along these lines it is interesting to note that the major thesis of this essay, while applied to psychoanalytic studies of Hinduism, could easily be extended to Buddhism. Among the early theorists, Jung engaged in a dialogue with Buddhism during his period of mourning and creative response. One also finds elements of mourning and personal experience in midcentury theorists such as Karen Horney, Erich Fromm, and Harold Kelman, as well as in the recent studies of a new cadre of clinician scholars, such as Jack Engler, Jeff Rubin, and Mark Epstein.

28. Parsons, "Ability to Mourn," 5.

29. See, for example, Kripal, *Roads of Excess*.

DIANE JONTE-PACE

Melancholia and Religion in French Feminist Theory

FRENCH FEMINIST theory has become increasingly significant for religious studies in recent decades.[1] Although scholars in this discipline have used this material in many different ways, the increasing presence of this perspective can be attributed to two primary factors. First, like the work of some of the scholars investigated in this volume, the work of the French feminists embodies or illustrates the mourning of religion in modernity. Second, scholars of religion have been attracted, consciously or unconsciously, to this body of literature because of the explicit attention in the work of the French feminist theorists to the individual and cultural processes of mourning in relation to religion.

What is French feminist theory? Although "French feminism" is a contested term, the following description is widely accepted: the French feminists include a group of theorists working in France and focusing on gender, most of whom are indebted to (but critical of) the psychoanalytic work of Jacques Lacan, and most of whom have been affiliated with the *Psych et Po* (*Psychanalyse et Politique*) movement that emerged in Paris in the aftermath of a series of social and political protests in 1968.[2] In addition to Julia Kristeva, Luce Irigaray, and Hélène Cixous, the group includes Catherine Clément, Monique Wittig, and others. Although there are common themes and concerns in the work of these theorists, there is also great diversity in their approaches: they do not constitute an ongoing "movement" per se. Yet collectively they have constructed, in the words of Joy, O'Grady, and Poxon, a "vocabulary and direction for a detailed and complex analysis of religious institutions."[3]

In this essay I draw upon the work of several scholars in religious studies whose writings have been influenced by these theorists, but I do not attempt to document the impact of the French feminists on religious studies in a comprehensive way. Instead, I focus primarily on the analysis of mourning and religion in the work of Julia Kristeva. Kristeva's work is particularly valuable for religious studies. She explores loss, grief, and mourning, not only by reflecting on how mourning works but also by analyzing how traditional monotheisms effectively structure and symbolize death and loss in the West, and how cultures and individuals mourn or fail to mourn in modernity when religious symbols are unable to provide a frame for the experiences of death and loss.

Let us begin with a brief survey of mourning and melancholia in the writings of some of Kristeva's psychoanalytic conversation partners, Sigmund Freud, Hélène Cixous, and Catherine Clément. Freud's famous essay of 1917, "Mourning and Melancholia," differentiated two approaches to loss: the first, a successful encounter involving conscious acknowledgment of the loss, a period of grief, and a phase of recovery; the second, melancholia, described as a more problematic response involving the unconscious and consisting of an entrapment in grieving or an inability to mourn. Freud specified that mourning and melancholia could emerge not only "in reaction to the loss of a loved person" but also in reaction to the "loss of some abstraction . . . such as one's country, liberty, an ideal."[4] And he suggested that grief could have a collective expression: whole cultures could experience a sense of loss, whole cultures could grieve, mourn, or experience melancholia. Thus, according to Freud, mourning and melancholia are both psychological and cultural; they are both individual and collective. And, as others have pointed out, these cultural "abstractions" or "symbolic losses" often include religion.[5]

Memory is important in Freud's understanding of how mourning works, both for individuals and for cultures. Supported by cultural rituals and structures, memory assists in the working through of loss and grief. The process is "carried out bit by bit" as the lost object is remembered and the affect associated with it is transformed: the "memories and expectations by which the libido is bound to the object" are recalled, "hypercathected," and gradually "detached." When the work of memory and mourning is complete, "the ego becomes free and uninhibited again."[6] In melancholia, however, the process of remembering and working through is disrupted. The ego cannot achieve the desired freedom but is imprisoned in (or by) trauma. We cannot remember, or we cannot stop remembering.

Hélène Cixous and Catherine Clément have drawn upon the Freud's understanding of mourning and melancholia to ask important questions about religion, gender, and culture in the modern world. In their view, depression is a widespread experience in the modern, industrialized West due to the ubiquity of alienation, injustice, and suffering. Mourning is necessary for the healing of this depression. For both theorists, religion, in the form of mysticism, initiation, trance, ecstasy, or "writing" (which, for Cixous, is a form of mysticism) is what makes mourning possible, leading to a cure. These mystical experiences of the sacred "allow for a renegotiation with both loss and destructive traces, and a return to life."[7] Ideally depression "precedes a rebirth" and can be compared to "an initiation": it has positive possibilities, including an entrée to the sacred and to transformative, life-enhancing experiences. But mourning, according to Clément and Cixous, is difficult today precisely because of the paucity of rituals through which depression can be resolved. Under these conditions depression often lingers and becomes melancholic. In Clément's words, "the void of the sacred becomes lost in a chasm and rebirth does not come about."[8]

Amy Hollywood, a religious studies scholar and interpreter of the French feminists, discusses Clément's and Cixous's interest in mourning and mysticism. She suggests that both writers see the work of mourning as related to the work of encountering death and "perhaps inevitably religious." According to Hollywood, mysticism, for Clément, is "a way of encountering and working through death that enables a return to life." Similarly, for Cixous, a "mystical mode of writing [is] a way to apprehend and resolve loss, particularly that brought about by the death of the other."[9] Cixous speaks of the "[w]rites of mourning [and] points to the necessity of catharsis particularly for women who need to mourn both religious and political losses."[10] And both insist, as Hollywood points out, that mourning is a "particularly crucial task for women at this point in human history . . . still so often burdened with the work of mourning and so often the victims of the greatest material and spiritual losses."[11]

Julia Kristeva

Julia Kristeva's writing on religion, mourning, and melancholia shares a great deal with the writings of Cixous and Clément.[12] She has even published a collaborative epistolary volume with Clément on the feminine and the sacred.[13] However, her analysis differs in a number of ways from theirs. She is not convinced, for example, that mysticism or "the sacred" is inevitably a healing force for depression: mysticism is instead a type of depression or melancholia in Kristeva's reading. She seems to suggest, as I show below, that the study of religion, rather than the experience of religion, can serve as a "counterdepressant." And she devotes more attention than they to the way that traditional religious symbols can contribute to mourning. Nevertheless, her work extends their psychoanalytic readings into deeper explorations of both mourning and melancholia in relation to religion.

I have argued previously that Kristeva's oeuvre can be seen as a systematic rewriting of Freud's major works on religion.[14] Kristeva's *Powers of Horror* reworks *Totem and Taboo* by postulating matricide and the abject, not incest and patricide, as the origin of culture.[15] Similarly, *In the Beginning Was Love* represents a revision of *The Future of an Illusion* through a reinterpretation of illusion as a "glorious" fiction that nevertheless "gives an accurate representation of the reality of its subjects' desires."[16] *Strangers to Ourselves* contains echoes of *Civilization and Its Discontents:* it asks how it is possible to live in culture and community given the inevitability of xenophobia and aggression.[17] And Kristeva's analysis of the sources of anti-Semitism in abjection in *Powers of Horror* and other texts consciously echoes Freud's speculations on the same topic in *Moses and Monotheism.*

I argue here that Kristeva's *Black Sun,* along with portions of *New Maladies of the Soul,* represents a rewriting of Freud's famous essay "Mourning and Melancholia." Kristeva draws this connection herself, taking Freud's text as her point of departure. In *Black Sun,* she states: "I shall examine matters from a Freudian point of view . . . in bring[ing] out from the core of the melancholy/depressive composite . . . a common experience of object loss and of a modification of signifying bonds."[18] She contrasts Freud's complex explanation of mourning and melancholia with words he had written just a year earlier "to the psychologist, mourning is a great riddle."[19] Her rereading of "Mourning and Melancholia" represents an exploration of that "great riddle": an inquiry into the intersections of these forms of grief with religion through an expansion of Freud's theory into the territories of death, loss, and the maternal.

Speculating on cultural dimensions of health and pathology, Kristeva suggests that traditional Christianity offered an effective and powerful discourse of mourning and loss. She explores ways that we are all melancholic today, in ways that religious symbols, practices, and ideas fail to provide support for the melancholia we experience. She focuses particular attention on the response to the changes or losses associated with religion that accompany modernity. Kristeva's central diagnostic and therapeutic questions focus not only on whether we mourn or are melancholy but, acknowledging the impossibility of a completed sense of mourning within the context of modernity, whether we can be creatively melancholic or are fated to be defensively unable to mourn. These are our choices, from a Kristevan perspective. She devotes particular attention to the role of religion in the origins of mourning and in religious studies as a constructive way of addressing melancholia in modernity.

Mourning

Christianity, Kristeva argues, "supplies images for even the fissures in our secret and fundamental logic."[20] Dawne McCance summarizes Kristeva's view: it is the genius of the Christian construct that it "facilitates perfectly the structural requirements of signification."[21] In Kristeva's reading, the crucifixion, the center of Christian theology, doctrine, and liturgy, functions in two ways for believers and, indeed, for all who are touched by the discourses of the Christian tradition. First, the crucifixion contains a set of symbols that help us negotiate loss and death. Second, the crucifixion articulates the experience of loss and division associated with the origin of the speaking self, the necessary sacrifice marking the developmental shift from preverbal immersion in the maternally linked semiotic (the imaginary) to the realm of the father associated with the entry into subjectivity and language (the symbolic). The crucifixion retraces the birth of the "subject in process" in the separation from the archaic maternal realm.

What does she mean by this? One of Kristeva's interpreters explains: "Christianity has, through facilitating an imaginary identification with the death of Christ, provided a means of bringing death into the symbolic [i.e., into language] or at least it has provided a way for enlarging the imaginary and symbolic means available for coping with death."[22] It embodies the deep sense of division we experience as we are torn from a pre-linguistic state, close to the mother, as we enter the paternal territory of language, in Lacan's terminology, the "nom" or "non du père." It traces the "essential alienation that conditions our access to language in the mourning that accompanies the dawn of psychic life, the death that marks our psychic inception."[23] Christianity thus shapes the Western psyche, providing structures, symbols, and words for the encounter with loss. It shows us how to mourn by retracing our primary mourning of the mother at the birth of the speaking self. Christ's death and resurrection function as a paradigm for the experience of maternally inflected loss-grief-recovery that constitutes mourning. Kristeva's concern about modernity and melancholia begins with this paradigm and its absence in the contemporary world.

Melancholia

In *Black Sun*, Kristeva develops an account of melancholia as post-religious depressive despair. "Never before in the history of humanity," Kristeva states, "has this exploration of the limits of meaning taken place in such an unprotected manner, and by this I mean without religious, mystical or any other justification."[24] The "unprotected" quality of psychic life in modernity is a central concern of Kristeva's. She is particularly interested in the loss of the viability of religious images and symbols and the ubiquity of melancholia. In her interpretations of the contemporary era she explores the question of how we engage in a discourse of death without a discourse of resurrection. In her analysis of the psychodynamics of atheism, she examines the religious art of the early modern period, tracing the beginnings of the loss of a sense of transcendence, a sense of death without resurrection, of loss without hope, and of the absence of God. In addition, she directs her attention to the dramatic effects, on women's lives especially, of the loss of the symbolism of the virgin mother, a symbolism that intricately intertwines sex with death.

In *Black Sun*, Kristeva develops an account of melancholia as post-religious depressive despair. Speaking in the first person, she describes an experience of an "abyss of sorrow," of "not knowing how to lose," of being "unable to find a valid compensation for loss." She concludes that the depressed or melancholic person is a "radical and sullen atheist," whose atheism is symbolic and semiotic as well as theological; close to a sense of "asymbolia" wherein all meanings are lost.[25] Kristeva's work has commented on the psychology of atheism in a number of texts, always with a critical view. As McCance explains, "for Kristeva, this asymbolic atheist is not just someone who has been stripped of all religious conviction"; it is a kind of "semiotic atheism, a condition where all faith and values are undone, all signs are emptied of their significance, when the promise for meaning of any kind has been revoked."[26]

In an effort to uncover what anticipates contemporary melancholic atheism and the contemporary absence of a vocabulary for death, Kristeva looks at the early modern period. Hans Holbein's 1522 painting *The Body of the Dead Christ in the Tomb* provides an entrée into a historical moment of transition to modernity. Painted "on the threshold of the modern, as metaphor of the collapse of the Christian story,"[27] the work emerges at a dramatic critical moment of modernity when the transcendent properties of the Christian narrative are threatened. Kristeva describes the painting, emphasizing Holbein's minimalism: the "empty stare . . . the dull blue-green complexion, are those of a man who is truly dead, of Christ forsaken by the Father ('My God, my God, why have you deserted me?') and without the promise of Resurrection."[28] Holbein's bleak Christ, like the contemporaneous Protestant iconoclasm "with its extreme simplicity of signs,"[29] is almost devoid of all affect. Christ is portrayed as dead and alone, with an expression of a hopeless grief. The painting is a vivid representation of melancholia: isolated, affectless, lacking any hint of passion or idealization. There is "no coded rhetoric . . . to alleviate the anguish induced by the intimation of death. . . . [It is a] representation of the complete absence of affect in signs which characterizes the melancholic's position."[30] This powerful and painful embodiment of melancholia portrays, in Kristeva's words, "a melancholy moment (an actual or imaginary loss of meaning . . . or despair, an actual or imaginary razing of symbolic values including the value of life)." Holbein, she concludes, leads us "to the ultimate edge of belief, to the threshold of nonmeaning."[31]

Theologian Grace Jantzen articulates clearly the question that Kristeva is asking in her work on Holbein: "If we are irretrievably post Christian how shall we, as individuals or society, do the death-work that does not go away with the demise of Christendom?"[32] Although Kristeva herself does not always insist that we are "irretrievably post Christian" (indeed, she finds traces of belief even in the most secular psyche, arguing that "believers . . . amount to almost everyone, in spite of what we might think"[33]), Jantzen's framing of Kristeva's question is indeed central for our era—and it is related to the question of the mother, for in the Christian narrative and the Western unconscious, mother and child, birth and death, are inseparable.

One of Kristeva's most frequently quoted texts, "Stabat Mater," poses a number of questions about the fantasy that for centuries upheld the symbolic economy of the West and its underlying grand narrative, the notion of a virgin mother who gives birth to (and mourns the death of) a special son. "These," she states, "are a few questions among others concerning a motherhood that today remains, after the virgin, without a discourse."[34] What does it mean to lack a discourse of motherhood, to be living "after the virgin"? The Marian discourse is rich and complex. The most significant element is the paradox of virginity and motherhood in relation to sex and death: eternally a virgin, eternally untouched by sex, Mary is also, whether through theologies of "dormition" or "assumption," untouched by death. Traditional Christianity constructs an ideal of the woman who is a sexless immortal mother: the fantasy functions, in Kristeva's words, to "tame the maternal." Although this idealization of a virginal motherhood has exacted a harsh toll on women's lives for many centuries, it has also nevertheless functioned as a cultural code providing a vocabulary and container for the feminine and the maternal.

The collapse of this symbolism leads to what Kristeva calls the psychic sore of modernity. Like the loss of a discourse of death, the loss of the cultural discourse of the ideal form of the maternal can push us toward melancholia. The draw of melancholia is doubly strong "after the virgin" because of the roots of mourning and melancholia in the loss of the archaic mother at the birth of the self. McCance even suggests that the form of Kristeva's text "Stabat Mater" is a subtle echo of the content of "Mourning and Melancholia" where Freud referred to melancholia as an "open wound": the split columns of the essay "oscillate on a symbolic-semiotic borderline, alluding perhaps to Freud's 'Mourning and Melancholia,' the sight of a wound or scar."[35]

If, as Kristeva suggests, melancholia is a ubiquitous feature of the contemporary landscape, our entire culture may be in serious danger. "In the flight from dogma and the impossible precariousness of faith," Lechte thus asks, "may we in the west not be risking collective suicide, or at least a symbolic death?" His answer is bleak: "For Kristeva, the answer seems to be Yes."[36] In Kristeva's analysis, the current fragility of religious discourses of death and the maternal leaves us in a melancholic position: "after the virgin," and without a vocabulary for sex and the maternal, and after the crucifixion, without a vocabulary for hope in the wake of death and loss, we are vulnerable or "unprotected" in an unprecedented way. The loss of all possibility of meaning and the inaccessibility of affect are serious risks. And yet Kristeva is not despondent; she does not exhibit a defensive "inability to mourn," she does not suffer from an inability to remember or to stop remembering. Instead she offers tentative responses to this melancholia, suggesting two possible paths within and through the "abyss of sorrow": psychoanalysis and postmodern writing. I believe that she also hints that the study of religion is the sort of response to melancholia that may "open up the closure" of melancholia.

I want to describe these Kristevan paths through melancholia, but it is important to emphasize first that Kristeva's sense of an opening beyond melancholia through postmodernism or psychoanalysis is circumscribed, tentative, ambiguous, limited. Her goal is not to find a final fix or a permanent cure; she does not seek a return to transcendence. Rather, she seeks a way to live with melancholia, to live with ambiguity as "subjects in process, ceaselessly losing our identity."[37] She seeks ways to allow melancholia to be creative rather than defensive. She even hesitates to use the term "hope": the "ambiguous position of the analyst," she says, "bases itself not on hope but on the fire of tongues." The "fire" is sparked by a self-reflexive, interpretive, metacognitive "combustion," a "three-way loop"[38] involving a hermeneutical stance of reflection upon one's own psychic process.

One path through melancholia named by Kristeva is psychoanalysis. She begins *Black Sun* with a chapter called "Psychoanalysis: A Counterdepressant." Elsewhere she had argued that it is only through psychoanalysis that "we know that we are foreigners to ourselves and it is with the help of that sole support that we can attempt to live with others."[39] She is clear that psychoanalysis avoids the nihilism of an excessive rationality: "psychoanalysis viewed as a theory of knowledge of psychic objects is part of the nihilist effort to objectify man's being. Nevertheless . . . the analytic process is first and foremost an unfolding of language prior to and beyond all unification, distantiation, and objectification." In her words, psychoanalysis is the "modest if tenacious antidote to nihilism."[40] And it leads through and beyond atheism: "atheism is repressive, whereas the experience of psychoanalysis can lead to renunciation of faith with clear understanding."[41]

For Kristeva, another path through melancholia is postmodern writing and literature: she asks whether postmodern "ecriture" is the breakthrough many have been waiting for; whether it represents an attempt to open up the closure of melancholia. For Kristeva, like Cixous, writing takes on a creative force and a powerful luminosity. Kristeva herself explores this option, attempting to "write in the face of a post Christian enigma or void" with what McCance calls a "borderline writing," a writing that walks the "fine edge of melancholic grief and opens itself to an important other or outside of language." Postmodern writings work close to the "thick film of language . . . where moods such as melancholia leave their remains."[42]

Kristeva's understanding of psychoanalysis and postmodern writing as potential paths beyond melancholia leads her directly into the field of religious studies. In this volume the contributors ask whether religious studies as a discipline represents a kind of mourning of religion in the Western world. Following Kristeva, we might nuance this question to ask whether melancholia provides a better frame for this question than mourning. Does the discipline of religious studies embody a path through the melancholia produced by religious changes and losses in modernity, a path that allows us to find a way to live and work creatively within melancholia?

A specific discussion of religious studies can be found in a chapter in Kristeva's *New Maladies of the Soul* called "Reading the Bible" where she reflects on her interest in biblical texts, religious studies, and the interpretive process. She asks "why is it that ever since Freud analytic attention has invariably focused on the sacred, and more specifically, on the biblical sacred?"[43] She cites directly a number of scholars of religion whose work has been important to her—Mary Douglas, Jacob Neusner, and Evan Zuess in the *Journal of the American Academy of Religion*—and she refers explicitly to the discipline of religious studies, noting, for example, that Douglas was "working independently from specialists in religious studies (116)." The essay "Reading the Bible" can be read as a meditation on Kristeva's own longtime interest in sacred texts and their interpretations; it can also be read as a reflection on religious studies in relation to the "new maladies" (such as melancholia) of modernity.

Kristeva begins the essay by differentiating her own psychoanalytic inquiry into biblical texts from the methods and assumptions more typical in religious studies. While religious studies engages in semiological, structural, and functional analyses, posing questions about "the logic or rhetoric of the text," her own work poses questions about the "linguistic subject of the biblical utterance . . . and its addressee: who is speaking in the bible? for whom?" This perspective leads her to the "intra or infrasubjective dynamics of the sacred text" (115–17). She retraces her own answers to these intra- and infrasubjective questions in texts published over several decades: she found the abjection of the mother in the "Levitical rules ('the object excluded from these rules . . . is ultimately the mother')"; and she found the father of personal prehistory in the unrepresentability of God (118, 122). Her approach, in other words, asks about interpersonal dynamics and unconscious fantasies woven through sacred texts; her analysis creates a hermeneutical space attentive to subjectivity: "interpreting these dynamics would require that we recognize a new space, that of the speaking subject . . . who opens himself . . . to analyzable spaces" (117–18).

Although Kristeva differentiates the "intra or infrasubjective" approach of psychoanalytic interpretation from the more typical approach in religious studies—the inquiry into the "logic or rhetoric of the sacred text"—those of us who work in the subfield we call "Religion and Psychological Studies" or "Psychology and Religion" will recognize the intersubjective and hermeneutic questions she poses. Her approach will also be recognized by theologians, philosophers of religion, historians of religions, biblical scholars, and others: the intersubjective is often addressed in contemporary religious studies. Most of her analysis, in fact, is as relevant to religious studies as it is to psychoanalytic interpretation: both fields balance on the tightrope between belief and interpretation, hoping that their analyses will, in Kristeva's words, "guide them toward the mechanism—if not the enigma—of what is seen as holy" (115).

Let us read Kristeva's words with this in mind: She states, "Psychoanalytic interpreters [and, I suggest, interpreters in the field of religious studies] are obliged to distance themselves from Faith in the Goddess of Reason as well as from religious Faith" (123). She proclaims, "Interpretation is an imaginary discourse that serves as truth [and] makes no attempt to hide its status as fiction, as a text" (124). Her words point to the luminosity—even the "combustibility" noted earlier—of the interpretive process that we find in the best work in religious studies. She suggests that psychoanalysis (read: religious studies) is "neither biblical, rationalistic, religious, nor positivist, the place of the analyst is always elsewhere and deceptive. . . . This ambiguous position generates an ethics of construction if not of healing" (125).

Religious studies represents, in a sense, a cultural process of "remembering, repeating, and working through," to use Freud's words, a process "carried out bit by bit," engaging the work of memory and interpretation around religious images, symbols, and practices. This work of memory, Freud argued, is crucial to the work of mourning. Kristeva, with her frequent forays into the history of art and religion, helps us see that it is central as well to the ongoing—or interminable—work of melancholia. For like analysis itself, melancholia is interminable. We are never finished with the remembering, the mourning, the working through.

Freud's acknowledgment that analysis is "interminable" is echoed by Kristeva, who refers to "the serene delicacy of the never attained end of analysis," which, she says, is "analogous to the logic of the Bible" (125–26). Kristeva concludes her essay "Reading the Bible" with these words: "We should read the bible one more time: to interpret it, of course, but also to let it carve out a space for our own fantasies and interpretive delirium" (126). With the interpretations that make up our field we acknowledge that religion "can be made into an object of analysis" at the same time that we "admit . . . that it conceals something that cannot be analyzed" (115).

Religious studies is thus part of the treatment that Kristeva recommends for cultural melancholia, this "new malady of the soul" so widespread in modernity. Thus Kristeva rewrites "Mourning and Melancholia," expanding the analysis into the realms of culture, religion, and gender. Religious studies as a discipline embodies precisely what Kristeva articulates as a creative if interminable response to melancholia. In spite of her respect for traditional religious codes, she does not yearn nostalgically for a return to premodern religious discourses of transcendence, nor does she submit to the fantasy of a "sublime other [who] promises the melancholic absolute meaning—the fantasy of a literalist or fundamentalist absolute" (140). Nor does she promote atheism. Kristeva's psychoanalytic work, like religious studies at its best, recommends "a renunciation of faith with clear understanding,"[44] neither atheist/secularist, nor religious/mystical, but rather, open to the play of interpretations, memories, and meanings within melancholia. This is a melancholia involving a sense of both resignation and reclamation, and an acknowledgment that we are all in some sense melancholy but not despairing, both post-religious and believers still.

Notes

1. See the articles and bibliography in several anthologies: Morny Joy, Kathleen O'Grady, and Judith L. Poxon, eds., *French Feminists on Religion: A Reader* (London: Routledge, 2002); Joy, O'Grady, and Poxon, eds., *Religion in French Feminist Thought: Critical Perspectives* (London: Routledge, 2003); David Crownfield, ed., *Body/Text in Julia Kristeva: Religion, Women, and Psychoanalysis* (Albany: State University of New York Press, 1992); C. W. Maggie Kim, Susan M. St. Ville, and Susan M. Simonaitis, eds., *Transfigurations: Theology and the French Feminists* (Minneapolis: Fortress Press, 1993); and Martha Reineke, *Sacrificed Lives: Kristeva on Women and Violence* (Bloomington: Indiana University Press, 1997).
2. Joy, O'Grady, and Poxon, introduction to *French Feminists on Religion*, 1–7.
3. Ibid., 9.
4. Unless otherwise noted, references to the work of Sigmund Freud are from *The Standard Edition of the Complete Psychological Works of Sigmund Freud*, trans. and ed. James Strachey (London: Hogarth Press, 24 vols., 1966–1974). Sigmund Freud, "Mourning and Melancholia," *Standard Edition*, 14: 243 (first published 1917).
5. Peter Homans, ed., *Symbolic Loss: The Ambiguity of Mourning and Memory at Century's End* (Charlottesville: University Press of Virginia, 2000); Diane Jonte-Pace, *Speaking the Unspeakable: Religion, Misogyny, and the Uncanny Mother in Freud's Cultural Texts* (Berkeley: University of California Press, 2001); Erich Santner, *Stranded Objects: Mourning, Memory, and Film in Postwar*

Germany (Ithaca, NY: Cornell University Press, 1990); Alexander and Margaret Mitscherlich, *The Inability to Mourn: Principles of Collective Behavior* (New York: Grove Press, 1975).

6. Freud, "Mourning and Melancholia," 245.
7. Joy, O'Grady, and Poxon, introduction to *Religion in French Feminist Thought*, xxiv; Amy Hollywood, "Mysticism, Death and Desire in the Work of Hélène Cixous and Catherine Clément," in Joy, O'Grady, and Poxon, *Religion in French Feminist Thought*, 145–61.
8. Clément in Catherine Clément and Julia Kristeva, *The Feminine and the Sacred* (New York: Columbia University Press, 2001), 147.
9. Hollywood, "Mysticism, Death and Desire," 148.
10. Joy, O'Grady, and Poxon, introduction to *Religion in French Feminist Thought*, xxiv.
11. Hollywood, "Mysticism, Death and Desire," 156.
12. Hélène Cixous and Catherine Clément, *The Newly Born Woman* (Minneapolis: University of Minnesota Press, 1986).
13. Clément and Kristeva, *Feminine and the Sacred*.
14. Diane Jonte-Pace, "Julia Kristeva and the Psychoanalytic Study of Religion: Rethinking Freud's Cultural Texts," in *Religion, Society, and Psychoanalysis: Readings in Contemporary Theory*, ed. Janet Jacobs and Donald Capps (Boulder, CO: Westview Press, 1997); also Jonte-Pace, "Situating Kristeva Differently: Psychoanalytic Readings of Woman and Religion," in *Body/Text in Julia Kristeva: Religion, Women, and Psychoanalysis*, ed. David Crownfield (Albany: State University of New York Press, 1992), 1–22.
15. Julia Kristeva, *Powers of Horror: An Essay on Abjection* (New York: Columbia University Press, 1982).
16. Julia Kristeva, *In the Beginning Was Love: Psychoanalysis and Faith* (New York: Columbia University Press, 1987), 11.
17. Julia Kristeva, *Strangers to Ourselves* (New York: Columbia University Press, 1991).
18. Julia Kristeva, *Black Sun: Depression and Melancholia* (New York: Columbia University Press, 1989), 10.
19. *Ibid.*, 98.
20. Kristeva, *In the Beginning Was Love*, 42.
21. Dawne McCance, "Kristeva's Melancholia: Not Knowing How to Lose," in Joy, O'Grady, and Poxon, *Religion in French Feminist Thought*, 139.
22. John Lechte, "Art, Love, and Melancholy in the Work of Julia Kristeva," in *Abjection, Melancholia, and Love: The Work of Julia Kristeva*, ed. John Fletcher and Andrew Benjamin (London: Routledge, 1990), 36–37.
23. Kristeva, *In the Beginning Was Love*, 41.
24. Julia Kristeva, "Postmodernism," in *Romanticism, Modernism, Postmodernism*, ed. H. R. Garvin (Lewisburg, PA: Bucknell University Press, 1980), 141, cited in McCance, "Kristeva's Melancholia," 135–36.
25. Kristeva, *Black Sun*, 3–5.
26. McCance, "Kristeva's Melancholia," 139.
27. Kristeva, *Black Sun*, 110.
28. Ibid.
29. Lechte, "Art, Love, and Melancholy," 36.
30. Ibid., 36–37.
31. Kristeva, *Black Sun*, 135.
32. Grace Jantzen, "'Death, Then, How Could I Yield to It?' Kristeva's Mortal Visions," in Joy, O'Grady, and Poxon, *Religion in French Feminist Thought*, 123.
33. Kristeva, *In the Beginning Was Love*, 26.
34. Julia Kristeva, "Stabat Mater," in *The Kristeva Reader*, ed. Julia Kristeva and Toril Moi (New York: Columbia University Press, 1986), 160–86.

35. McCance, "Kristeva's Melancholia," 139.
36. Lechte, "Art, Love, and Melancholy," 39.
37. Kristeva, *In the Beginning Was Love,* 9.
38. Julia Kristeva, *New Maladies of the Soul* (New York: Columbia University Press, 1995), 125.
39. Kristeva, *Strangers to Ourselves,* 182.
40. Kristeva, *In the Beginning Was Love,* 60–63.
41. Ibid., 21–27.
42. Joy, O'Grady, and Poxon, introduction to *Religion in French Feminist Thought,* xxiii; McCance, "Kristeva's Melancholia," 141.
43. Kristeva, *New Maladies,* 123; hereafter cited in text.
44. Kristeva, *In the Beginning Was Love,* 27.

PART II

MOURNING THE
(DIS)CONTENTS OF
RELIGION

WILLIAM B. PARSONS

Psychologia Perennis and the Academic Study of Mysticism

CONTEMPORARY understandings and uses of the term "mysticism" are the product of a long history of development. Louis Bouyer notes that the origin of the word is to be found in the Greek Mystery religions.[1] At first, *mystikos,* derived from the verb *muo* ("to close"), lacked any direct reference to the transcendent, referring only to the hidden or secret elements of ritualistic activities. However, picked up by the early Church Fathers, it migrated in a new direction, being defined with respect to three interrelated contexts: biblical, liturgical, spiritual. Implicit in the Christian terms "mystical theology" and "mystical contemplation" is the notion that mystical experience brings one into contact with a transcendent reality and, furthermore, that such experiences can be accessed only through the auspices of church and tradition. For them mystical experience signified the presence of an objective reality above and beyond the wholly subjective. Mysticism was "the experience of an invisible objective world: the world whose coming the Scriptures reveal to us in Jesus Christ, the world into which we enter, ontologically, through the liturgy."[2] Contrary to modern, Western psychological expectations, their interest lay not in championing the individual and personal experience but in promoting the teachings of the church.

A new migration occurred during the sixteenth and seventeenth centuries. As Michel de Certeau has catalogued, one finds the emergence of mysticism as a substantive (*la mystique*), the delineation of the topic in terms of a subjective "experience" divorced from church and tradition, and the investigation and interpretation of such experiences from a scientific perspective. A new discourse was created: the reconceptualization of ecstatic and contemplative religious figures as social types found within a particular tradition ("the mystics"). A new understanding of the sacred was found: the mystic's "Absolute" was framed in generic terms "as an obscure, universal dimension of man, perceived or experienced as a reality (*un reel*) hidden beneath a diversity of institutions, religions, and doctrines."[3] These two moves allowed for another, namely, the "psychologization" of mystical experiences and states. The latter made "a nonreligious exegesis of religion possible" and gave rise "to a reintegration that eradicates the past without losing its meaning."[4] Extending de Certeau's initial observations in his survey of religious texts during the eighteenth and nineteenth centuries in Great Britain and North America, Leigh Schmidt delineates the influence of numerous factors, notably liberal Protestant thought, in both securing the widespread use of the substantive "mysticism" and "inventing" its modern form, understood as "ahistorical, poetic, essential, intuitive, and universal."[5]

Both Schmidt and de Certeau note how central psychological figures of the late nineteenth and early twentieth centuries reflect developments in the term mysticism. A paradigmatic case is that of William James, who framed mysticism in a way diametrically opposed to that found in Bouyer's survey of the early Church Fathers. For example, James states that in his *Varieties* he is "treating personal experience as the exclusive subject of our study," defining religious experience, of which mysticism is the deepest form, as "the feelings, acts and experiences of individual men in their solitude, so far as they apprehend themselves to stand in relation to whatever they may consider the divine."[6] Tradition and its accouterments, by which James meant theology, philosophy, liturgy, ritual, and the various aspects of church organizations, all crucial for access to the presence of God for the Church Fathers, were understood by James as secondary phenomena unessential for access to the divine.

Schmidt also thinks that modern construals of mysticism have paved the way for the popular, contemporary conflation of the terms "mysticism" and "spirituality."[7] There is much evidence to buttress this assertion. The Pauline *spiritus* ("breath") characterized a person guided by the spirit of God. It was growth in the spirit, which included the development of virtues, dispositions, and ideals in the striving toward Christian perfection, that was emphasized.[8] To be sure, through the centuries there were deviations along the way (at one point spirituality came to denote ecclesiastical property and persons who exercised ecclesiastical jurisdiction), but in the main spirituality held fast to its moral, psychological, and religious meanings.[9] Adhering to its biblical roots, much of current spirituality in theological literature refers to religious growth within a particular tradition (e.g., the "spirituality" of St. Teresa of Avila). In this way "classic spirituality" (as some refer to it) and what we referred to above as the project of articulating a "mystical theology" are commensurate: they both refer to growth and mystical experiences within a total religious matrix.

However, alongside this "classical spirituality" one finds a form of "modern" spirituality that, like modern mysticism, can be alternately referred to as non-institutional, nontraditional, or, if speaking directly to its specifically Christian roots, unchurched.[10] Like classical spirituality, modern forms of spirituality are fixated on religious experience and the development of the self. The major dividing point concerns allegiance to a particular religious tradition. Conforming to the well-known public/private split, this new, modern spirituality often portrays institutional religion as the enemy, a place where authoritarianism, mendacity, and dogmatism have replaced authentic, living religious experience. Adherents are notably eclectic, adopting a supermarket approach to religious traditions and practices, constructing a highly individualized private spirituality that is decidedly psychological and holds to a conception of the Divine as innate and within. Robert Fuller sees modern spirituality as part of a long unchurched religious tradition with roots in the Western past (e.g., Unitarianism, Theosophy, Spiritualism, mesmerism, transcendentalism, New Thought, Swedenborgianism, and Jungian, humanistic, and transpersonal psychologies).[11] Framed in this way, one can see how "modern" mysticism and "modern" spirituality have become interchangeable terms (mystical experiences are seen as part of, indeed the denouement of, the spiritual path). Many people (recent estimates are as high as 21 percent) now prefer to express their religious sentiments along the lines of an unchurched mysticism and spirituality divorced from religious institutions and their accoutrements. As the saying goes, "I'm spiritual, but not religious." This unchurched spirituality, then, is highly individualized, very psychological, and predictably capitalistic in its stress on human potential and techniques for growth. With respect to the thesis advanced in this essay, one could say that spirituality is a form of "disenchanted" mysticism; spirituality is "mysticism" mourned.

Acknowledging the fact that multiple cultural strands have played a factor in the rise and dissemination of an unchurched mysticism and spirituality, this essay focuses on the contributions of one such cultural strand, which I call "psychologia perennis" (the perennial psychology). The latter term refers to the collective body of religious psychologies and affirms how such psychologies have become a way for many to express and monitor issues pertaining to existential meaning, wholeness, numinous mystical experiences, and individuation. The argument proceeds by way of linked vignettes, depicting what amounts to historical snapshots pertaining to the origin, development, and cultural impact of certain psychologies on the development of an unchurched mysticism. Put together, a portrait of this important phenomenon begins to develop.

The first vignette ("Psychologia Perennis: The Product of Mourning") proceeds by way of a series of abbreviated case histories designed to show how a process of mourning was involved in the creation of an unchurched, religio-mystical psychology. The second vignette ("The Cultural Dissemination of Mourned Mysticism") turns to a related issue: how did this religious psychology move from the initial, sometimes rudimentary formulations of individual theorists to a way of expressing religious sentiments common to large groups of people? The answer to this question is complex and demands the articulation of several interrelated sociocultural mechanisms. We shall rest content in narrowing our focus to one such mechanism. Following Weber, we aim to show how the "great ideas" of creative psychologists were fruitfully mediated through institutionalized, therapeutic functionaries, thus facilitating the widespread preponderance of the psychologia perennis and the rise of a new social type (the "inner-worldly mystic"). The arguments of the first two vignettes are indispensable for the analysis undertaken in the final vignette ("Cultural Mourning and the Academic Study of Mysticism"). Banking off the conclusions of the previous two sections, this last section assumes that the concept of mourning applies not simply to isolated individuals but to entire cultures. That is to say, the popularity of a modern, unchurched psychological form of mysticism is an indication of cultural mourning at work. With this in mind, the final section unpacks how the fertile psychosocial soil seeded by the proponents of the psychologia perennis played a determinative role in the production of classic and recent debates in the academic study of mysticism. Although most scholarly analyses of these debates have rightly highlighted noteworthy advances with respect to issues of an epistemological, comparative, and theological nature, our efforts are designed to reveal that these debates indicate not simply a clash of ideas but also a clash of cultures—that of a more traditionalistic way of viewing the particularity and integrity of individual religions versus the promotion of a transcultural, universal, psychologically sophisticated, unchurched mysticism.

Psychologia Perennis: The Product of Mourning

While de Certeau has nothing to say about the figures, characteristics, and subsequent career of unchurched mysticism during the course of the twentieth century, he does make note of what he refers to as "a significant debate," namely, that between Sigmund Freud and Romain Rolland. Rolland was a French novelist, musicologist, social critic, and mystic who, in a letter dated December 5, 1927, had asked Freud to analyze what he referred to as an "oceanic feeling." Freud responded in *Civilization and Its Discontents* by interpreting it as a vestige of the primary state of narcissism. Rolland protested, seeing mysticism as evidence of a universal religious unconscious dimension common to all men, apart from and yet simultaneously the source of religious institutions and their accouterments, which could be analyzed, accessed, and cultivated. De Certeau finds in Rolland evidence of one aspect of the historical trend he attempts to delineate: the shift away from defining mysticism solely with respect to a particular religious matrix. But Rolland's attempt to promote a mystical psychoanalysis and a "universal science-religion" are more interesting—and more symptomatic of a cultural and historical trend—than de Certeau ever imagined. In the development of Rolland's mysticism one finds a microcosm of the processes and characteristics that define the historical emergence of an institutionalized, psychologically informed, unchurched mysticism.

In illustrating the transition from a churched to an unchurched, psychologically informed mysticism in the person of Rolland we utilize what Peter Homans calls the psychology *and* religion approach. A psychology-and-religion approach seizes on biography and personal experience "in context" by taking as its micro-sociological unit the complex interplay in individuals between religion (the cultural dimension), secularization (sociohistorical factors), and development (psychological factors). The key to linking psychological with sociohistorical processes is a Weberian "double" ideal type: the tension between analytic access and a common culture. Analytic access simply refers to an individual's introspective activity and depth-psychological probes. It is in "tension" with what Talcott Parsons refers to as a "common culture" for, sociologically speaking, analytic access always takes place at the margins of culture. The double ideal type thus presupposes an inclusive concept of "mourning," one that is defined with respect to the psychological concept of disillusionment or de-idealization, involves both the cognitive and affective dimensions of the psyche, and extends what is mourned to social and cultural "objects" such as values, ideals, and symbols. In an ideal-typical sense, the process is envisioned as starting when the power of a religious worldview or common culture to command allegiance wanes and symbols "die" (disenchantment, as Weber would have it). What was previously idealized, and hence believed or given allegiance to, becomes de-idealized. This loss leads to mourning, a regressive process that involves, to various degrees depending on the person, an introspective engagement with unconscious contents. This is so for the unconscious, previously worn "on the outside"—that is, projected onto, hence contained and monitored by, religious ideation and dealt with in an "experience-distant" manner—no longer finds nourishment on the collective level. Such loss loosens unconscious contents, including in some cases unchurched mystical experiences. The dramatic upsurge of the unconscious may result in breakdown, despair, or cynicism. However, it also provides an opportunity for individuation, which is to say the process of growing out of the social womb and the integration of previously unmonitored unconscious contents—a process that can result in a response to the loss of religion in the form of the creation of new ideals and symbols, one of which is the formation of the psychologia perennis. And, as evinced by the latter, such ideas usually display some form of connection with the religious past. While de-idealized and in some sense rejected, religion is never wholly left behind but rather repudiated and assimilated in varying degrees and proportions. In a very real sense, religion "lives on" in psychology. It is this sense of historical continuity that is responsible for the oft-repeated apprehension of psychology "as" a religion.[12]

Applied to Rolland, we can first note that widespread social and historical circumstances (pluralism, empiricism, secularization) pervaded his efforts to articulate and promote a psychologia perennis. On the personal level, Rolland became disillusioned with institutional religion, was beset by powerful unchurched mystical experiences, and ultimately gravitated toward psychological method. Rolland moved from the confines of a particularistic, revealed religion animated by a Divinity (Catholicism) to an idiosyncratic, unchurched mystical worldview animated by a philosopher (Spinoza) to a desire to create a social space for an unchurched, mystical psychology. These three phases of Rolland's life can now be examined in more detail.

Romain Rolland (1866–1944) claimed he was socialized and participated in organized Catholicism for the greater part of his youth. As he puts it, he was "born Catholic, in a Catholic family, in a Catholic town"[13] (Clamency, in western Burgundy on the Yonne River). The impact of this initial exposure to organized religion never wholly left him. He never ceased corresponding with Catholic friends such as Paul Claudel and Louis Gillet, had positive opinions of Catholic thinkers such as Teilhard de Chardin and Henri de Lubac, and, late in life, even expressed an "instinctive preference" for Catholicism. Indeed, a barometer of the lasting imprint of Catholicism on the life, thought, and behavior of Rolland is revealed in Freud's association of him, in *Civilization and Its Discontents,* with the love command.

The second phase ushers in Rolland's move from Catholicism to an unchurched mysticism. It was his family's move from Clamency to Paris that proved to be the initial precipitating factor in this change. At the tender age of fourteen he was whisked off to Paris for what was to become a future career as an academic. However, as a student at the Ecole Normale superiere he met with a culture that clearly showed the influence of secularization: "God was dead . . . the whole moral atmosphere of Paris around 1880 was deicidal."[14]

Under the influence of the surrounding intellectual culture the young Romain formally renounced his ties to organized Catholicism. Put psychologically, the rich symbolic universe of Catholicism, mediated, internalized, and maintained through saintly and priestly intermediaries and the integrative power of rituals, had, to that point in Rolland's life, been able to engage unconscious contents enough to ward off meaninglessness and suffering, monitor instinctual eruptions, and maintain psychic equilibrium. Deprived of this cultural narrative, Rolland was thrown back on himself, there to be subject to a series of mystical experiences. It was these "brief and staggering contacts with the Unity," writes Rolland about his adolescent years, that "were the key to the spiritual world where I lived for the next forty years."[15] In his *Mémoires* Rolland describes how his notes were full of such experiences during the 1880s. In one such note he recalls how he "was possessed by Nature like a violated virgin. For a moment my soul left me to melt into the luminous mass of the Breithorn. . . . Yes, extravagant as it may sound, for some moments I *was* the Breithorn."[16] Rolland was also to describe these experiences in terms that prefigured his account to Freud: "The entire universe is one unique, immense sound from which burst, like a ripe pomegranate, billions of harmonics, all composing one same oceanic harmony."[17]

These experiences became the existential basis for a philosophical statement he termed the *Credo Quia Verum.* The latter, penned in 1888, is nothing less than a working mystical theology constructed from the mix of religious ideation extant in fin-de-siécle Parisian culture. Its content revolves around religio-philosophical issues concerning the nature of God, self, world, and other.[18] Most important, the *Credo* indicates a repudiation of a specifically Christian ideology. The very title ("I believe because it is true"), which refers to seeing over believing and mystical experience over doctrine, seems directed against the more familiar claim of Tertuillian (*Credo quia absurdum*). As such, it is not surprising that the figure who animates the *Credo* is not Christ but Spinoza. Forty years later, Rolland wrote how Spinoza "still remains sacred to me, like the Holy Scriptures for those who believe in them; I never touch those volumes except with reverence."[19] What Spinoza did was to mediate to Rolland a conception of God that resonated with the reality he had met in his mystical experiences. What Rolland advocated in the *Credo* was nothing less than a nature-based mysticism.

Thirty years passed before the third phase commenced, a time in which Rolland was to reflect once again on the meaning and import of mysticism. The precipitating event was the calamity of the Great War, which signified for Rolland the coming collapse of Western culture and the waning ability of institutionalized Christianity to monitor man's antisocial proclivities. One could justifiably say that this was a period during which Rolland was subject to a massive de-idealization with every phase of Western civilization. His earlier disillusionment with Christianity now became total: "Christians of this war have distanced me from Christianity forever."[20] As one commentator put it, Rolland's comments about Christianity reflect "the spasm that seizes a man in the face of the ruins of his faith."[21] Presented with this cultural disaster, Rolland followed a pattern endemic to many disillusioned religious intellectuals: he turned to other cultures and to the past. Looking to the East and its rich mysticism, he found his own past. In a letter to an Indian friend, Dilip Kimar Roy, Rolland related how he discovered, in the works of Sri Aurobindo "just what I myself had found, unaided, at the age of twenty, when I wrote the same thing in my Credo Quia Verum."[22] It was the mystical experiences of his youth, he went on to say, that brought him "singularly near to the spirit of India when I later came to know it."[23]

Rolland went on to contact many religious intellectuals in India, including Gandhi and Tagore, and to pen his now classic biographies of Ramakrishna and Vivekananda. His inquiry into Eastern civilization led him back to his own *Credo*, to the mystics of the Western past, and finally to the conclusion that there existed a deep, universal, and mystical dimension of the human soul that could be an invaluable source for the regeneration of a decaying Europe. In synthesizing mysticism East and West he took as his starting point the two principal ideas behind neo-Vedantic philosophy: the essential spirituality of life and the divinity of man. These ideas, thought Rolland, could be found in all cultures, religions, and philosophies. Neo-Vedantic philosophy merely cataloged what was a universal, innate feature of consciousness. The fundamental source of religion was dynamic in character, a free and vital becoming that, given the proper individual and social conditions, "spontaneously" manifested itself and eventually solidified into discernible religious forms. As Rolland put it: "mysticism is always and everywhere the same."[24]

This unchurched perennialism can be found in Rolland's pivotal letter of December 5, 1927, to Freud. After noting his research into the East and coming biographies of Ramakrishna and Vivekananda, Rolland described the "oceanic feeling" as "completely independent of all dogma, all credo, all Church organization . . . the true source of religious energy which has been collected, canalized and dried up by Churches to the extent that one could say it is inside the Churches that one finds the least true religious feeling."[25] But what motivated Rolland's letter to Freud was not simply to elaborate on the deepest sources of religious feeling. He wrote to ask Freud to subject mysticism to psychoanalytic scrutiny. Why? In his biographies of the Hindu saints, Rolland had cited psychological studies by Morel, James, Myers, Starbuck, Flournoy, Leuba, and others, expressing confidence that the "modern psycho-physiologist, armed with all the latest instruments of the new sciences of the soul," would be able to "attain to a full knowledge" of the workings of the mystical subconscious.[26] Rolland hoped Freud would join him in this cultural agenda, which consisted in nothing less than what he referred to in his biographies of the Hindu saints as a "universalistic science-religion" and "mystical psycho-analysis." This "rationalistic religion" would be that "religion of the future" upon which "the salvation of Europe depends."[27] This alarmed Freud who, as de Certeau notes, could only be reminded of another advocate of a religious psychology who played an important role in his life: Carl Jung.

Jung, of course, has been often cited as not simply a psychologist *of* religion but one who actively promoted a religious psychology. And, as he himself notes, the roots of his psychology go well back into his childhood. Although Jung was socialized into Protestantism, his relationship to Christianity was tenuous. As cataloged in his *Memories, Dreams, Reflections,* Jung became disillusioned with

Christianity through a series of dreams (e.g., the dream of the Phallus and subterranean God), fantasies (notably the Cathedral fantasy), and disappointing experiences with the Church (communion), all filtered through a distant father ambivalent about his faith and status as a Protestant pastor. The choice for him became that between the experience-near subterranean God found in his introspective moments and the remote, experience-distant God of institutionalized Christianity. It was the former that became the basis for an unchurched psychological religion.

Jung's initial disillusionment with Christianity played no small role in leading him as an adolescent to Nietzsche, to the psychiatric profession, and then to Freud. However, friction slowly accrued between Freud and Jung, and by 1914 their split was final. It is in one of the reasons for their split that we find more analogies between Jung and Rolland. Like Rolland, Jung wanted to enlist Freud in the creation of a religious psychology. In a letter of January 19, 1909, Jung had already related to Freud how attractive he had found, in the figure of the Protestant pastor Oskar Pfister, the "mixing of medicine and theology."[28] By February 11, 1910, he was openly declaring to Freud the need for a religious psychology: "Religion can only be replaced by religion . . . 2000 years of Christianity can only be replaced by something equivalent . . . I imagine a far finer and more comprehensive task for psychoanalysis."[29] Freud was more sanguine, responding that psychoanalysis was not "a substitute for religion; this need must be sublimated."[30] But the damage was done. The two men eventually filed for divorce, a decision that led Jung to be seized by a period of personal disintegration and a series of visions that, in his autobiography, he describes as that "confrontation with the unconscious" that gave him "the *prima materia* for a lifetime's work."[31] Acknowledging the impact of cultural and developmental forces on his psyche, Jung begins his account of his entry into the unconscious labyrinth by stating how the "Christian myth" no longer possessed him: "In what myth does man live nowadays? In the Christian myth, the answer might be. 'Do *you* live in it?' I asked myself. To be honest, the answer was no. . . . 'Then do we no longer have any myth?' No, evidently we no longer have any myth."[32] The existential issue facing Jung was thus how to find (or create) his own "personal myth."

It was through his encounter with fantasy figures such as Salome and Philemon/Elijah and the spontaneous emergence of mandala figures that Jung found his personal myth. Later, as articulated most clearly in what is now known as his *Two Essays on Analytical*

Psychology, he gave theoretical sophistication to his introspective probes: the process of individuation, the notion of the collective unconscious and delineation of its archetypes, the objectivity of the psyche, active imagination, and so on. These formulations rendered religion, its myths, and symbols as nothing more than "cultural containers" for the eruptions of the collective unconscious. Like James and over against the Church Fathers, Jung saw the church and its inventory of myths and symbols as derivative, defining them as "codified and dogmatized forms of original religious experience."[33] Indeed, Jung advocated a psychologia perennis based on his own mystical experiences (that is, in drawing upon Otto, the numinosity of the archetypes), his turn to the mysticism of the East and West, and the universality of the unconscious. All this rendered the individual a temple unto himself, a veritable congregation of one. Unlike Durkheim, who thought religion was "eternal" because people were social animals, Jung posited the same because the collective unconscious was dynamic and the therapeutic process theogonic in nature.

The above indicates that Jung, like Rolland, formed his theory in a state of mourning. Homans has indicated that in Jung one can clearly see the threefold process of de-idealization, introspective probes, and creative response at work.[34] It was the early de-idealization of his father, valued cultural symbols (Protestantism), and finally Freud that led Jung to first enter the psychiatric profession, then experience a long period of the eruption of the unconscious, including the all-important numinous encounter with the Self archetype, which in turn led to his exploration of other cultures and a psychological perennialism based on the archetypes and the collective unconscious. What was at first "on the outside" in the form of culturally legitimated symbols, myths, rituals, and narratives (i.e., Protestantism) later became elaborated "on the inside" in terms of a religiously toned unconscious. It is this continuity that legitimates the characterization of Jung's theory as not only a psychology "of" religion but psychology "as" religion.[35]

Aside from Jung and Rolland there are other seminal and originative figures in the history of psychology during the course of this century who reflect in part or whole the shifts in the study of mysticism noted by de Certeau as well as the further development of the formation of a socially viable unchurched mysticism. For example, continuing with the early psychologists and going back to James, it is clear that the latter never went so far as to promote an institutionalized, psycho-mystical religion. His was an exercise in the psychology *of* religion, not psychology *as* religion. A different story emerges, however, with respect to his correspondent and fellow psychologist Richard Maurice Bucke. James had taken a special interest in Bucke as a result of his book *Cosmic Consciousness.* James cited the latter in his *Varieties,* later writing to Bucke that it was a work of "first rate importance" in conveying the characteristics of the mystical consciousness and that Bucke's efforts made him "a benefactor of us all."[36]

Like Jung, Bucke had broken with institutional Christianity as a youth. Deeply philosophical, he had at a young age come to the conclusion that Jesus was a great and spiritual man but not God. Then, in 1872, at the age of thirty-six, Bucke had a mystical experience, an instance of what he later called "cosmic consciousness," which changed the course of his life. Bucke relates how after a pleasant evening with friends reading poetry he found himself on the ride home in a state of quiet, passive enjoyment. Being suddenly surrounded by a flame-colored cloud, he had an "intellectual illumination" that, as a salute to the growing pluralism of his day, he refers to as "one drop of Brahmic Bliss," through which he came not simply to *believe* but to *know* that "the Cosmos is not dead matter but a living Presence, that the soul of man is immortal . . . that the foundation principle of the world is what we call love and that the happiness of every one is in the long run absolutely certain."[37]

In *Cosmic Consciousness* Bucke elaborated on the ramifications of his experience in three important ways. First, with respect to religion, he claimed it was the "common-core" upon which a perennialism could be established. It was the limitations of language, diversity of cultures, tradition, and other intermediaries that accounted for what otherwise could be shown to be the essential unity of the world's religions. Like James, Bucke listed a variety of universal "marks" or characteristics that he thought constituted a genuine instance of cosmic consciousness, such as intellectual illumination, moral elevation, sense of immortality, and loss of fear of death (316–17).

Second, he interpreted cosmic consciousness as essentially a psychophysiological phenomenon. Cosmic consciousness was defined as that type of consciousness that "intuits" the "life and order of the universe" and is to be distinguished from the simple (perceptual/receptual) consciousness of animals and the reflective, conceptual self-consciousness of humans (9). Cosmic consciousness entailed a move from states of fear and hate to love and faith—a move rooted in the evolution of the nervous system. Developmentally, Bucke claimed that a strong and athletic mother, a father of superior physical and spiritual powers, parents with diverse temperaments, a perfect blending of diverse parental characteristics in the child, and a particular life stage (middle thirties) were determinative factors favoring the move to cosmic consciousness.

Finally, Bucke set out a social agenda in which the above facets of cosmic consciousness were seen in the context of history and evolution. Shifting to a prophetic voice, Bucke held that through time one saw an increasing number of humans being endowed with moments of cosmic consciousness. This step in evolution was such that "men with the faculty in question are becoming more and more common" and that "our descendants will sooner or later reach, as a race, the condition of cosmic consciousness" (317–18). Cosmic consciousness places the individual "on a new plane of existence," elevates his moral and intellectual stature, and renders him "a member of a new species" (2). It is this "new race" that is "in the act of being born from us" and that will, in the "near future," inhabit the earth (318). Then, becoming more specific, he called attention to the "three revolutions" now facing mankind: (1) the establishment of "aerial navigation" and its socio-material consequences, (2) the abolition of private property and move to a socialist economy, (3) the religio-psychical revolution as detailed in his book. These three will, according to Bucke, lead to "a new heaven and a new earth." The result is nothing less than unchurched mystical man in a socialist state.

The early theories of Jung and Bucke are commensurate with later developments in the psychologia perennis. One such example is Roberto Assagioli, the author of *Psychosynthesis* and founder of the Institute for Psychosynthesis, who incorporated into his psychology Freud's personal unconscious, Jung's collective unconscious, and a "higher unconscious" or "superconscious." The aim of Assagioli's psychology is to activate superconscious energies and innate intuitive capacities. These reorder the "lower" elements of the psyche and ignite mystical experience, higher moral faculties, creativity, and contact with a transpersonal realm.

More representative theorists can be found in those associated with humanistic and transpersonal psychologies. Abraham Maslow was the driving force behind both psychologies. Above and beyond physiological, safety, belongingness, and self-esteem needs, he posited that of self-actualization. And it is the well-developed self-actualizer who ends up having "peak-experiences." Peak-experiences are synonymous with mystical experiences and can be defined with respect to a laundry list of characteristics: unity, transcendence of space and time, awe, wonder, loss of fear. More importantly, Maslow sees peak-experiences as that common core around which all religions are built: "to the extent that all mystical or peak-experiences are the same in their essence and have always been the same, all religions are the same in their essence and always have been the same."[38]

In a refrain now familiar, Maslow goes on to distinguish between two religious social types: the "mystics" (those granted peak-experiences) and the "legalists" (the non-peaker church bureaucrat). The latter tries through the accouterments of church tradition and theology to communicate the original insight of the mystic, an effort Maslow thinks is all too often in vain. Indeed, for Maslow "all the paraphernalia of organized religions . . . are to the "peaker" secondary, peripheral, and of doubtful value . . . each peaker discovers, develops, and retains his own religion."[39] It is psychology that has divested religion of its supernatural character and put mysticism in its rightful place as an object of scientific study.

To this end Maslow instituted transpersonal psychology, which is concerned with the scientific study of "unitive consciousness, peak experiences, B values, ecstasy, wonder," and so on.[40] While the theorists and agendas that are covered by the banner of transpersonal psychology are numerous and varied, four aspects of this movement are germane to the argument at hand. First, there is the stress on immediate, firsthand unchurched mystical experience. This is true with regard to the ultimate aim of its practitioners and analysands as it is for theory building. Second, as concerns the *study* of mysticism, transpersonal psychology has championed a wide variety of types of scientific investigation, notably studies of meditation from experimental, neuro-physiological and bi-hemispheric perspectives (exemplified in studies by Arthur Deikman, Robert Ornstein, and Roland Fischer), empirical research into the effect of drugs and altered states (Stanislav Grof), and psycho-physiological analyses of near-death experiences (NDEs). Third, with respect to transpersonal therapy, the paradigmatic framework is that of the "spectrum of consciousness," an idea best articulated in the work of Ken Wilber. Briefly put, the underlying assumption is that of what he explicitly refers to as the "perennial psychology"—that is, the "universal view as to the nature of human consciousness which expresses the very same insights as the perennial philosophy but in more decidedly psychological language."[41] The view of consciousness and therapy is a highly eclectic one, drawing from the map of consciousness found in Western psychotherapies and the world's mystical traditions (with a seeming emphasis on Eastern mysticism). There exists, then, a spectrum of consciousness in which the human personality is seen as "a multi-leveled manifestation or expression of a single consciousness" ranging from "the Supreme identity of cosmic consciousness" through multiple layers down to "egoic consciousness." Each "level" of mind, be it the "shadow level," "existential level," or "cosmic consciousness," has a corresponding therapeutic technique through which it can be accessed, worked through, and developed. This is a technological, therapeutic-access view of mysticism. Finally, although the social agendas of the transpersonalists vary, it is fair to state that all would be sympathetic to the psychologist and NDE researcher Kenneth Ring's notion of "homo noeticus." The latter, states Ring, is an "emerging form of humanity" that seeks a "culture founded in higher consciousness, a culture whose institutions are based on love and wisdom, a culture that fulfills the perennial philosophy."[42]

What, then, do we have in Rolland, Jung, Bucke, Assagioli, Maslow, and the transpersonalists? Despite some real differences in therapeutic technique and metapsychology, there are some general but fundamental characteristics that unite them as members of the psychologia perennis: a championing of the individual as an unchurched locus of religiosity and veritable congregation of one; a valorization of personal testimony of unchurched mystical experiences; an advocacy of perennialism; the search for mysticism and its origins in the unconscious; the discernment of innate, intuitive mystical capacities; the development of a technology of altered states; the institutionalization of psycho-mystical therapeutic regimens; and a social vision consisting of the emergence of *homo mysticus.* In sum, a reversal of the Church Fathers' understanding of mysticism—emphasizing as they did a general reluctance to valorize their own personal mysticism, the development of religious virtues, and the accouterments of church and tradition: the need for mediation, the gift of grace, liturgy, and the sacraments.

The Cultural Dissemination of Mourned Mysticism

If one accepts the conclusion that, for the first time in history, the twentieth century has seen widespread formulations of an unchurched psychological mysticism, then a related issue is its cultural dissemination. As Max Weber would have it, how do we move from the formulations of "isolated individuals" to "a way of life common to whole groups?"[43] Certainly the social mechanisms through which the ideas of the perennial psychologists have come to be disseminated through culture at large are multiple and complex. One such mechanism can be fruitfully explored by utilizing Weber's analysis of how ideas, even if misunderstood, lead to cultural change. As is well known, Weber promoted this approach most forcefully in *The Protestant Ethic and the Spirit of Capitalism*. His sociological observations amounted to a "trickle-down" theory starting at the level of the cultural elite and "idea men" (the Protestant reformers and theologians) whose seminal formulations about the nature of man and his relation to God was mediated to the "masses" (believers) through the auspices of institutions and their idealized functionaries (ministers and pastoral counselors, the pulpit and the sermon).

This line of argument is commensurate with Philip Rieff's observations on the rise of what he terms "negative communities."[44] Indeed, one can frame Rieff's analysis as proceeding along essentially Weberian lines. For Rieff what "came before" were the Protestant reformers and the emergence of inner-worldly asceticism. Like all religious communities, the latter constituted a "positive community." The defining characteristic of such communities consists in the elaboration of a cultural symbolic in which controls and restraints on behavior outweigh permissions and an ethic in which the group takes precedence over the individual. In such communities there exists a "language of faith" that is deemed authoritative; a cultural super-ego that is idealized and internalized and that serves to keep the "lower" socially disruptive instinctual forces (sex and aggression) in check through repression and guilt. Represented institutionally by the "Church" and the "Party," positive communities reintegrate the anomic/neurotic through what Rieff calls "commitment therapies." The latter are those therapies, typical of all forms of religious healing, that enable the afflicted to encounter their unconscious in what Kohut terms an "experience-distant" manner. This is so for the language of sin and redemption, and the multiple symbols, myths, and narratives that invariably accompany the healing ritual are seen, at least from a psychodynamic perspective, as cultural dreams, being disguised projections of the unconscious. This religious language, mediated through rituals and the commanding, idealized figure of a religious functionary, serve to edify and release aggressive and sexual tensions, further allowing for the reenactment of the internalization of the cultural super-ego. In short, "commitment therapies" are "suggestive-supportive" in nature, being in the service of the reigning cultural symbolic.[45]

Negative communities, on the other hand, are of recent historical vintage and find their origin in a new cultural elite championing a psychological and therapeutic mode of self-relating. This new mode of therapy is not so much "suggestive-supportive" but "analytic" and "uncovering" in nature. In the case of Freud and his psycho-analytic followers the point is to engage the unconscious directly ("where id was, there ego shall be"), thus widening the ego and a sense of one's unique individuality. Indeed, cultural forms such as religion and politics are rendered suspect, being understood as sym-bolic manifestations of unconscious contents. An "analytic attitude" of observation, detachment, and tolerance of psychical discontents replaces the "language of faith" and the command to repress. The result is "deconversion" in the sociological sense, that is to say, the collapse of the cultural super-ego and the replacement of the Church and Party with the "Hospital" and "Theater" (as normative institutions), as well as the valorization of the individual over the group and the emergence of a therapeutic character type, "psycho-logical man."[46] Insofar as the concept of "negative communities" is designed to show the shift from the social hegemony of religion, the group, and "therapies of commitment" to the rise of the individual and analytic access, it gives psychosocial depth to the corresponding shift away from tradition-based mysticism that we have cataloged starting with de Certeau.

The perennial psychologists, now understood as a particular group of theorists within the more general category of those championing a therapeutic culture, can be further specified and defined with respect to the degree of de-idealization and the double act of repudiation and assimilation that they exhibit. Freud and his followers de-idealized religious forms of ideation and behavior to a deeper degree. As a result, it is harder to see anything in psychoanalysis that overtly resembles a "religion." On the other hand, while Jung, Rolland, and the perennial psychologists were similarly disillusioned with tradi-tional forms of religion, they were more likely to assimilate idealized forms of religious ideation into their respective psychologies. The mythic is in some sense present and pronounced. Religion "moves" from public, socially shared "containers" to the hidden ground of a religious or sacred unconscious. Hence it is that the perennial psy-chologists exhibit the form: psychology "as" a religion.

The fundamental means through which the new form of sociality advocated by the perennial psychology and implicit in the concept of negative communities is internalized and hence widely dissemi-nated is, as with positive communities, the ritual. But in religious rituals, be it the Eucharist, the confessional, or the hajj, the world-view mediated to one (that is, models "for" and "of" reality as Geertz would have it) always serves to reinforce the primary characteristics and values of a positive community. Psychological rituals (e.g., the therapeutic session and weekend retreat) operate by virtue of withdrawal into a liminal space that instills the values of negative communities. The door that marks off the "sacred space" of the room of the therapeutic session represents the "repression barrier" and the cultural super-ego. Once one is safely behind that door a different set of social rules is operative: the repression barrier is lifted, and one gains analytic access to the unconscious, as well as a new form of sociality that valorizes the individual, one's relation to the unconscious, and the subsequent awareness of one's uniqueness over against the sociopolitical and religious whole. Moreover, unlike the Catholic confessional, the institutional basis of psychological forms of therapy must be seen in that modern context to which Freud alluded when he called for the establishment of a secular cure of souls. In contrast to the traditional, religious stress on localized, permanent congregations enjoining regular ritual attendance, the therapeutic culture caters to the individual, existing in a "private sphere" on a consumer basis. "Membership" is casual and often transient, while any "group" formation lacks the binding historical force associated with a tradition. As seen earlier, the individual picks and chooses from a variety of different kinds of therapies and introspective technologies, constructing a worldview suited to their tastes and preferences. In the absence of one overarching, hegemonistic worldview, the arduous task of identity formation is thrust ever more directly in the hands of the individual. Truly here is the psychological version of being a congregation of one.

Commensurate with this analysis is the twentieth-century rise and development of what Weber termed the "inner-worldly mystic." While Weber had little to say about this social type, recent sociological studies have made clear the contemporary pervasiveness of inner-worldly mysticism.[47] The sociologist Roland Robertson, for example, takes his cue from Troeltsch's observation that a modern, non-institutional, individualistic form of mysticism was emerging. Then, drawing on Weber's concept of the inner-worldly mystic, Robertson expands on this ideal type by linking it to the rise of individualism, pluralism, rationalization, a scientific-bureaucratic ethos, and various modern introspective techniques for the realization and actualization of "the self" as found in the transpersonal and human potential movements.[48] In analyzing this new form of self-cultivation, Robertson notes that it is, in fact, socially engaged, being a modern form of social adaptation that seeks to synthesize that ethos which champions an orientation toward work in the world, societal involvement and social "perfection," and the inner injunction to seek wholeness, self-realization, and "self-perfection." The modern mystic is a psychologically informed individual seeking self-fulfillment in a capitalistic, bureaucratic society.

To take this a step further, we mentioned at the outset that the psychologia perennis constitutes but one cultural strand among the historical many (e.g., transcendentalism, Theosophy, New Thought, Eastern religions, Native American traditions, monastic enterprises), all of which have helped the inner-worldly mystic ascend to a place of social prominence and have contributed to the changing nature and definition of the broad terms "mysticism" and "spirituality" during the course of the twentieth century. Although a full exploration of these cultural strands and their relation to one another is beyond the parameters of this study, it is of more than passing interest to note that the results reached here are commensurate with those reached by recent studies similarly invested in contemporary construals of mysticism, spirituality, and the New Age. Indeed, many of the defining characteristics Melton and Lewis have cited as paradigmatic of the New Age (e.g., the stress on religious experience, healing, individual as well as societal transformation, the use of scientific terminology, optimism, social realization of a golden age) are similarly typical of the proponents of the psychologia perennis.[49] Along these lines Catherine Albanese argues for a new definition of mysticism as "a metaphor for inwardness, direct experience, and metaphysical empowerment in material life (all of which, it seems to me, mysticism is in the American context) . . . [American] mysticism ties together self, God and nature in a religious expansionism that has refused to go away."[50] So defined, and as illustrated in multiple and diverse forms of the contemporary religious life, Albanese sees mysticism as "a key distinguishing characteristic of the emerging American ethnos," a claim she links with the early researches of Ernst Troeltsch, tracing its historical development as far back as Emerson and the transcendentalists and analyzing its contemporary status in religious forms such as the New Age movement.[51] Then, drawing on Scholem's claim that modern forms of mysticism have attempted "to bring back the old unity which [institutional] religion has destroyed, but on a new plane, where the world of mythology and that of revelation meet in the soul of man," Albanese posits that the New Age has served to re-create the "diffused religion of the mythic age" alongside "the revelation of the institution through its appeal to a continuing inner voice." As such, what we find in the New Age is a "reprimitivized" religious situation: "what can be read from one point of view as secularity may be seen from another as the diffuse-ness of a "reprimitivized" religious situation."[52] Again, although Albanese's wide-ranging survey goes well beyond the parameters set in this study, her presentation of the prevalence of mysticism in American culture has a general affinity with the development of an unchurched, individualistic, psychologically informed mysticism as traced in this essay.

Cultural Mourning and the Academic Study of Mysticism

If one accepts the conclusions of the preceding two sections, then the concept of mourning applies not simply to individuals but to entire cultures as well. It is this wider understanding of mourning, both individual and cultural, that forms the basis for the new task at hand: the analysis of academic debates on mysticism. Contrary to most scholarly controversies concerning mysticism, which have rightly unearthed a spectrum of epistemological, theological, and comparative issues, the analysis undertaken in this section asks a different sort of question: to what extent is that cultural soil, seeded though mourning and its creative product (that is, the dissemination of the psychologia perennis and the rise of inner-worldly mysticism), responsible for the production of noteworthy academic debates on mysticism? The question is not designed to undermine in any way the importance of epistemological, comparative, or theological de-bates. It is, however, designed to draw attention to an ignored cul-tural context that has played a role in fermenting the considerable interest and anxiety that mark some of the scholarly controversies over mysticism. Specifically, we illustrate this with respect to two major debates, one classic and one contemporary, which continue to command the attention of scholars working in the field.

R. C. Zaehner's *Mysticism Sacred and Profane* has been taken within academia to be an account over whether mysticism is mani-fold or unitary. As is well known, Zaehner's classic study was in-stigated by Aldous Huxley, who, through his mescaline-induced visions, had become a proponent of perennialism. This grated on Zaehner's Catholic sensibilities, leading him to offer a threefold ty-pology of nature, monistic, and theistic forms of mysticism that were cross-culturally universal. But another reading can be promoted. This reading is possible because Huxley's perennialism was not doc-trinaire but idiosyncratic and highly psychological. And Zaehner's response constituted more than a simple threefold typology based on a comparative analysis of mystical traditions.

From the perspective of culture studies, what makes *Mysticism Sacred and Profane* a classic is *not* so much its typological schema as its status as a symptomatic expression of profound social conflict and upheaval. It spoke not to dry academic issues but to deeply held religious values that were undergoing a significant process of change and renewal. One must remember that the development of humanistic and transpersonal psychology, those very psychologies that championed the turn to "experience" and entheogens as advocated by Huxley, Leary, and Alport, occurred during the countercultural movement that defined the 1960s. This movement attacked reigning forms of (Christian) heteronomous morality and religion; looked toward Eastern religions for help; promoted introspective techniques and authentic experience; and impacted traditional conceptions of government, politics, work, gender, equality, race relations, and sexual orientation. This was a time of massive and culture-wide de-idealization; a time in which a "rhetoric of liminality" pervaded the sociocultural milieu. Zaehner's defense of Christianity and Huxley's "deconversion" and turn to Eastern religions, advocacy of altered states, freedom of expression, and anti-institutional sentiments fit hand in glove with the tensions surrounding the rise of a cultural rhetoric of liminality. What Zaehner found objectionable about Huxley was his debasement of the theistic (read: Christian) mystical tradition that denied the need for mediation and grace in favor of a narrative of human potential and self-actualization. And behind Huxley lay an entire cultural movement that attacked Christian moral codes and their social representatives.

Zaehner's depiction of Huxley's psychological state is commensurate with a culture pervaded by disillusionment. Zaehner tells us that Huxley shared the culturally popular view of the 1950s that viewed Christianity as synonymous with a heteronomous ethical code. For Huxley and others of his generation, that code was sexually, politically, and economically oppressive. So it is that Huxley became disillusioned and, being disillusioned, anomic. In other words, Huxley de-idealized his Christian culture and its social representatives. Indeed, Zaehner characterizes Huxley and his search for a "new religion" as motivated by psychological difficulties: feelings of meaninglessness, personal disintegration, and a desire to escape from selfhood. What Huxley wanted was authentic religious experience, a sense of wholeness and meaning, and an ideology he could live by. His wish was realized in the classic texts of Buddhism and Hinduism, where he found an emphasis on experience over ethics, authenticity over social convention, introspection over belief. And he came into firsthand contact with the essential experiential reality of these religions through mescaline.

Huxley's creative response to disillusionment and mourning took the form of an idiosyncratic, psycho-mystical, and highly eclectic perennialism. Aside from taking bits and pieces from Buddhism and Hinduism, in describing his mystical experiences, Huxley conceptualized his drug-induced reveries with respect to the Bergsonian concept of "Mind at Large." As Zaehner points out, Mind at Large is heavily psychological. And he thinks the psychologist to whom Huxley comes closest is none other than Jung. For Zaehner, Mind at Large is but a rudimentary version of Jung's concept of the collective unconscious. In other words, Huxley, far from promoting a doctrinaire Hindu or Buddhist agenda, presented an individually specific, quite modern, Westernized version of the perennial *psychology*. Disillusioned with traditional religion, Huxley took his own drug-induced mystical experiences, ran them through the concepts available to him in his culture, created a rudimentary religio-psychological theory to explain mysticism and religion in general, then offered it to a generation disillusioned by traditional, institutionalized religion. Given this, and in light of what we have learned about the relation between de-idealization, mourning, creative response, and the rendering of the psychologies advocated by Jung and Rolland, it does seem that one can justifiably extend the same analysis, as well as its conclusions, to Huxley.

Zaehner's response to Huxley is equally illuminating. He admits early on that his outrage is based on his Catholic faith.[53] In responding to Huxley, however, Zaehner did far more than simply offer a mystical typology that championed theism. Zaehner adopted a psychological-developmental stage approach to mysticism that engaged Huxley on his own terms. In other words, far from arguing simply on the level of typologies, Zaehner wanted to show a type of religious, mystical subjectivity that was qualitatively different from that depicted by Huxley. This subjectivity presupposed and transcended the level of Jungian psychological individuation. Zaehner was echoing the early Church Fathers' call for a type of mystical subjectivity that was based on grace and could not be reached without active participation in Church and Tradition.

In Zaehner's view the psychology of Jung is the paradigmatic example of a rationalized nature mysticism. At the same time, Jung's psychology, viewed in the classic sense as a psychology "of" religion, also becomes the interpretative lens through which Zaehner evaluates the various cases of what he portrays as Huxley's nature mysticism. The unitive experience with all of creation or nature is interpreted by Zaehner as signifying "inflation," the experience of the Self archetype and the foretaste of the more permanent state to which the ego is privy when fully individuated. It is the felt glimpse of what such a psychologically integrated state would be like—a state in which the ego does not cease to exist but is displaced from its central position by the timeless, deeper Self. This means that for Zaehner, as for Jung, the process of individuation is more important than mystical experience per se. Indeed, the latter is valuable only if it helps one individuate. Underneath the high visibility of Zaehner's stress on mysticism as experience, then, lies a view of mysticism as "process" (i.e., individuation), which is far closer to the true aim and spirit of his inquiry.[54]

But Zaehner does not stop with Jung. For him a "fully individuated" person is commensurate with Oscar Wilde's "true personality of man" and the Christian view of Adam before the Fall. But individuation is only the first stage on the theistic mystic's path to his ultimate destination, union with God. Jung and his theories apply only to nature mysticism and "pan-en-henic" experiences. Beyond this stage, states Zaehner, "religious or theistic mysticism begins."[55]

While nature mysticism is unchurched, promotes individuation, and can be interpreted through a Jungian psychological model, theistic Christian mysticism presupposes individuation and is dependent on a transcendent Therapist beyond our control. Thus it is that alongside Zaehner's phenomenological distinctions between nature, monistic, and theistic mysticism lies a psycho-religio stage theory of mysticism that, while incorporating and utilizing Jungian psychology, ultimately reserves an explanation of its highest stages for that conceptual scheme endemic to traditional religious theism. It is in this way that Zaehner reaffirms the Christian message, complete with its focus on ethics, grace, and the need for participation in liturgy and the sacraments in light of the threat posed by a countercultural movement that, in the form of Aldous Huxley, fit hand in glove with the rhetoric of liminality and the promotion of an unchurched mysticism.

In a slightly different way one can see the tension between churched and unchurched mysticism at work in a more recent controversy. The essence of the rather long-running debate between Steven Katz's contextualists (or constructivists) and Robert K. C. Forman's essentialists (or perennialists) has been framed as that between those that argue for a kind of experience that is non-intentional and lacks specific cultural and ideological content (a "pure conscious event" or PCE) and those who characterize all forms of experience, including mystical experience, as mediated. Eschewing the attempt to isolate a common core to all religions, the contextualist argues for specifying only institutional types of mysticism (Christian, Islamic, Jewish, Hindu, etc.). The constructivist approach to mysticism (and with regard to this particular point one should also include Zaehner) is far closer to Bouyer's observation about early Christian mysticism: it needs to be seen as part of a total religious matrix.

Forman's project, as many have noted, is more indebted to the apophatic tradition as found in neo-Advaitan forms of mysticism (Forman is an admitted practitioner of Transcendental Meditation) and its Western counterparts. His challenge to the claims of Katzian constructivism concerning pure conscious events and perennialism has been primarily of a comparative and philosophical/epistemological nature.

The thrust of our narrative proposes a new understanding of this debate. While Forman's essentialism and stress on the apophatic may have some root in traditional Eastern and Western religions, it is more accurate to read his project as a product of those cultural and historical forces that, as we have argued, ushered in the psychologia perennis. This becomes particularly evident when one sees Forman's academic project as part of his larger social agenda, which consists in a program for "spirituality and change" that he calls the Forge Institute. The institute's mission is "to help promote a spiritual renaissance in society." The "type" of spirituality it champions is not traditional but, as stated in a recent newsletter, is "transtraditional" and, further, an "inclusive spirituality or open ended and continual spiritual growth." Forman explains that "we are trying to find the best way to describe the spirituality that cannot be captured in any one system, is interdependent and relational, is willing to truly listen to others, that is growing and 'experience-able' as contrasted with a more static belief system."[56] Along with the Forge Institute, Forman has attempted to develop university-based contemplative studies programs (aided by transpersonalists such as Ken Wilber) and was instrumental in the formation of the *Journal of Consciousness Studies*. The latter is devoted to the study of consciousness "of all types" but particularly altered states as found in meditative and contemplative traditions. It aims at explaining such states with respect to psychological and neurophysiological models. It is, in other words, a renewed attempt to energize those studies of the 1960s as found in Arthur Deikman, Robert Ornstein, Roland Fischer, Charles Tart, and others, which were co-opted by the transpersonalists in their desire to conceptualize and provide access to the "spectrum of consciousness." Indeed, Forman's own notion of a PCE is nontraditional, framed as pointing to innate mystical capacities, and accessible to scientific and psychological probes.[57] It is further noteworthy that many of the members of the advisory board of the Forge Institute (a list that includes Roger Walsh, Francis Vaughn, Charles Tart, and Ken Wilber) are explicitly associated with transpersonal psychology. In other words, Forman's academic project is guided by a social objective that aims at creating a public space for an unchurched, scientific, psychological mysticism. It is, in many ways, continuous with the project championed by Huxley. And both deserve to be seen in the tradition of the psychologia perennis.

Notes

1. Louis Bouyer, "Mysticism: An Essay on the History of the Word," in *Understanding Mysticism*, ed. Richard Woods (Garden City, NY: Image Books, 1980).
2. Ibid., 52–53.
3. Michel de Certeau, "Mysticism," *Diacritics* 22, no. 2 (1992): 14.
4. Ibid., 24.
5. Leigh Eric Schmidt, "The Making of Modern Mysticism," *Journal of the American Academy of Religion* 71, no. 2 (June 2003): 288.
6. William James, *The Varieties of Religious Experience* (New York: Modern Library, 1929), 370, 31–32.
7. Walter Principe, "Toward Defining Spirituality," *Studies in Religion* 12, no. 2 (1983): 127–41.
8. David M. Wulff, *Psychology of Religion: Classic and Contemporary*, 2nd ed. (New York: John Wiley and Sons, 2000), 8.
9. Principe, "Toward Defining Spirituality."
10. M. MacDonald, "Spirituality," in *The Encyclopedia of Religion*, ed. Lindsay Jones, 2nd ed. (New York: Macmillan, 2005), 8718–21.
11. Robert Fuller, *Spiritual but Not Religious* (New York: Oxford University Press, 2001).
12. The formulation presented here follows the work of Peter Homans. See Homans, *The Ability to Mourn: Disillusionment and the Social Origins of Psychoanalysis* (Chicago: University of Chicago Press, 1989); Homans, *Jung in Context: Modernity and the Making of a Psychology* (Chicago: University of Chicago Press, 1979). See also my interview with Homans: William B. Parsons, "The Ability to Mourn: Disillusionment and the Social Origins of Psychoanalysis: A Conversation with Peter Homans," *Criterion* 30, no. 1 (1999).
13. Romain Rolland, *Le voyage intérieur* (Paris: Éditions Albin Michel, 1959), 176. Much of this summary of Rolland is culled from a more extensive, detailed treatment found in William B. Parsons, *The Enigma of the Oceanic Feeling* (New York: Oxford University Press, 1999).
14. Romain Rolland, *Journey Within*, trans. Elsie Pell (New York: Philosophical Library, 1947), 85.

15. Romain Rolland, in Louis Beirnaert, "Romain Rolland, Les derniéres etapes du voyage intérieur," *Etudes* 44 (1945): 250–56.
16. Romain Rolland, *Mémoires et fragments du Journal* (Paris: Albin Michel, 1956), 23.
17. Ibid., 23–25.
18. Romain Rolland's *Credo Quia Verum* is to be found at the end of volume 4 of *Cahiers Romain Rolland* (Paris: Éditions Albin Michel, 1949).
19. Rolland, *Journey Within*, 17.
20. Romain Rolland, *Au Seuil de la dérniere porte* (Paris: Les Éditions de Cerf, 1989), 23.
21. William Thomas Starr, *Romain Rolland and a World at War* (Evanston, IL: Northwestern University Press, 1956), 175–76.
22. Dilip Kumar Roy, *Among the Great: Conversations with Romain Rolland, Mahatma Gandhi, Bertrand Russell, Rabindranath Tagore, Sri Aurobindo* (Bombay: N. M. Tripathi, Nalanda, 1945), 71–72.
23. Romain Rolland, *The Life of Vivekananda and the Universal Gospel*, trans. E. F. Malcolm-Smith (Calcutta: Advaita Ashrama, 1965), 176–77.
24. Ibid., 348 n. 1.
25. See Rolland's letter to Freud of Dec. 5, 1927, in Parsons, *Enigma of the Oceanic Feeling*, 173–74.
26. Rolland, *Life of Vivekananda*, 346ff.
27. Ibid., 259.
28. Sigmund Freud, *The Freud-Jung Letters: The Correspondence between Sigmund Freud and C. G. Jung*, ed. William McGuire, trans. Ralph Manheim and R. F. C. Hull (Princeton, NJ: Princeton University Press, 1974), 197.
29. Ibid., 293–94.
30. Ibid., 295.
31. Carl Jung, *Memories, Dreams, Reflections* (New York: Vintage, 1961), 199.
32. Ibid., 171.
33. Carl Jung, *Psychology and Religion* (New Haven, CT: Yale University Press, 1977), 6.
34. Homans, *Ability to Mourn*, 144–52.
35. For insights into how Jung's psychology has become institutionalized as a veritable mystico-therapeutic regimen, see Richard Noll, *The Jung Cult* (New York: Free Press, 1994).
36. Quoted in R. May, *Cosmic Consciousness Revisited* (Rockport, MA: Element, 1991), 19.
37. Richard Maurice Bucke, *Cosmic Consciousness* (New York: Citadel Press, 1993), 8; hereafter cited in text.
38. Abraham Maslow, *Religions, Values and Peak-Experiences* (New York: Penguin Books, 1976; first published 1973), 19–20.
39. Ibid., 28.
40. Anthony J. Sutich, "Transpersonal Psychology: An Emerging Force," *Journal of Humanistic Psychology* 8 (Spring 1968): 77.
41. Ken Wilber, "Psychologia Perennis: The Spectrum of Consciousness," *Journal of Transpersonal Psychology* 7 (1975): 105. I am indebted to Wilber for my own use of the term "psychologia perennis."
42. Kenneth Ring, "Near-Death Experiences: Implications for Human Evolution and Planetary Transformation," in *The Near-Death Experience: A Reader*, ed. Lee Bailey and Jenny Yates (New York: Routledge, 1996), 194.
43. Max Weber, *The Protestant Ethic and the Spirit of Capitalism*, trans. Talcott Parsons (New York: Charles Scribner's Sons, 1958), 55.
44. See Philip Rieff, *The Triumph of the Therapeutic: Uses of Faith after Freud* (New York: Harper, 1966).
45. Ibid.; see esp. chap. 3.

46. Ibid.
47. See Roland Robertson, *Meaning and Change: Explorations in the Cultural Sociology of Modern Societies* (New York: New York University Press, 1978); Philip Wexler, *The Mystical Society: An Emerging Social Vision* (Boulder, CO: Westview Press, 2000); Alton B. Pollard, *Mysticism and Social Change: The Social Witness of Howard Thurman* (New York: P. Lang, 1992); Harry T. Hunt, *Lives in Spirit: Precursors and Dilemmas of a Secular Western Mysticism* (Albany: State University Press of New York, 2003).
48. Robertson, *Meaning and Change.*
49. See James R. Lewis and J. Gordon Melton, eds., *Perspectives on the New Age* (Albany: State University Press of New York, 1992).
50. Catherine Albanese, "Religion and the American Experience: A Century After," *Church History* 57 (1988): 345.
51. Ibid.
52. Ibid., 346. Albanese has written at length on the cultural origins and status of the New Age. See, for example, Albanese, "The Magical Staff: Quantum Healing in the New Age," in Lewis and Melton, *Perspectives on the New Age;* Albanese, "The Subtle Energies of Spirit: Explorations in Metaphysical and New Age Spirituality," *Journal of the American Academy of Religion* 67, no. 2 (1988): 305–26.
53. R. C. Zaehner, *Mysticism Sacred and Profane* (New York: Oxford University Press, 1980), xiii.
54. Ibid., 94, 106, 110–11, 118, 148.
55. Ibid., 118, 150.
56. From a newsletter entitled "first formal update" of the Forge Institute (February 1999).
57. See, for example, Robert K. C. Forman, ed., *The Innate Capacity: Mysticism, Psychology, and Philosophy* (New York: Oxford University Press, 1997).

ERNEST WALLWORK

Mourning Modern Ethics on the Couch

FOR MANY individuals today, the losses that accompany moral change are different from, but no less important than, losses associated with changes in religion. This essay uses psychoanalytic theories about grief, mourning, and loss to better understand what is at stake psychologically and morally as individuals in our society move away from their internalizations of received moral traditions.[1] It also uses psychoanalytic theory and case studies to critique certain widely read theories that address sociocultural shifts in morality. Drawing on my clinical work as a psychoanalyst with patients struggling over moral issues, I explore various problems that individuals experience in seeking to live moral lives. I use psychoanalytic theories to illuminate what has been lost morally, whether or not this is a good or bad thing, and how what has been lost can be productively mourned in order to produce a deeper sense of self, leading to the creation of new moral meanings and behaviors.

Mourning Modern Ethics on the Couch

As I listen to my psychoanalytic and psychotherapy patients talk about their lives in the deep, uninhibited ways that they do in the privacy of the consulting room, I do not hear much evidence of the radical narcissistic individualism lamented by the Rieff-Lasch-Bellah school of cultural interpretation.[2] My patients, far from being the narcissistic libertarians discussed in Bellah's *Habits of the Heart*, typically feel guilty when they fail to fulfill a promise, say, to come for an appointment at a particular time (even if they end up paying for it anyway), or when they lie or cheat. They even feel guilty when they try but fail to tell their analyst the full emotional truth about some deeply conflicted issue. In short, most patients seem to assume the validity of what some contemporary ethicists call "the common morality," without worrying very much about its philosophical underpinnings. Those who disregard moral conventions do not usually represent cutting-edge changes in culture, but rather are casualties of profound developmental failures that have left them with deeply flawed personality structures.[3]

What, then, has been lost morally in the lives of most of our contemporaries in post-industrial societies? One answer, proposed by Alasdair MacIntyre in *After Virtue*, holds that we have lost rational ways of resolving our most serious moral disagreements.[4] Contemporary arguments about abortion, war, and justice go on interminably, MacIntyre argues, because, ultimately, we lack the shared ways of thinking ethically that enabled our ancestors to resolve moral disputes. When we argue, we end up reaching incommensurable basic premises that turn out to be incapable of further rational support. For this reason, MacIntyre declares that contemporary morality is in a state of "grave disorder." We possess only fragments of a once coherent moral universe. To be sure, moral discourse goes on today, as it always has, as if our moral judgments are—or could be—backed by impersonal objective reasons. However, when push comes to shove, MacIntyre avows, we possess no shared definitive meta-decision procedure, meta-principle, or meta-theory with which to defend even our ordinary moral beliefs. Thus, we turn out to actually "use" moral language as emotivists such as C. L. Stevenson proposed in the middle of the last century. That is, the sole final defense of our moral standards turns out to rest with emotional approval, which is conjoined with the desire that others approve of these standards as well.[5] Simply put, MacIntyre's argument is that the emotivists were wrong about the meaning of moral language, but, nevertheless, right about how we actually use moral discourse.

MacIntyre, like Robert Bellah and his coauthors in *Habits of the Heart*, addresses public (not private, intra-psychic) changes. He mourns the passing of the traditional communities that legitimated the allegedly coherent moral cultures of predecessor ages. Even though *After Virtue* is clearly a work of mourning, MacIntyre's solution to what he views as the catastrophic collapse of ethical foundations lies in retrieving an Aristotelian understanding of virtues—that is, virtues embedded in practices within moral traditions—insofar as this is possible within the conditions of post-industrial societies.

MacIntyre does not expect help from psychotherapy for this work of retrieval because, in his view, the practice of psychotherapy is inexorably tied up with the deepest moral deficiencies of our era. Psychotherapy, in MacIntyre's caricature, is an expression of emotivist culture that rests morality on instrumental reasoning about arbitrarily chosen ultimate ends of action. "The therapist . . . treats ends as given, as outside his scope; his concern . . . is with technique, with effectiveness in transforming neurotic symptoms into directed energy, maladjusted individuals into well-adjusted ones."[6] What is needed to counter moral erosion, MacIntyre contends, is to rediscover and re-invigorate (1) communal virtues, (2) the social practices within which they are cultivated, and (3) the moral traditions that back them up.

If MacIntyre's analysis of the collapse of once coherent moral cultures was accurate, we would expect some collaborative evidence from the couch in the form of mourning the loss of traditional moral communities or anger about the prevailing manipulative uses of moral discourse. But there is little evidence of this. The only patient I have treated in the past twenty years who has mourned the loss of traditional morality suffered from the telltale borderline symptom of thinking in all-or-nothing terms. At one point in our work, this patient became extremely agitated by the thought that if my interpretations of the defensive nature of his impossibly idealistic moral beliefs were to be believed, the whole of morality would collapse, leaving only Nietzschean nihilism. "If you're right," he groaned, "there's no way to criticize Hitler's final solution." These persecutory anxieties dissipated, later in the analysis, not because he found a rationally defensible ethic or a close-knit community, but after he had become aware of how his predilection for either/or and all/nothing binaries precluded thinking about subtler moral possibilities. In Kleinian terms, his anxieties about the entire collapse of moral culture shifted when he moved from the paranoid-schizoid position to the "depressive position," which enabled him to think about morality in both/and instead in either/or terms.

What patients most mourn morally, I find, is neither MacIntyre's traditional moral world nor the republican and biblical traditions that Bellah and his coauthors would revive; rather, they mourn the simple fact that the Western moral traditions no longer work very well for those striving to live morally within the complexities of contemporary existence. Our options today not only far exceed anything our forefathers imagined, but we possess multiple conceptual schemes for describing and evaluating the choices we confront. The simplifying meta-narratives proffered by Rieff, Lasch, Bellah, and MacIntyre fail to shed sufficient light on the problem of choice under the conditions of contemporary existence or to proffer adequate remedies, largely because they couch the difficulty at too abstract a level of generality (at the level of meta-narratives), when, in fact, the chief difficulties lie nearer at hand. The Rieff-Lasch-Bellah-MacIntyre cultural meta-narratives partake of the problems that bedevil the leading ethical theories; they end up offering impractical, simplifying solutions (such as reviving dead cultural legacies or hunkering down in "new . . . communities within which the moral life can be sustained through the new dark ages which are already upon us")[7] when remedies are needed that provide guidance about how to go about thinking reasonably well about the multiple levels of meanings, affects and consequences of the very particular practical dilemmas that bedevil us.

A large part of the problem ordinary people have with being moral is simply the difficulty of judging moral situations in their full, unique complexity. Ethical theories offer insufficient help not because they cannot be justified (MacIntyre) or because they commend radical individualism (Bellah) but because they oversimplify the relevant facts of most actual moral dilemmas. Abstracting from the complexities of a particular situation, a Kantian or utilitarian ethic tends to highlight some aspects of complex cases at the expense of others, yielding solutions that fail to fit the full range of facts that need to be considered and evaluated for a viable ethical resolution of the case at hand.

An entrenched cultural fantasy holds that good people know spontaneously or intuitively the right thing to do, without much effort, thereby obscuring the difficulty of making really good moral judgments.[8] The psychic fallout of this fantasy includes anxiety about making mistakes, self-doubting, intolerance of delay, mistrust of others and oneself, and compensatory dogmatism combined with a tendency to shift the blame elsewhere. It is not easy to constrain these disruptive affects and defenses long enough to make room for the difficult task of thinking about the many issues that go into making the best moral decisions.

The Psychoanalytic Approach to Moral Decision Making

Against the fantasy that the moral life is easy, psychoanalysis pleas for a measure of skepticism about what we know and how we know it. Unlike the single motive theory of moral conduct that modern moral philosophers prefer, psychoanalysis specializes in searching for multiple interpretations of the same action, yielding an approach to ethics that calls for a blending of evaluative considerations rather than subsuming a case under a single principle. Too frequently, ethics texts subsume novel situations under abstract rules or paradigmatic cases that either do not apply or apply poorly because they were constructed for completely different circumstances. On issues such as care of the terminally ill and aggressive treatment of seriously defective newborns, one-size-fits-all cookie-cutter solutions seldom work. What a doctor said in jest to me recently, as he handed me a blue paper disposable dressing gown, applies to many ethical generalizations: "One size fits no one!"

Although most contemporary Americans need to mourn the failings of their inherited moral tradition, individuals differ significantly with respect to precisely what moral simplifications need to be mourned. For some people, traditional rules are too rigid to permit the mental space necessary for thinking creatively about the complexities of particular cases and relationships. For others, the received moral tradition sets forth ideals of perfection against which almost all decisions and actions fall woefully short, often giving rise to an agency-sapping depression that cuts the ground from under the moral life. For others still, not only does the moral tradition fail to envision many pressing moral situations (for example, a gay lifestyle, same-sex marriage, or withholding nutrition and hydration from individuals in persistent vegetative states), but the resources the tradition does offer are unhelpful, if not actually offensive, and in need of considerable amplification from elsewhere.

Mourning the failure of a moral tradition entails a work of cultural critique, such as that pursued by postmodernists, postcolonialists, feminists, and queer theorists, but it is also a highly individual work of self-exploration, one that requires each individual to recognize where the received morality fails intra-psychically and what might be done about it. The psychoanalyst's consulting room is one place in contemporary culture where this kind of work of "moral mourning" is routinely done; though, curiously, psychoanalysts, for a variety of reasons, do not often imagine their work in explicitly moral terms.[9]

A number of leading psychoanalysts have interpreted mourning as a process of relinquishing self or object representations at various stages of development.[10] Examples include Klein's "depressive position," Mahler's concept of separation-individuation, Kohut's view of de-idealization, Joffe and Sandler's depiction of the child's relinquishment of longing for "ideal states of self,"[11] and Loewald's views of the oedipal stage as a mourning process. When mourning does not take place or gets bogged down, the options include sadistic violence or pathological mourning, both of which retard further psychic growth and the discovery of new creative outlets.

Since each individual has something different to mourn when the received moral tradition fails, identifying what it is that one has lost—or imagines one has lost—is indispensable to getting on with the mourning process and, eventually, finding creative solutions to the moral difficulties of daily living. The clinical vignettes below highlight some differences among individuals who experience the failures of the received moral traditions in radically diverse ways. Although these cases are representative of some typical problems, each is also unique.

Case 1. Mourning Fixed Moral Guideposts

Beth was a forty-two-year-old, widowed mother of three when she started her analysis. The problems she presented seemed the reverse of MacIntyre's portrayal of our moral plight. For most of her life, Beth had no problem making moral decisions in the clear light of the conservative Calvinist values of the rural community in which she was raised. If she had read MacIntyre's *After Virtue*, she would have rejected the idea that we live in a state of serious moral disarray or that we are unable to resolve major moral disagreements. She would have said that her personal life and that of her neighbors is fairly well ordered morally. As for the seemingly unsolvable dilemmas that MacIntyre cites, she would have claimed that conscience is a reasonably reliable guide for most well-intentioned people most of the time.

The problems that brought Beth to my office were not the result of any fissures in her moral world. Rather, her problems derived largely from the rigidity of the moral framework that had sunk deep taproots in her psyche. The inflexible absolutism of her internalized moral code made it impossible for her to acknowledge the many subtle moral distinctions that were required for good decision making at her place of work and in her private life. Although Beth had left the small town in which she was raised for a suburb on the fringe of a modestly sized urban area in the Northeast, she continued to rely on the morality she had internalized during her childhood, the one that was preached at her church on Sundays. She thought most of the other elementary school teachers with whom she worked ascribed to a like set of values. Her moral code was expressed and reinforced by the many bromides by which she lived: "A stitch in time saves nine." "Waste not, want not." "Pride goeth before a fall."

Beth sought therapy for chronic depression that included painful feelings of despair, loneliness, low self-esteem, depleted interest and energy, as well as a pattern of self-defeating conduct and under-achievement in her career, vocational activities, and romantic life. She wanted to get more out of life and to do more, but she found herself struck by paralyzing inertia whenever she contemplated "coming out of hiding."

Beth experienced her subjective thoughts, decisions, and actions as if they were micromanaged by a complex set of internalized rules and bromides that made her feel guilty, whatever she decided to do. If she tried to avoid being late when taking her children to school by leaving a bed unmade, she harassed herself until she made the bed, worrying all the while about being late. "There are so many rules," she moaned.

"I'm caught, coming and going. As I'm beginning to get just enough outside them here to see them, I'm shocked how complicated things can be when they don't need to be. Just yesterday I was dealing with the birthday present for a colleague. I'd bought her a perfectly fine present that I thought she'd like, but then doubling back on my-self and second-guessing my selection, I started thinking it might be taken as demeaning her. I was afraid she'd be insulted, if she saw the gift as implying she's an infirmed old woman who needs an aid like this. It was supposed to be a little funny, but I thought she might take it as cruel and humiliating. . . . But, you know, there really isn't anything wrong with this present. It doesn't need to take so much of my time. This is just one of many little things I've been trying to do today. Struggles go on non-stop in my head and they're wearing me out. I live, exhausted, in a jungle of rules—'don't do this, don't do that, this isn't good enough, you're mean, thoughtless, cruel, cheap,' on and on—it's never ending. I can't go on living like this!"

It slowly became apparent that beneath her humble compliance, Beth hid genuine abilities and, indeed, accomplishments. She was terrified of her strengths. Associating to what her success would mean, Beth expressed fear that if she let her talents loose, her father, brothers, aunts, mother, and analyst would be consumed by envy and spoil what she had done, as her parents did when they ridiculed her starring performance in a sixth-grade school play. She, therefore pro-tected herself by knocking herself down before someone else could and by appearing meek, dumb, and subservient. In lieu of valuing her strengths, she undervalued and hid them, even from herself.

The self-sabotaging nature of Beth's defenses found outward sym-bolic expression one day when, coming into her living room, she was suddenly envious of the beautiful flowers that had blossomed on a couple of tropical plants she had meticulously cultivated. Feeling acutely her own shortcomings in comparison with these plants and, at the same time, imaging visitors envying her horticultural achievement, she hacked the blossoming plants down with a large butcher's cleaver, metaphorically reenacting what she had done with accomplishments most of her life: destroying her budding achievements. She could take little pleasure in genuine accomplishments at work and in raising her children as a single mom or with her secret writing project—largely because she thought of herself as thoroughly inadequate.

In the course of her analysis, Beth came to appreciate how trying to follow the many inflexible rules that encumbered her internal world seriously undercut not only her self-esteem but also her efforts to live morally. For example, her preoccupation with trivial duties, such as washing the dishes after every meal or maintaining a meticulously neat classroom, often led to the neglect of more important responsibilities, such as attending to a child's needs. As she became increasingly aware of these and other moral failures, Beth began to doubt and then to criticize the moral order that had been a major source of security throughout her life. Eventually, she abandoned and mourned the loss of the fantasy that she was good only to the extent that she followed the many rules that she had been taught. Although she had thought of the rules as encouraging altruism, she discovered that maintaining them was actually selfish in the sense that it was done for her own peace of mind and often at the expense of the needs of others. Indeed, she often hurt her own children and those in her charge by punishing them too severely for petty infractions.

Criticizing the old morality was particularly problematic for Beth because it seemed to her to involve thinking too much about herself. Yet, as the analysis unfolded, she also became increasingly aware of how failing to attend to her needs, as the older morality dictated, really did not work well for others either:

Last night, when Frank [a man she was dating] dropped by, we had a really nice talk over a snack. He'd been working late and hadn't gone home yet. Seeing my car in the carport, he'd decided to stop in. He had said when he walked in, "when you need to go to bed, let me know." I was again able to break a family rule, the one that says "never ask a guest to leave." At 10:30, I told him I was exhausted suddenly and he was fine with it. After all, he'd asked me to let him know when I got tired. Later, I worried that I'd done a bad thing, asking him to leave. For awhile I felt guilty, but, then, I thought that that's Dad's code and it really doesn't work all that well.

Mourning loss of the fantasy that she was good insofar as she lived by the rules that she had been taught, Beth gradually came to appreciate in sessions like the one above that she possesses the ability to analyze complex moral dilemmas and to arrive at conclusions based on taking into account multiple, incommensurable values and the effects of various options on the lives of herself and others. As she underwent this moral transformation, she moved emotionally from depression (melancholia) through mourning the loss of the security of her father's moral world to a newfound delight in her own moral creativity when challenged by difficult dilemmas.

The following vignette from late in Beth's five-year analysis shows how far she progressed from dutiful compliance to a fixed set of rules to a form of critical reflection that enables her to navigate more satisfactory resolutions among conflicting currents of thoughts, feelings, and motivations. Beth's decision in this situation is controversial, but there can be no doubt that she has been freed by analysis for a much richer and more creative kind of moral reasoning than she had been capable of previously.

I had a couple of challenges on Saturday regarding Dad's morality, and I became newly aware of some things. I was able to stay with making thoughtful choices. First, my friend Marcia left her briefcase at my house when she stopped by Friday night. She called to ask as if I could drop it off at her place over the weekend, assuming I'd be in her neighborhood. In the past, I would have said, "of course," and then bent myself out of shape to drive the briefcase over to her house. But I avoided getting into that old self-sacrificial mode. I said I didn't expect to be in her part of town anytime in the next week, so it might be better, if she needed the briefcase sooner, to come over to pick it up. Of course, she did. But, I suspect I've been such a pushover in the past that Marcia and other friends think I'm a doormat, that I'll always go out of my way to do things for them, regardless of the inconvenience to me. This time I was clear about my limits and everyone got their needs met. Marcia got her briefcase, and I didn't expend a lot of my limited time and energy going overboard helping her out.

Beth's case shows the difficult struggle involved in mourning the loss of a once secure moral world. It also highlights how good moral decisions involve a complex balancing of incommensurable values in light of concrete particulars, not compliance with a priori abstract general principles. As Tim's case below shows, Beth's problem with inflexible moral standards is only one reason why the received morality does not work well for people today. The received moral tradition does not work well for Tim either, but for different reasons. What he needs to mourn differs as well.

Case 2. Mourning Impossible Ideals

The losses Tim is mourning are very different from Beth's. Tim has not been encumbered by too many rules but by too few. Since junior high school, Tim has flagrantly opposed most social conventions in his choices of clothes, jobs, friends, and recreational activities. A perpetual rebel who spent his high school years dressed in gothic black, Tim has been fighting "the system" for most of his life. In contrast with Beth, who always sought to be a "good girl" by following familial-religious rules, Tim was a very "bad boy" with a defiant "attitude," who, by breaking rules, managed to elicit enormous rage and despair from his parents, teachers, coaches, and a long list of bosses and lovers. He has been punished harshly over the years for his many transgressions (including jail time) but without much effect on his willingness to comply the next time around. Yet, for all his manifest unwillingness to conform, Tim is a decent, kind, and generous man, the kind of rough-hewn, regular guy who will stop on a superhighway to help a total stranger repair a broken-down vehicle.

To his many acquaintances, Tim seems to be a remarkably free spirit, with few worries. He approaches most new friends with bravado. "I've always lived life the way I've wanted, without any regrets," he told a new barstool companion recently. But actually, Tim is chronically depressed and anxious. For as long as he can remember, he has unsuccessfully sought a deep, affectionate bond with men and women, which has always eluded him. In one of his earliest (screen) memories, he is crying hysterically in his crib, feeling totally abandoned, desperately alone, and utterly terrified, until wheezing, gasping for breath, unable to breathe, he passes out from exhaustion. Apparently, his parents had been told that crying strengthens character, rather than weakens it. As a punishment for his annoying hyperactivity, Tim's mother locked him in his room alone for hours. Retaliating self-destructively, Tim smashed his toys until he had none left, soothing himself for their loss by banging his head against the walls or pillows.

Freud's "Mourning and Melancholia" highlights the importance that anger at unavailable objects plays in Tim's psychic life. Furious at his aloof, emotionally absent parents for rarely making emotional contact (both Tim's parents appear to have been too narcissistic and severely depressed to empathize with their only child), Tim blamed and punished himself. In some ways, his self-punishments were worse then his parents' penalties, because there was nowhere he could hide from his own self-punitive ruminations.

Convinced that he was to blame for his parents inability to connect emotionally, Tim tried unsuccessfully to make restitution after he graduated from college by moving back in with them, hoping against hope that his parents would warm up to him emotionally. Unfortunately, both his parents were killed in a freak automobile accident a few months later. Unable to mourn their deaths productively, Tim mourned pathologically by identifying with the hated objects and directing even more rage against himself.

Desperate to keep alive the fantasy of some real connection with his parents, Tim packed his small house with the contents of their much larger one. He hoped that by possessing his lost parents' possessions, he would feel more deeply connected to them.

Tim's immense unconscious guilt about his failed relationship with his parents and his inability to mourn them was generated in three different ways.[12] First, Tim's guilt sprang from a more or less realistic appraisal of the part he himself played in the failure to connect with his parents. He had been a difficult child, and as he grew older he deliberately provoked his already-stressed parents, leading them to distance themselves ever further from him. This component of Tim's guilt was recognized by Freud in discussing the self-reproaches of melancholics: "a few genuine self-reproaches are scattered among those that have been transposed back."[13] Second, Tim suffered from the more irrational guilt that arises from knowing that even if he was not in reality responsible for their lack of love and untimely deaths, he had often hated his parents and wished that they would die. Much of his neurotic guilt after his parents' deaths appears to be of this character. Finally, Tim experienced unconsciously the wholly irrational guilt that arose from turning the enraged criticisms he had aimed at his parents toward himself. Tim's sense that whatever he did he was a failure derived in large part from this guilt. As Bowbly notes, "It was one of Freud's great discoveries to recognize that psychotic guilt is to be accounted for by a shift of this kind."[14]

Tim's pathological mourning had persisted for two decades when we began analysis, after other therapies failed to help. By that time, Tim's pathological mourning had been repeatedly reinforced by vain efforts on his part to repair the damaged love at the heart of all his relationships, most especially his relationships with women with whom he imagined creating a family of his own. His mostly brief relationships ended in failure because, in a perverse repetition of his childhood, he found women who turned out to be emotionally distant like his mother, despite initial impressions of liveliness. Finding himself emotionally abandoned yet again with each new girlfriend, Tim repeatedly blamed himself, without appreciating the emotional void, usually due to depression, in the objects of his affection. Eventually, Tim's mounting despair hurt the relationship, and he or his girlfriend fled, leaving him once again in grief over yet another abandonment.

This destructive pattern came to an end after the analysis restarted the mourning process. One mutative component was free association, which allowed Tim to openly express both his infantile yearning for his absent parents as well as angry reproaches against them. Another mutative aspect of Tim's analysis was his realization that while he had contributed to the serious estrangement with his parents during his openly rebellious high school years, his rebellion was based on prior frustration and anger at his aloof parents. A third mutative aspect of the analysis came with Tim's realization in the transference that he irrationally blamed and punished himself for the analyst's unavailability. He was not really responsible, he came to realize, for driving his analyst away when the analyst was lecturing in a distant city. After Tim put himself in real danger several times when his analyst was absent—for example, by driving at high speeds "under the influence" and by nearly severing a finger in a boating "accident"—the unconscious roots of Tim's early, persistent self-inflicted punishments could be analyzed as not only his way of expressing anger but also, paradoxically, a way of connecting with those he loved. Tim's self-destructive conduct managed to grab his parents' attention, as it later did his analyst's, in ways that made emotional contact, albeit negatively and at considerable cost to Tim.

What Tim had to mourn was the impossibility of ever finding the idealized love he had longed for as a child. In doing so, he became more realistic and satisfied with the ordinary human loves that are available, without trashing himself or the relationship for falling short of perfection.

One might think that Tim's struggle was less with the received moral tradition than with private frustrations, but for him the two were deeply intermeshed emotionally. For example, Tim had transferred onto society his bitter struggle with his parents. Chafing under social restrictions and deprivations, he dreamed of utopian socialist compensations. When Tim's psychic economy changed, so did his approach to conventional morality. What changed in Tim was not his moral indignation at social inequities or at environmental degradation, but, rather, his way of thinking about these issues. Less consumed by rage at social power elites or at himself, Tim was able to think more deeply about the social and psychological sources of major social problems and to direct his energies more strategically toward realizable goals. Less convinced that the world was governed by either totally good guys or totally bad guys, Tim was able to differentiate more subtly between the good and bad in various reformers, politicians and causes.

Case 3. Mourning the Loss of an Ego Ideal

Dan was a twenty-three-year-old recent college graduate in a corporate executive training program when he sought psychotherapy for some vague psychological complaints that were not initially clear to his therapist. An impressive athlete in several sports in both high school and college (he had been captain of several teams), Dan had not tried to be either a "good boy" who always followed the rules, like Beth, nor a "bad boy" who usually defied them, like Tim. Instead, Dan respected societal standards as necessary for cooperation and fair play, just as he respected the rules of the sports he played. He played hard to win within the rules, without worrying about hurting a competitor's feelings on the one hand or failing to get what he wanted on the other. He was used to winning.

What Dan needed to mourn, it turned out, was that he was not, and could never be, the "macho heterosexual guy" he wanted to be. No one knew, because he had not told anyone before his therapist, that he had suddenly realized, while lifting weights in ninth grade, that the reason he felt uncomfortable bantering with other guys about the cheerleaders was that he liked guys. For Dan, who, unlike many gays, had never felt different growing up, acknowledging his sexual orientation was profoundly traumatizing. Feeling ashamed, humiliated, and frightened, he "fell apart" emotionally and academically for most of his ninth-grade school year before realizing that he could keep his "dirty secret" to himself and that no one need ever know. When his many efforts to force himself to be straight (by dating girls) failed, Dan directed his considerable rage on himself. Projecting his self-contempt outward, his fear of being discovered and ridiculed kept him in constant inner torment. He had been the guy in middle school who had cruelly mocked nerds for being "gay"; now he found himself fighting off bouts of severe persecutory anxiety.

His compromise solution was to throw himself into sports, where he cultivated a masculine identity that effectively shielded his inner life from being known by anyone—including, even, himself.

Over the course of his intensive psychotherapy, which followed a period of deep depression during which he came close to suiciding, Dan mourned the loss of his ideal facade, the "hetero-guy" self, and faced up to being "gay" and what it meant to him.[15] Giving up this hetero-ideal was especially difficult because that ideal protected him from an unarticulated dread of being vulnerable, which, to him, included openness to any emotional states not entirely under his control. It took a long time for Dan to begin to tolerate emotions other than anger, but as he did so, in the safe holding environment created by his therapist, Dan's self-recriminations decreased in ferocity as he started to tolerate thinking differently about himself. He became more open to being vulnerable, beginning with exposing himself to the intense grief and disappointment he felt about himself and his life circumstances. With this new openness, Dan became noticeably more empathic, caring, and kind. His therapist could feel it in the transference. Whereas Dan had previously taken his therapist for granted, he now began to notice and express sympathy when his therapist looked especially tired; on one occasion, he offered to cut a session short when his therapist was sick.

Even Dan's ethics of fair play proved to be caught up in the ego's defensive use of conventional social morality. The shift that Dan experienced in therapy is designated by Lacan as the ethical fulcrum of psychoanalysis, namely, a shift in Dan's *desire*. For Dan, this basic change in his desire opened up a realm of feelings below conventional morality. It's not that Dan changed his moral standards. He continued to value cooperation and fair play, but therapy had a profound impact on how Dan subsequently went about being moral, especially the emotional depth of the way he relates to himself and to others. Less in need of protecting a citadel self, Dan became open to a richer range of emotions within himself that has enabled him subsequently to respond with greater empathy to the emotions, needs, and desires of his many close friends and family members.

Conclusion

All three of these very dissimilar cases involve mourning some perceived failure in the internalized moral tradition. The nature of that failure differs from case to case, but all share the sometimes painful realization that clear ethical resolutions are not always readily available and that it is often extraordinarily difficult to discern the difference between the right and the wrong course of action. Each patient has had to struggle with the failure of some focal desire, whether it be for the security provided by a reliable set of stable rules (Beth), for the affects connected with romantic love (Tim), or for the sense of self-esteem tied to realizing a specific ideal self-state (Dan). Each of these focal desires proved dysfunctional in part by pervading the individual's thinking with a single-minded, one-dimensional, exclusionary, and tyrannical angle of vision. But each patient discovered, after mourning a specific failure, more creative ways of being moral. For example, Beth discovered that the conventionally right way may be wrong, everything considered, and that it is preferable to consider multiple moral meanings in trying to figure out what to do. Tim learned, by modifying the rage aroused by anything less than perfection, to be more engaged in "good enough," partially successful cooperative actions. Dan found in himself a range of unexpected moral emotions, including tenderness and sympathy, that helped him to better process moral choices and to act on moral decisions more humanely.

Taken together, these insights point toward the kind of postmodern, psychodynamically informed ethic I think we see emerging today from a variety of cultural sites. Previous ethical theories tried to codify morality in some final, permanent form that would always and everywhere tell us what we ought to do. My patients implicitly realize that ethical action requires an open-ended approach, involving multiple meanings and interpretative possibilities, as well as emotional engagement and tolerance of otherness, and that, in consequence, the outcome may never be "quite right."

Notes

1. The term "mourning," for psychoanalysts since Freud, refers to the affects and mental processes following significant losses, including the loss of significant beliefs and ideals. Like depression, mourning entails "a profoundly painful dejection, cessation of interest in the outside world, loss of the capacity to love, inhibition of all activity, and a lowering of the self-regarding feelings." Unless otherwise noted, references to the work of Sigmund Freud are from *The Standard Edition of the Complete Psychological Works of Sigmund Freud*, trans. and ed. James Strachey (London: Hogarth Press, 24 vols., 1966–1974). See Freud, "Mourning and Melancholia," *Standard Edition*, 14: 244 (first published 1917). Normal mourning, unlike pathological depression, is usually a transient reaction that is followed eventually by acceptance of the loss and the emotional freedom for reinvestment in new relationships and projects. Melancholia (depression) has a variety of neurophysiological and psychodynamic causal

antecedents, but anger at a lost object that has been redirected at the self is a primary factor in neurotic depression. "Through a fusion of self and object representations, aggression originally directed toward the object has been turned against the self." See Burness Moore and Bernard Fine, eds., *Psychoanalytic Terms and Concepts* (New Haven, CT: American Psychoanalytic Association and Yale University Press, 1990), 53.

2. Philip Rieff, *Freud: The Mind of the Moralist* (Garden City, NY: Doubleday/Anchor Books, 1961); Rieff, *The Triumph of the Therapeutic: Uses of Faith after Freud* (New York: Harper and Row/Harper Torchbooks, 1968); Christopher Lasch, *The Culture of Narcissism* (New York: W. W. Norton, 1979); Robert N. Bellah et al., *Habits of the Heart* (Berkeley: University of California Press, 1985).

3. That these characters are not the product of post-industrial societies is indicated by their frequent appearance in Shakespearian plays and Victorian novels. Consider, for example, George Eliot's powerful depiction of Casaubon's obsessive compulsive borderline personality traits and Rosamond's narcissistic character in *Middlemarch*. And, as numerous commentators have noted, St. Augustine's struggle in the *Confessions* revolves around a variety of deep-seated narcissistic issues that did not have to await our "culture of narcissism."

4. Alasdair MacIntyre, *After Virtue: A Study in Moral Theory*, 2nd ed. (Notre Dame, IN: University of Notre Dame Press, 1984).

5. Charles Stevenson, *Ethics and Language* (New Haven, CT.: Yale University Press, 1944).

6. MacIntyre, *After Virtue*, 30. Elsewhere I have argued that MacIntyre presents a caricature of the ethical aspects of psychoanalysis: see Ernest Wallwork, "Psychodynamic Contributions to Religious Ethics: Toward Reconfiguring Askesis," *Annual of the Society of Christian Ethics* 19 (1999): 169. I have also published an interpretation of psychoanalytic theory and practice as a moral undertaking that differs from MacIntyre's portrayal: see Wallwork, "A Constructive Freudian Alternative to Psychotherapeutic Egoism," *Soundings* 69 (1986): 145–64; Wallwork, *Psychoanalysis and Ethics* (New Haven, CT: Yale University Press, 1991); and Wallwork, "Ethics in Psychoanalysis," in *The American Psychiatric Publishing Textbook of Psychoanalysis*, ed. Ethel Spector Person, Arnold M. Cooper, and Glen O. Gabbard (New York: International Universities Press, 2005), 281–97.

7. MacIntyre, *After Virtue*, 263.

8. The prevalence of this fantasy is evidenced by the political belief that politicians posses moral "integrity" when they stand by fixed "principles," regardless of their inappropriateness to the situation at hand. Conversely, the public outcry that commonly occurs when public officials try, but fail, even for understandable reasons, to make good decisions relies on the background assumption that a good person should be able to avoid mistakes. The result is that ideologues get praised, while conscientious decision makers are often condemned for taking the time to be reflective or for not knowing what could not have been known as clearly at the time of the decision. Public acknowledgment of the difficulties of making decisions among incommensurable values under conditions of imperfect knowledge and uncertainty is rare in American public life.

9. See Wallwork, "Constructive Freudian Alternative"; Wallwork, "Ethics in Psychoanalysis"; Wallwork, *Psychoanalysis and Ethics*; Wallwork, "Psychodynamic Contributions."

10. I am employing the concept of mourning in an expanded sense, much like the formulation found in Peter Homans, *The Ability to Mourn: Disillusionment and the Social Origins of Psychoanalysis* (Chicago: University of Chicago Press, 1989). This formulation includes reactions to the loss not only of a person through death but losses of beliefs as well, especially convictions that

are constitutive of one's identity, such as the moral standards by which one attempts to live.

11. W. Joffe and J. Sandler, "Notes on Pain, Depression, and Individuation," *Psychoanalytic Study of the Child* 20 (1965): 394–424.

12. John Bowlby, "Pathological Mourning and Childhood Mourning," *Journal of the American Psychoanalytic Association*, 11 (1963): 510–11.

13. Freud, "Morning and Melancholia," 248.

14. Bowlby, "Pathological Mourning," 511.

15. Dan suffered from what I call "moral depression," defined as the hopeless realization that one lacks the inner resources with which to realize some core, idealized aim having to do with moral character. The concept includes Freud's general point about the role of the "ego ideal" in depression, but it lays the stress less on the superego's self-condemnation, as in "moral masochism," and more on the sense of hopelessness about ever being able to live up to the standards of the ego ideal or ideal self. The "self-I-want-to-be" is the cumulative construction of the child's successive attempts during the stages of childhood, including the Oedipal stage, when things go badly, to restore the satisfactions of the primary narcissistic mental states of early infancy with a compensatory fantasy.

HARRIET LUTZKY

Mourning and Immortality

RITUAL AND PSYCHOANALYSIS COMPARED

RELIGION IS often thought to be intimately linked to the problem of mortality. It is no surprise that the earliest indication of religious thought is found in ritual burial, which suggests beliefs about an "afterlife," although it is not necessarily an indication of structured religion. The relation between religion and mortality was formulated by early scholars of religion, such as Ludwig Feuerbach, who saw man's tomb as "the sole birthplace of the gods," and William Robertson Smith, who saw the tomb as precursor of the temple, the god's home.[1]

In examining the relation between religion and mortality, I see one question as primary. Whose mortality is at issue, that of the self or of the other? Freud claimed that humanity has a dual attitude toward death, both acknowledging and denying it. While the death of strangers is readily admitted, the possibility of one's own death is denied. Freud said, "in the unconscious every one of us is convinced of his own immortality."[2] In his view, the problem of death arises only with the death of a loved one, who is part of oneself and yet, in a sense, a stranger. In this the two attitudes toward death converge.

The philosopher Emmanuel Lévinas also saw the problem of death as a relational one, defining it in terms of the "non-response" of the other, rather than of the "non-being" of the self.[3] The death of the other is, he believed, a more primary issue than the death of the self—"to be or not to be" is "probably not the question *par excellence.*"[4]

From this perspective, then, the fundamental problem that death poses to humanity is not the existential problem of the end of one's own existence but the relational problem of the loss of a loved one. The problem of death would thus epitomize the more general problem of loss or separation. Mourning, which occurs on both the ritual and intrapsychic levels, is the process of dealing with such loss.

The Problem of Psychological Separation

The aim of mourning has been called the separation of the living from the dead.[5] However, from some psychoanalytic perspectives, separation on the psychological level is not possible. Freud claimed that "we can never give anything up; we only exchange one thing for another. What appears to be a renunciation is really the formation of a substitute or surrogate."[6] D. W. Winnicott, reformulating Freud's thought in attachment terms, asked how it is that the separation of subject and object seems to occur "in spite of the impossibility of separation."[7] His answer was that this is a paradox and, as such, cannot be resolved, but must simply be tolerated.

Winnicott claimed that as the child develops from merger with the mother to seeing the mother as a person in her own right, what results is not a separation per se but "an infinite area of separation," not an actual space between the two but "a potential space."[8] Thus, potential space appears when the threat of actual space (that is, separation) looms.

The concept of potential space is an extension of Winnicott's concept of transitional experience, which describes an intermediate area of experience between the subjective sense of the other as being created by the self, and the objective sense of the other as being given in reality. Transitional experience is, on the one hand, a way-station on a (maturational) path leading from the predominance of the former position (the other as part of self) to the predominance of the latter one (the other as separate from self). On the other hand, the two apparently contradictory relations to the object co-occur, and this is the paradoxical aspect of transitional experience. The object is experienced at one and the same time as created by the self (and thus, since part of self, eternally present) and as given by reality (and thus, since other than self, potentially absent).

For Winnicott, transitional experience persists throughout life as an intense type of experiencing that he sees as the hallmark of creative living, manifested in artistic and scientific creativity, in the imaginative life, and in religion (here tacitly considered a creative phenomenon)—in short, as the "location of cultural experience."[9] Of particular interest for the present inquiry is Winnicott's notion that because potential space is the locus of creative living, it is, for the individual, "sacred."[10]

Two Models of Mourning

Bearing in mind Winnicott's thoughts on the impossibility of psychological separation, both maturationally and in the case of loss, and its consequent replacement by paradoxical, transitional phenomena, I compare two models of mourning. On the one hand is the study of death symbolism carried out by the French anthropologist Robert Hertz, and on the other, certain psychoanalytic theorizing on intrapsychic mourning. There is, however, no claim being made here that these models, or ideal types, are necessarily applicable to all cultures or to all individuals.[11] In particular, I focus on three issues. First, both approaches explicitly or implicitly identify the essential characteristic of the mourning process as the merger (symbolic or psychological) of the subject with the lost object, in which the absence and (felt) presence of the departed other are experienced simultaneously. Second, both approaches see the resolution of the mourning process as consisting in the transformation of that merger. Third, the absence and (felt) presence of the object are ultimately experienced on different planes, as there emerges a new and permanent status for the departed one, possibly an enriched self for the bereaved, and hence a new relation between the two.

Death Symbolism in the Thought of Robert Hertz

Robert Hertz was one of the most brilliant scholars in the French sociological school of Emile Durkheim.[12] His major work, "A Contribution to the Study of the Collective Representation of Death," published in 1907, is considered a classic study of death symbolism and "one of the most original analyses pertaining to death written in [the twentieth] century."[13] In the Durkheimian school, the main focus of which was on social solidarity (or integration), Hertz's contribution was unique in its analysis of forces, such as death, which threaten that solidarity, and of society's response when solidarity is actually broken.[14] He studied both the social and individual aspects of problems without assuming a "disjunction between social facts and inner states."[15] Hertz is held to be the principle theoretician of the notion of death as a process of transition.

In many cultures, death is conceived of as a gradual process occurring over time. During this process a transition takes place, the passage of the deceased from one status to another, from one world to another. Hertz analyzed the transition using the example of the ritual of "double burial," which, though not of high frequency, is found worldwide. For example, the Jewish ritual of the anniversary unveiling of the tombstone is considered a vestige of the double burial rite. His analysis, constructing an ideal type, is of structural significance for understanding interpretations of death as passage or transition even in the absence of the double burial ritual itself. The model of transition that Hertz proposed involves three parties, the corpse, the "soul" of the deceased, and the mourners.

The corpse, which arouses a feeling of dread, is considered to be afflicted with "death pollution" (as it is also in societies without double burial), one of the most widespread and gravest forms of ritual pollution. In traditional societies, the pervasive concept of impurity, also referred to as pollution, defilement, or contamination, does not refer to a physical condition or ethical issue but rather to ritual status—one that dictates that the impure object or person may not be approached with impunity. Therefore, there is a "ban" on (or taboo against) contact with the corpse. The impurity of the deceased is thought to be due to their transitional position suspended between two worlds, the world of the living and that of the dead. The deceased exist in both statuses, which are mixed within them. In the typical double burial ritual, there is first an initial, temporary burial of the corpse.

In this model, the soul does not reach its final destination immediately after death any more than does the body. It too goes through a period of transition, during which it exists on the margins of two worlds, hovering around the body, possibly threatening the bereaved in its anger at being excluded from society.

The third term in this transition is the ritual mourner.

Entry into the Ritual Mourning Status

In Hertz's analysis, the ritual mourners go through a process paralleling that of the body and soul of the deceased. In traditional societies, the ritual status of death pollution affects not only the corpse of the deceased but his or her (socially defined) kin as well. The ban on the community's contact with the deceased also applies to contact with the ritual mourners. In some cultures there is even relational pollution, so that regardless of physical proximity, death pollution spreads throughout the kin group; the more closely related to the deceased, the more polluted.[16]

Mary Douglas described the function of ritual impurity as the establishment or reinforcement of boundaries.[17] The impurity of the ritual mourners has several significant boundary repercussions. One, the shared death impurity of deceased and kin, and the resulting ban on the community's contact with the kin, have the effect of binding the kin to the deceased,[18] thus temporarily reestablishing the identity of the kin group in face of the threat to its integrity. Fusing the ritual statuses of bereaved and deceased, the ban on the mourners creates an obligatory solidarity between them as well as an obligatory participation of the mourners in the state of being of the departed one. Two, as the bereaved are segregated by the ban from the rest of the community, their involvement in their everyday lives is temporarily suspended. Three, the ban on contact with the polluted kin prevents the highly "contagious" death pollution from spreading throughout the community. The barrier that it creates protects the community as a whole from the threat of disintegration aroused by the death of one of its members.

According to Hertz, the ban placed on the ritual mourners is what constitutes "compulsory institutional mourning" and is its defining characteristic. Institutional mourning is "the direct consequence in the living of the actual state of the deceased," what Aristotle called the "'homoeopathy' of the mourner with the departed."[19] Ritual mourning is thus symbolic death in which the mourners join their departed kin. The initial impact of loss through death is, paradoxically, to intensify the relation of the living and the dead, rather than to separate them.

The merger of the ritual statuses of deceased and mourner corresponds to transitional experience as described by Winnicott. For the mourner, the deceased is part of self and therefore present, at the same time that he or she is, in reality, separate from self and gone. This temporary, transitional, ritual merger, lasting while the mourner moves toward the new reality, has been described by other anthropologists as well.

Arnold van Gennep's classic study of rites of passage (more correctly translated as "rites of transition")[20] followed upon Hertz's work. Gennep drew attention to the fact that what predominates in funeral rites is the issue of transition in the state-of-being of the bereaved as he or she moves toward a new state, rather than the more obvious issue of separation from the deceased. During the period of the ban, the dead are not yet dead and the living are not really living, but the two "constitute a special group, situated between the world of the living and the world of the dead."[21]

Victor Turner described his concept of liminality in virtually the same terms as those used by Winnicott to describe transitional phenomena: "This coincidence of opposite processes and notions in a single representation characterizes the peculiar unity of the liminal: that which is neither this nor that, and yet is both."[22] Turner saw liminality ("crossing an abyss") as an essential aspect of all social transition, including the adjustment to the death of another,[23] seeing the deceased and the mourners as "betwixt and between" life and death, each participating in both states as together they cross the abyss. He considered liminality "sacred" (or usually so).[24]

Transformation of the Ritual Mourning Status

The socially determined transitional period of the ban is accompanied by changes in all three parties: the body of the deceased disintegrates, leaving only the bare bones; the deceased's soul becomes pacified and ceases to hover around its kin; and the ritual mourner sheds his or her polluted ritual status and gradually prepares to take leave of the departed kin and return to everyday life. This may also entail a change in social status. Finally, the relation between mourners and deceased is transformed as well.

Exit from the Ritual Mourning Status

In the double burial ritual, when the disintegration of the body is complete, the bones are disinterred and ritually purified, such as by washing. This purification profoundly alters the ritual status of the deceased. Only then may he or she be worthy of entering the company of the ancestors and, in the final rites, be reburied among them.

After disintegration of the body, special rites are performed, parallel to the reburial rites, which alter the ritual status of the deceased's soul. Only then, and only because of the ritual action of the living, may the soul leave this world definitively and, as a "shade," enter the world of the afterlife to join the immortal community of ancestors. Death ritual, in this model, structurally integrates the soul of the departed into the cosmos of the bereaved mourner.

The rituals that put an end to the transitional process of death for the body and soul of the deceased also end the ritual mourning period, effecting a profound change in the status of the living. As the ban on the bereaved is lifted, they may take leave of their relative. Thus the rite that ultimately permits the deceased to join the immortal society of ancestors parallels that which permits the bereaved to rejoin the society of the living. To quote Hertz, the rite concluding the period of ritual mourning "is one and the same act of liberation applied to two different categories of persons."[25]

The kin then often assume new and more mature transformed roles, as occurs in the paradigmatic mourning situation, the passing of the older generation, which leads to an assumption of authority by the succeeding generation.

As the deceased and bereaved separate to join (or rejoin) their respective communities, a new, and even in part obligatory, relation may be established between them. The new relation to the lost loved one may be, in the words of Piers Vitebsky, "combined with, or even conceived as, a continuing interaction which is somehow qualitatively transformed."[26] The relation to the now immortal ancestor often remains a permanent part of the religious life of the bereaved, especially in cultures where the dead may continue to demand attention from the living, as well as protecting and guiding them. Everyday life may involve a ritualized relation between them, including prayers, food offerings, and anniversary celebrations.

The Community in Mourning

Mourning as an institution also deals with the loss to the community as a whole, for the individual is both constructed by society and an integral part of it. Death rituals provide a way for the community to relinquish one of its members and gradually reorganize itself, carrying out the dual process of disintegration of the former social reality and reintegration of the new.[27]

A number of distinctions between institutional and personal mourning should be noted. Institutional mourning is a compulsory condition imposed by the society on the socially defined bereaved, usually members of the deceased's kin group as specified by the kinship pattern of the culture. Society may define the length of the mourning period and require specific practices, such as particular clothing, rites, or periods of abstention. The image of ritual mourners tearing out their hair or ripping their clothes is a familiar one. But the violently self-destructive ritual mourning behavior may be compulsory and does not necessarily represent the individual's true feeling. Ritual mourning behavior must rather be explained in terms of its symbolic value.[28] It may *represent* what is known of the feeling of grief, rather than expressing the actual, lived feeling of the moment. In this sense, I propose that ritual mourning resembles artistic creation, described by Suzanne Langer as "the symbolic expression of an artist's knowledge of feeling (a very different thing from symptomatic expression of currently felt emotions)."[29]

While the aims of ritual and intrapsychic mourning are held to be essentially the same, ritual mourning does not have exactly the same meaning for the individual as does the intrapsychic mourning process. Therefore, ritual mourning cannot be characterized simply as a collective form of individual mourning, even though thinkers such as John Bowlby and Edmund Leach locate its origin in the personal reaction of the individual.[30]

Mourning in Psychoanalytic Thought

How do the features of the ritual mourning process compare with psychoanalytic understanding of mourning? Whereas the former involves three parties, the latter involves the inner world of the subject and an intrapsychic mourning process.[31]

Entry into the Psychological State of Mourning

One initial feature of the intrapsychic mourning process is the withdrawal of interest from the outside world. This has the effect of distancing the mourner from involvement in everyday life, a phenomenon that is generally accepted as normal by the mourner's entourage. Freud cited such withdrawal as evidence that work is going on, which he termed "the work of mourning."[32] Another initial feature of the mourning process, a counterpart to the withdrawal of interest, is an inward focus, an absorption in the internal world that appears to involve centering on an internal object and one's relationship to it.

Characterizing the initial relation to the internal object in mourning has been problematic in psychoanalytic theory and has slowly evolved since Freud's early formulations. The essential feature has gradually come to be seen as an unconscious regressive return to a lower level of subject-object differentiation, carried out in the service of the ego without relinquishment of reality testing and usually conceptualized as "identification." This concept generally refers to a psychological process in which "the subject assimilates an aspect, property or attribute of the other and is transformed, wholly or partially, after the model the other provides."[33] Identification is now seen both as one of the main processes by which the subject is initially constituted and as a regressive response of the already constituted subject to loss, permitting reconstitution. This regressive identification, contingent upon loss, in which the subject confounds self and other while at the same time acknowledging the reality of the other, bears great similarity to transitional experience and processes.

In his earlier thinking, Freud had considered mourning to be governed by reality testing, which demanded separation from the departed object, since it no longer existed.[34] The work of mourning would then come to an end when the subject gave up its "attachment to the object which has been abolished."[35] At that time, Freud saw the process of identification, in which "the shadow of the object fell upon the ego," as occurring only in melancholia (or depression), which he considered a pathological form of mourning.[36]

But Karl Abraham, basing his thinking on Freud's writings on object loss in general, suggested that identification, albeit temporary, played a consoling role in mourning as well as in melancholia, with the distinction that the normal mourner never loses consciousness of the reality of the loss.[37] And Freud himself ultimately came to affirm identification as the primary means for dealing with object loss: "If one has lost a love-object, the most obvious reaction is to identify oneself with it, to replace it from within . . . by identification."[38]

Explicitly linking her work to Freud's and Abraham's, Melanie Klein expanded on Abraham's idea that archaic psychological processes are involved in mourning. She saw mourning as a regression to the depressive position that permits a reliving and reworking of problems encountered at that developmental level, when the threat of separation and loss is first experienced.[39] The pain of the current loss of the external object is intensified by the accompanying unconscious fantasy of having lost the internal (good) object as well, especially when this is felt to be due to one's own aggression. Mourning offers the opportunity to repair damage felt to have been done to the internal object. Therefore, when the lost loved object is reinstated in the ego, the (good) object, internalized during early development but now also experienced as destroyed, is reinstated as well. Klein called this "setting up the lost object inside [of one's self]."[40]

Mourning is thus a repeat, a process of "*recovering* what [the mourner] had already attained in childhood" and of reworking and consolidating it. It is this reparation of the inner world that, for Klein, "characterizes the successful work of mourning."[41] Klein saw reparation as a creative process operative not only in the depressive position but also in the cultural domain of art and religion. She made an explicit connection between the reparative work of mourning and the afterlife by relating reparation to "heaven," a place of harmonious reunion of the family, with love prevailing over hate and life (i.e., the life instinct) triumphing over death (i.e., the death instinct).[42]

D. W. Winnicott elaborated on the issue of aggression, seeing the mourning process as involving the working through of guilt, the sense that one's own destructive wishes, inevitably mixed with love, are responsible for the death.[43] (In death symbolism, these unconscious aggressive wishes may be projected onto the "soul" of the deceased, which is then felt to hover around the living, wishing to do them harm, as in the cultural belief systems discussed by Hertz and Gennep.)

Michael Balint has described trauma as producing a need to cling, which, expressing both fear of abandonment and defense against that fear, aims to restore proximity and contact.[44] I think that identification in mourning, as a regressive, dedifferentiating, transitional response to traumatic loss, could be understood as a form of clinging. In that case, the identification/clinging would express separation anxiety, "an appropriate response to the threat of loss, but also present, perhaps even predominant, at some point in the mourning process."[45] It may be this underlying separation anxiety that is responsible for rendering separation psychologically impossible. Of interest in this connection is the fact that older forms of the word "mourn" are related to the meaning "be anxious."[46]

Transformation of the Self and the Relation to the Lost Object

Freud and his followers Abraham and Fenichel eventually came to think that while introjection of and subsequent identification with the object might in fact be the unique condition for renunciation of the object, it was, however, a temporary one. In this view, "Mourning consists of two acts, the first being the establishment of an introjection, the second the loosening of the binding to the introjected object."[47] Between these two acts, there is held to take place a process of compromise.

Though Freud did not formulate the concept of transitional experience, he did make the observation that the gradual nature of the process of mourning (carried out "bit by bit, at great expense of time and cathectic energy") reflects the fact that compromise between two positions is taking place.[48] There is a compromise solution to the cognitive conflict between the wish to deny the loss and the necessity of accepting its reality, that is, between the desired presence and the real absence.[49] There is also a compromise solution to the affective conflict between an original tendency to express raw emotion and the postponement of this expression, a postponement that seems to be an essential component of grief.[50]

However, to some later psychoanalytic thinkers, the work of mourning results neither in the earlier formulated severing of the "attachment to the [real] object that has been abolished" nor in the later formulated "loosening of the binding to the introjected object," but rather in a restructuring of the relationship.

Exit from the Psychological State of Mourning

Roy Schafer said that Freud had "implied a relation between identification and the object's psychic immortality." For Schafer, "the transitional work of mourning" transforms the original, introjected object into an identification. Thereafter, the object is no longer experienced as an object but is preserved by integration into the "subjective self and systemic organization."[51]

Hans Loewald also emphasized the lasting and transformative impact of object loss.[52] For him, as for Klein, a developmental model of the process of separation is pertinent to the analysis of separation due to loss. He suggested that the resolution of the Oedipus complex (with the relinquishment/loss of the parent as object of desire, and consequent establishment of the super-ego) might be a prototype of the mourning process. In the subject's dealing with loss, the process of identification involves the identity, merger, or confounding of subject and object, or aspects of them, thereby erasing difference. Such identifications may be "way-stations on the road to internal, psychic structure." This reconstitutes the subject on a higher level of organization, transforming the relationship to the object "into an internal, intrapsychic, depersonified relationship, thus increasing and enriching psychic structure."[53]

Peter Homans believes that the process of mourning, which he considers a transitional disillusionment, may transform the subject. The creative outcome of mourning is greater individuation, which in turn permits the subject to create new meaning in his or her life, "new structures of appreciation born of loss."[54] Homans also identifies "symbolic loss," the disenchantment with the symbol system that had previously given structure and meaning to life. This loss, in contrast to personal loss, might be dealt with by transformation of the lost symbolic world into an object of analysis.[55]

Other contemporary authors, such as Robert Gaines and John E. Baker, also emphasize the continued existence of the internal object after loss, albeit in a new form.[56]

Thus, a number of psychoanalytic thinkers believe that the mourning process permanently integrates the lost object into the psychic structure of the subject in a new way. This pertains both to the constitution of psychic structure that results from maturationally appropriate separation from the object and to the reconstitution that is elaborated on the basis of later experiences of separation due to loss.

Comparison of the Ritual and Psychoanalytic Models of Mourning

The hallmark of mourning is an initial intensification of the relation between deceased and bereaved. On the ritual level, in Hertz's analysis, the ban on the kin withdraws them from the world and creates a temporary and mandatory intensification of the involvement of the mourner with the deceased, now identified with each other through the confounding of their (polluted) ritual statuses, suspending them together between life and death. This ban is the sine qua non of ritual mourning and its defining characteristic. On the intrapsychic level, in the theories reviewed here, there is the subject's initial withdrawal from the world and inner focus on the lost object, along with the intensification of the bond with the lost object in the subjective merger of identities (or of internal representations of self and other), conceptualized as (regressive) identification. Currently, unconscious identification with the lost object is generally held to be the defining characteristic of the intrapsychic mourning process. Furthermore, the co-occurrence of this merger of the symbolic ritual statuses of bereaved and deceased, and of the unconscious intrapsychic representations of subject and lost object, alongside the bereaved subject's acknowledgment of the deceased's absence in reality, describe a transitional phenomenon.

The intensified relationship is then transformed. It is within the segregated, transitional unit that the work of mourning is carried out. This work transforms the ritual or psychological status of the departed object, of the subject, and of the relation between the two.

The mourning process is exited when the lost one has achieved a permanent status in the world (cosmos or psyche) of the bereaved, and the bereaved has changed to accommodate the new reality. In ritual death symbolism, as analyzed by Hertz, acknowledgment of the permanent absence of the deceased from the everyday life of the community ultimately comes to coexist with belief in the permanent presence of the deceased—but now on another plane of experience, in the afterworld, part of the cosmos and the place to which the bereaved will ultimately repair. In some psychoanalytic thinking, at the end of the mourning period the lost object may be experienced as permanently absent from the everyday world and yet be permanently present in a transformed mode, integrated in a new way into the now permanently reconstituted internal world of the subject. Thus on both ritual and intrapsychic levels, at the close of the mourning period, the lost object has become immortal.

On the ritual level, when the ban is over and the bereaved are freed from mourning, they return (perhaps with new and more mature social roles) to a changed community. On the intrapsychic level, the new integration of the object into the subject's inner world may contribute to change and maturation. On both ritual and intrapsychic levels, the regressive passage through transitional self-object dedifferentiation (or to a lower level of differentiation) permits the emergence of a transformed and potentially enriched self.

The transformation of the status of the deceased and of the bereaved necessitates a transformed relation between them. On the ritual level, there may be a permanent relation between the two, as the survivors continue to minister to the needs of their deceased kin, while the deceased continue to watch over the living. On the intrapsychic level, departed loved ones may serve as a source of inspiration or solace, and aspects of their personalities and values may be integrated into the very self of the survivor.

Conclusion

Consideration of the nature of the connection between religion and mortality has usually focused on existential issues involved in feelings about the idea of the death of the self. In the present essay the connection between religion and mortality has been examined from the perspective of relational issues involved in feelings about the death of the other.

Mourning as the response to the death of another exists in two forms, ritual and intrapsychic. Here we have looked at the two together, what Homans has called working with a double ideal type.[57] This kind of comparison, which has also informed other work by the present author,[58] enriches our understanding of the essential contribution of the mourning process to religion.

Mourning is based on the impossibility of separation in a psychological sense, and on the transitional process that takes its place. The transitional work of mourning, transforming the culturally constructed soul of the deceased and the psychologically constructed internal object, establishes the immortal status of the departed one.

Transitional phenomena have religious features, according to some thinkers. For example, to the psychoanalyst D. W. Winnicott, transitional experience (potential space) is the locus of creativity and culture, including religion. To the anthropologist Victor Turner, transitional experience may be the essential aspect of all ritual (and to some scholars, ritual is the essence of religion).[59] To both, the transitional is sacred. Further, in the case of ritual mourning, it is not only the process but also the result of the sacred transitional process that may have a significant religious implication. It may be the institution of ritual mourning that has created the religious category of immortality.

As the intrapsychic work of mourning transforms the "shadow" of the object in the internal world, ritual action transforms the soul of the deceased into a "shade" in the afterworld. The mourning process thus transforms the "shadow" and creates the "shade"—the immortal twin heirs of the departed one.[60]

Notes

1. Ludwig Feuerbach, *The Essence of Christianity*, trans. George Eliot (New York: Harper and Row, 1957; first published 1841), 33; William Robertson Smith, *Lectures on the Religion of the Semites*, 2nd ed. (London: Adam and Charles Black, 1914), 156–57.
2. Unless otherwise noted, references to the work of Sigmund Freud are from *The Standard Edition of the Complete Psychological Works of Sigmund Freud*, trans. and ed. James Strachey (London: Hogarth Press, 24 vols., 1966–1974). Freud, "Thoughts for the Times on War and Death," *Standard Edition*, 14: 289 (first published 1915).
3. Emmanuel Lévinas, *God, Death and Time*, trans. B. Bergo (Stanford, CA: Stanford University Press, 2000), 9.
4. Emmanuel Lévinas, "Bad Conscience and the Inexorable," in *Face to Face with Lévinas*, ed. R. A. Cohen (Albany: State University of New York Press, 1986), 40.
5. Daniel Lagache, "Le travail du deuil," *Revue française de psychanalyse*, 10 (1938): 695.
6. Sigmund Freud, "Creative Writers and Day-Dreaming," *Standard Edition*, 9: 145 (first published 1908).
7. D. W. Winnicott, "The Place Where We Live," in *Playing and Reality* (Harmondsworth, UK: Pelican, 1974), 127.
8. Ibid., 126.
9. Winnicott, "The Location of Cultural Experience," in *Playing and Reality* (Harmondsworth, UK: Pelican, 1974), 121.
10. Ibid., 121.
11. See Peter Homans, following Weber, on ideal types, in introduction to *Symbolic Loss: The Ambiguity of Mourning and Memory at Century's End*, ed. Homans (Charlottesville: University Press of Virginia, 2000), 5.

12. Robert Hertz, "A Contribution to the Study of the Collective Representation of Death," in *Death and the Right Hand,* trans. R. Needham and C. Needham (Glencoe, IL: Free Press, 1960; first published in *Année sociologique* 10 [1907]: 48–137), 295.

13. Peter Metcalf and Richard Huntington, *Celebrations of Death: The Anthropology of Mortuary Ritual,* 2nd ed. (New York: Cambridge University Press, 1991), 33.

14. Robert Parkin, *The Dark Side of Humanity: The Work of Robert Hertz and Its Legacy* (Amsterdam: Harwood Academic Publishers, 1996), 25, 178.

15. Rodney Needham, "Robert Hertz," in *International Encyclopedia of the Social Sciences,* vol. 18 (New York: Macmillan, 1968–91), 297. See also Metcalf and Huntington, *Celebrations of Death,* 74.

16. Stanley Tambiah, "From Varna through Mixed Union," in *The Character of Kinship,* ed. Jack Goody (Cambridge: Cambridge University Press, 1973), 209; Metcalf and Huntington, *Celebrations of Death,* 82.

17. Mary Douglas, *Purity and Danger: An Analysis of the Concepts of Pollution and Taboo* (London: Ark, 1984; first published 1966).

18. Hertz, "Collective Representation of Death," 40.

19. Ibid., 50–51; Robert Parker, *Miasma: Pollution and Purification in Early Greek Religion* (Oxford: Clarendon Press, 1983), 64.

20. Arnold van Gennep, *The Rites of Passage,* trans. Monika B. Vizedom and Gabrielle L. Caffee (Chicago: University of Chicago Press, 1960; translation of 1909 ed.), 146–47. Gennep's term is more correctly translated as "rites of transition": see S. T. Kimball, introduction to Gennep, *Rites of Passage.*

21. Gennep, *Rites of Passage,* 148.

22. Victor Turner, "Betwixt and Between: The Liminal Period in *Rites de passage,*" in *Reader in Comparative Religion: An Anthropological Approach,* ed. William A. Lessa and Evon Z. Vogt (New York: Harper and Row, 1972; first published 1964), 341.

23. Victor Turner, "Liminality, Kabbalah, and the Media," *Religion* 15 (1985): 207; Turner, "Betwixt and Between."

24. Victor Turner, *Dramas, Fields, and Metaphors: Symbolic Action in Human Society* (Ithaca, NY: Cornell University Press, 1974), 273–74; Turner, "Liminality, Kabbalah, and the Media," 208.

25. Hertz, "Collective Representation of Death," 64.

26. Piers Vitebsky, *Dialogues with the Dead: The Discussion of Mortality among the Sora of Eastern India* (Cambridge: Cambridge University Press, 1993), 10.

27. Hertz, "Collective Representation of Death," 82.

28. Metcalf and Huntington, *Celebrations of Death,* 33.

29. Suzanne Langer, *Mind: An Essay on Human Feeling,* vol. 1 (Baltimore: Johns Hopkins University Press, 1967), xv.

30. John Bowlby, *Attachment and Loss,* vol. 3 (London: Penguin, 1991; first published 1980), 132; Edmund Leach, "Magical Hair," in *Myth and Cosmos: Readings in Mythology and Symbolism,* ed. J. Middleton (Garden City, NY: Natural History Press, 1967), 102.

31. For a review of the psychoanalytic literature on mourning, see George Hagman, "Mourning: A Review and Reconsideration," *International Journal of Psychoanalysis,* 76 (1995): 909–25. For treatments of other psychological issues in the field of mourning studies, see Bowlby, *Attachment and Loss;* David R. Dietrich and Peter C. Shabad, eds. *The Problem of Loss and Mourning: Psychoanalytic Perspectives* (Madison, CT: International Universities Press, 1989); George H. Pollock, *The Mourning-Liberation Process,* vols. 1 and 2 (Madison, CT: International Universities Press, 1989); and Mardi Horowitz, "A Model of Mourning: Change in Schemas of Self and Other," *Journal of the American Psychoanalytic Association* 38 (1990): 297–324.

32. Sigmund Freud, "Mourning and Melancholia," *Standard Edition*, 14: 245 (first published 1917).
33. J. Laplanche and J.-B. Pontalis, *The Language of Psycho-Analysis*, trans. Donald Nicholson-Smith (London: Hogarth Press, 1973), 205.
34. Sigmund Freud, "Inhibitions, Symptoms and Anxiety," *Standard Edition*, 20: 172 (first published 1926).
35. Freud, "Mourning and Melancholia," 255.
36. Ibid., 249.
37. Sigmund Freud on object loss: e.g., Freud, "Group Psychology and the Analysis of the Ego," *Standard Edition*, 18: 108; Freud, "The Ego and the Id," *Standard Edition*, 19: 29; Karl Abraham, *Selected Papers of Karl Abraham, MD*, trans. D. Bryan and A. Strachey (London: Maresfield Library, 1988; first published 1927), 435, 438.
38. Sigmund Freud, "An Outline of Psychoanalysis," *Standard Edition*, 23: 193 (first published 1940); also Freud, "New Introductory Lectures," *Standard Edition*, 22: 63 (first published 1933).
39. Melanie Klein, "Mourning and Its Relation to Manic-Depressive States," in *The Writings of Melanie Klein*, vol. 1 (Glencoe, IL: Free Press, 1975; first published 1940).
40. Ibid., 362.
41. Ibid., 362, 363.
42. Some religious implications of the Kleinian concept of "reparation" are discussed in Harriet Lutzky, "Reparation and Tikkun: A Comparison of the Kleinian and Kabbalistic Concepts," *International Review of Psychoanalysis* 16 (1989): 449–58.
43. D. W. Winnicott, "The Mentally Ill in Your Caseload," in *Maturational Processes and the Facilitating Environment: Studies in the Theory of Emotional Development*, 217–29 (New York: International Universities Press, 1965; first published 1963), 221.
44. Michael Balint, *Primary Love and Psychoanalytic Technique* (New York: Liveright, 1965).
45. C. M. Parkes, "Separation Anxiety: An Aspect of the Search for a Lost Object," in *Loneliness: The Experience of Emotional and Social Isolation*, ed. R. S. Weiss (Cambridge, MA: MIT Press, 1973), 53–55, 65–66.
46. See J. A. Simpson, and E. S. C. Weiner, eds., *The Oxford English Dictionary*, 2nd ed., 20 vols. (New York: Oxford University Press, 1989).
47. Otto Fenichel, *The Psychoanalytic Theory of Neurosis* (New York: Norton, 1945), 394.
48. Freud, "Mourning and Melancholia," 245.
49. Ibid.
50. The tendency to express raw emotion and the postponement of that expression are discussed by Fenichel, *Psychoanalytic Theory of Neurosis*, 21, 162; and Charles Darwin, *The Expression of the Emotions in Man and Animals* (London: William Pickering, 1989; first published 1872).
51. Roy Schafer, *Aspects of Internalization* (Madison, CT: International Universities Press, 1990; first published 1968), 226–27, 117, 235.
52. Hans W. Loewald, "Internalization, Separation, Mourning, and the Superego," *Psychoanalytic Quarterly* 31 (1962): 483–504.
53. Hans W. Loewald, *Papers on Psychoanalysis* (New Haven, CT: Yale University Press, 1980), 84, 83.
54. Peter Homans, *The Ability to Mourn: Disillusionment and the Social Origins of Psychoanalysis* (Chicago: University of Chicago Press, 1989), 263.
55. Homans, introduction to *Symbolic Loss*, 38.
56. See, for example, Robert Gaines, "Detachment and Continuity," *Contemporary Psychoanalysis* 33 (1997): 549–71; John E. Baker, "Mourning and the Trans-

formation of Object Relationships: Evidence for the Persistence of Internal Attachments," *Psychoanalytic Psychology* 18 (2001): 55–73.

57. Homans, *Symbolic Loss*, 5.

58. See the following works by Harriet Lutzky: "Reparation and Tikkun: A Comparison of the Kleinian and Kabbalistic Concepts," *International Review of Psychoanalysis* 16 (1989): 449–58; "The Sacred and the Maternal Object: An Application of Fairbairn's Theory to Religion," in *Psychoanalytic Reflections on Current Issues,* ed. Howard Siegel et al., 25–44 (New York: New York University Press, 1991); "Deity and the Social Bond: Robertson Smith and the Psychoanalytic Theory of Religion," in *William Robertson Smith: Essays in Reassessment,* ed. William Johnstone, 320–30 (Sheffield, UK: Sheffield Academic Press, 1995); "Desire as a Constitutive Element of the Sacred," *Archiv für Religionspsychologie* 25 (2003): 62–70.

59. Turner, "Liminality, Kabbalah, and the Media", 208.

60. The terms "shadow" and "shade" are variants of each other (*Oxford English Dictionary*) as are (according to the present essay) the concepts to which they refer.

PART III

MOURNING RELIGION
IN CULTURE

MARY ELLEN ROSS

Theology and Mourning in Film

LOSS AND REDEMPTION IN THE CINEMA OF KRZYSZTOF KIESLOWSKI

MOURNING IS almost always filled with ambiguity, even when the grief itself is experienced as one of abject loss and often, tragically, of multiple losses. But how we mourn—what Peter Homans has aptly called our "ability to mourn"—is conditioned deeply by our culture. Even in contemporary Western culture, which social theorists have described as alienating, existential, and radically individualistic, mourning, as Homans points out, does not take place in total isolation. Rather, we are all always both detached and connected to broader communities. And the privileged site of this "intermediate space" is, as Homans also argues, film. Mourning does not take place in pure isolation, even when we are alone. It also takes place in front of the screen (whether that of the cinema or of television) "on which each of us, alone and late at night, projects his own dreams." Taken in its broadest and most inclusive sense," Homans continues, "it is this socially shared screen which today has come to mediate between the contents of the individual person's unconscious inner world and the myriad productions of the various social orders of modern society."[1] The cinema represents our collective and individual mourning. Even more the cinema gives us, in a post-Christian culture, the ability to mourn.

In a brilliant psychoanalytic study on film and mourning, Erik L. Santner has shown how the postwar German cinema of Edgar Reitz and Jürgen Syberberg has "taken important steps in [the] labor of recollecting a cultural identity out of stranded objects of a poisoned past."[2] This is something we have come to expect of much European cinema. The Europeans, we might say, do not go to the movies; they go to the cinema; and their ritualized experience of cinema does not carry them away from their world, as do most Hollywood films, but into their world. But the project of understanding modern European experience can also look to the future, and this forward-looking effort at a redemption of European experience is nowhere more apparent than in the work of the Polish director Krzysztof Kieslowski.

Throughout his oeuvre, Kieslowski constantly came back to the problem, moreover, of mourning, of trying to locate a collective fantasized meaning that enables us to mourn our losses and continue on with our lives with some sense of meaning even as an old order (the Europe of the cold war) broke up and a new one (the Europe of the European Union) began to come into being.

While most U.S. commentators celebrated the development of the unification of Europe as an example of the progressive Americanization of the continent and the unleashing of individualistic and capitalistic energies, it is hardly surprising that many Europeans, especially those born in eastern Europe and inclined to gaze onto the "freedoms" of the West with some skepticism, had a far more ambivalent view. This is certainly the case with Kieslowski, whose cinema expressed deep anxieties about certain Western notions of freedom and, above all, a concern about the individual detached from all community and yet "unable to mourn." In no film does he offer a more profound examination of this dilemma than in *Blue* (1992), a work that constitutes a collective space for what Freud aptly called *Trauerarbeit*, the work of grieving, a process that always necessarily involves both an attack on the ego and, when successful, the reestablishment of identity through the retrieval of a meaningful past and the forging of new ties to a broader community. *Blue*, I am suggesting, not only chronicles the work of grieving, but it also offers a screen on which we as individuals are able to enter into a shared community, even when we watch the film in total isolation, the DVD casting up images, at once bright and shadowy, from a story that connects us to the larger world.

Blue begins with loss, horrific personal loss. The film's protagonist Julie survives a car accident that has taken the lives of her husband and their daughter. Julie is suddenly, unexpectedly, profoundly alone. And her isolation is compounded by the simultaneous absence and presence of her mother, who suffers from Alzheimer's disease. "My husband and daughter are dead," Julie tells her mother. "I have no home. I was happy. I loved them. They loved me. Now I have only one thing to do: nothing." The mother's blank, passive face redoubles Julie's pain.

The profoundly personal quality of the narrative of *Blue* has struck many reviewers as ironic.[3] Kieslowski's declared intent in the making of the film, after all, is political. In fact, *Blue* is the first part of a trilogy whose titles he connects to the symbolism of the French flag: blue for liberty, white for equality, and red for fraternity. As Anthony Lane remarked in his *New Yorker* review of the film, "if you're hoping for Gerard Depardieu to come bursting out of the Bastille with a ripped shirt, tough luck."[4] But Kieslowski, as I suggest above, is grappling with a less obvious dimension of liberty. Beneath the political freedoms he embraced, Kieslowski, like many other eastern Europeans, also perceived a profoundly individualistic, even atomistic culture in which the loss of one's immediate family could strip one of all social ties and plunge the individual into a virtually paralyzed abyss. Freedom in this sense is terrifying. Julie has lost everything.[5] Kieslowski's project is that of teasing out new notions of freedom that are dependent upon the individual's ability to connect past to present, to overcome the fractured temporality of trauma, and to establish new bonds that reconstitute ties that have been lost.

The dynamics of fragmentation—of a fragmented self—have played a major role in psychoanalytic thought throughout the twentieth century. Although Freud's celebrated essay "Mourning and Melancholia" has been a rich resource for many theorists, the description it provides of the underlying dynamics of mourning is sketchy at best.[6] It is my view that Melanie Klein's theory, although it is not framed as a contribution to the psychoanalytic theory of mourning, offers an insightful psychodynamic map of the mourning process. Though originally focused on infant development, Klein's analysis of splitting, the paranoid-schizoid position, and the depressive position—concepts I explicate below—can also be applied to a new context, specifically to the reaction to grief and loss in adulthood. Her theory, moreover, illuminates mourning as both an individual and cultural process. Thus Klein can help us understand more fully the mourning process and its vicissitudes that Freud outlined in his famous essay.

Within the psychoanalytic community Klein is the thinker who has done the most to capture the problem of ambivalence, especially the confusing experience of love and hate and their often startling and apparently paradoxical cohabitation in the same person and in that same person's feelings for a "loved" one. An exploration of Klein's thought, therefore, offers important insights not only into the personal narrative of Kieslowski's Julie but into his moral and political theory as well. Moreover, not only does Melanie Klein's thought illuminate the film, but the film illuminates certain aspects of Klein's thought. The film can enrich our understanding of some of Klein's insights, most notably by providing an imaginative depiction of the form that mourning and reparation may take in adulthood, a subject Klein addresses much less often than the topics of grief and restoration in infancy. Ultimately, the heroine's actions present a specific vision of moral character that enriches and refines Klein's own somewhat schematic concept of responsible adulthood.

At the beginning of Kieslowski's story, shortly after the car wreck, Julie begins to experience the ascendancy of what Klein calls "paranoid-schizoid" thought. We see this in Julie's growing sense of the fundamental hostility of the world and in her attempts to separate herself from it. According to Klein, the paranoid-schizoid position, which persists throughout life, emerges during the first three months of infancy. Ideally, in Klein's view, this position is eclipsed by further psychic development in the individual, though a traumatic event always has the possibility of forcing a regression to this state, as we see in the case of Julie and the tragic losses that she confronts. The term "schizoid" refers to the major defense that characterizes this position, that of splitting. The infant, a radical Manichean, simplifies the world by dividing it into good and bad. In Klein's view, this division finds its first representation in the mother's breast: the good breast is the one that nourishes and comforts; the bad breast is the one that the mother withholds. Lacking the cognitive and emotional abilities to perceive whole persons, newborns are unable to see their mothers as a whole but only as a collection of disparate parts—eyes, shoulders, hands, breasts. And it is within this context and the drive to have some control over the world that infants attach themselves passionately to the good breast, not only to relieve hunger but to find comfort and love. It is in this moment that the infant is most connected to another, most alive, most able to escape the terror of the radical individualism periodically forced upon him by the breast withheld, even when he cries out in hunger. Since the infant does not yet see his mother as a whole person, he further reassures himself by the process that Klein calls "splitting": the withheld breast is a different object from the breast that is offered. The baby tolerates no ambiguity, since this process of splitting allows him to sense that he can, in some small way, control his world by attaching himself passionately to the good aspects of his world and attempting to keep the frustrating and painful aspects at bay.

The paranoid-schizoid position takes its character from the fact that the infantile psyche is a battlefield on which the forces of love and hate play themselves out.[7] The infant loves the breast because it is the source of things essential to his well-being. But he also hates the breast, largely because in its absence it is a source of frustration: "The baby's first object of love and hate—his mother—is both desired and hated with all the intensity and strength that is characteristic of the early urges of the baby. In the beginning he loves his mother at the time that she is satisfying his needs for nourishment, alleviating his feelings of hunger, and giving him the sensual pleasure which he experiences when his mouth is stimulated by sucking at her breast. . . . But when the baby is hungry and his desires are not gratified, or when he is feeling bodily pain or discomfort, then the whole situation suddenly alters. Hatred and aggressive feelings are aroused and he becomes dominated by the impulses to destroy the very person who is the object of all his desires and who in his mind is linked up with everything he experiences—good and bad alike."[8] The fact that the mother's body contains the riches that the baby wants greedily to appropriate for himself enhances these strong destructive tendencies. Therefore, the infant is plunged almost immediately after birth into a state of terrifying anxiety, for he fears his aggressive, greedy impulses will destroy what he loves and needs.

Unable to tolerate this situation, the infant engages in some typical defense mechanisms. These include not only splitting but also projection and introjection. In splitting, the infant protects himself from inner turmoil and anxiety by dividing the breast into the good (gratifying and idealized) breast and the bad (absent and hostile) breast. The infant, motivated by envy of the riches of the mother's breast and the greedy desire to appropriate these for himself, fantasizes attacking the bad breast and then perceives it as torn to bits, each of which he views as a vengeful persecutor. In this way, the infant projects his own aggression outward onto the breast. The infant then introjects the good breast, which forms the basis of what Klein calls the good internal object, the foundation of the ego and the source of the baby's (and ultimately the adult's) resilience in the face of anxiety and stress. "This first internal good object acts as a focal point in the ego. It counteracts the processes of splitting and dispersal, makes for cohesiveness and integration, and is instrumental in building up the ego."[9] The process of introjection is thus often more benign than splitting and projection and provides a bridge between the paranoid-schizoid position and more mature forms of mental functioning. Through complex permutations of this basic scheme, the infant struggles to protect the good from the bad and control his fear that his own aggression has made him vulnerable to attack from the targets of his own aggression. He is anxious that his internal world may disintegrate due to the vengefulness of hostile forces. The perception that one has caused and is threatened by fragmentation is possible primarily because the infant does not see entities as whole and therefore cannot see that the good and bad mother are one, or that the aggressive and loving selves are one as well.

What we see in *Blue* is a study of a person who has suffered such a dramatic loss that much—although not all—of her relation to the world begins to take on the characteristics of the paranoid-schizoid position. In Kleinian terms, Julie's devastation has occurred because she has experienced a double loss: the loss of her husband and child, and the more subtle loss of the good internal object, the source of self-regard and hope, here underscored by the absence of her mother as well. Klein believes that the loss of a loved one is echoed internally and may result in the damage or loss of the beloved self. Julie's loss causes the rise of intense anger and anxiety that we sense simmering just beneath the surface.

To cope, even to survive, Julie begins to act out in terms that Klein would explain through the persistence of the paranoid-schizoid position into adult life. Julie, that is, begins to split or divide her world in the service of her survival. Kieslowski emphasizes Julie's efforts to separate herself from her past. He portrays Julie as a woman who wants nothing to do with the past and its reminders; now she can now only perceive it through a veiled grief. In fact, Julie is unable to mourn. Trying to protect herself and to gain some control over her fragmented internal state, she does everything in her power to detach her own history, infected with tragedy, from the empty but less painful present. Temporal splitting is a defense beyond the capacities of the young child, who has no clear sense of duration, and yet is available to the adult in times of crisis. Julie's view of past and present as separate is analogous to the infant's perception of self and objects as fragmented. Just as the infant must be able eventually to forge a coherent perception of self in order to engage in moral action, so the adult who regresses to the paranoid-schizoid position loses the ability to grieve and to act within a moral community. The capacity for moral agency depends on consciousness of the past and the ability to learn from it. In its subtle treatment of the various possible responses to time, *Blue* presents a helpful examination of the psychology of the experience of temporality and a welcome addition to the work of some of Klein's successors who have focused on the psychology of adulthood.[10]

The film reiterates various modalities through which Julie severs her connections with the past. In one of the first scenes following the depiction of the accident, we see Julie hurl an object through one of the hospital windows near the nurse's station. In this way, she hopes to create a diversion so she can slip unnoticed into a drug cabinet and swallow enough pills to kill herself. She will annihilate her past by annihilating herself. Julie grabs a handful of pills, puts them in her mouth, and after a long pause, spits them out. To the nurse who appears in the doorway, she says simply "I can't." Using Klein's vocabulary, one might say that the good internal object, established long ago in early childhood, has been so damaged by the loss that Julie seriously considers destroying herself. However, some of the object's resilience remains, for she cannot complete the act. This hopeful note foreshadows progress that occurs later in the narrative, when Julie begins to overcome her self-destructive denial of her own history.

But early on, Julie attempts to erase her memories and divorce herself from all familiar space and all material reminders of the past. Here we see her projection of her own anger and anxiety onto the world. Unable to assimilate her rage at her loss and her acute fear of her own mortality, she casts these sensations outward, onto the world, and the world takes on the character of a hostile, dangerous place. Once she is released from the hospital, she returns to the country home she has shared with her husband and daughter. She instructs her lawyer to sell everything and to use part of the money to provide for her mother, the maid, and the gardener. At another point, she throws the contents of her purse onto a bare mattress, one of the few remaining objects in her house.[11] Her purse contains small random bits of her history and symbolizes her old identity. Among the objects to fall is a piece of blue candy, no doubt something she had bought for her daughter. She devours the candy—an unconscious act of introjection that is itself a hopeful sign—and throws the other contents of her purse into the fire. Then she goes to Paris, finds an apartment building that doesn't allow children, and moves in.

Another act of destruction is a critical element around which much of the plot turns. At the time of his death, Julie's husband Patrice, a renowned composer, was working on a concerto to celebrate the unification of Europe. His work, now a genuinely collective product, was intended to be performed in the capitals of unified Europe simultaneously. Part of Julie's effort to erase the past entails her collecting the unfinished score from the archives of her husband's conservatory and throwing it into the back of a garbage truck. Here Kieslowski explicitly links Julie's fragmented state to the larger political context. Significantly, the object Julie seeks to destroy in this scene is itself a cultural product meant to be, like film, experienced collectively. The fragmented individual here appears to endanger the process of political unification itself.

Julie is determined not only to cut herself off from the material reminders of the past; she severs her ties with people as well. Projection of her own anxious and fragile inner state onto others has caused her to view all relationships as dangerous. As she says to her mother, "I don't want any belongings, any memories, no friends, no love. They are all traps." When she moves to Paris, she re-appropriates her birth name so that no one will find her. The person she seems most determined to escape is her husband's colleague Olivier, who loves her. Olivier had been among the first to visit her in the hospital, but she had refused to speak to him. Then the night before she left her home, she called him, asked him to come over, and made love to him. But this act was not intended to make a connection but a break. The next morning, she announces, "You see, I'm like any other woman. I sweat. I cough. I have cavities. You won't miss me." And it is after this act that she leaves her former home. Olivier ultimately tracks her down in Paris and asks her if she is running from him. She doesn't answer—she barely seems to notice him. Julie's spurning of Olivier is an indication of the cognitive distortions that accompany splitting and projection. She cannot recognize him for the loyal and devoted person he is, and initially rejects the opportunity to rebuild her life that he can provide. Olivier later becomes frustrated with her unemotional vagueness, and he pursues a drastic course in an attempt to evoke any type of response, whether positive or negative. Others notice the apparent inner emptiness as well: when Julie returns home from the hospital and finds her maid crying, she asks her why. The maid replies, "because you aren't." It would be a mistake to interpret Julie's impassive demeanor as a lack of feeling. Rather, it results from the splitting off of intolerable emotions, leaving the outward appearance of monotonous indifference to people and things.

At the height of this period of denial, Julie becomes thoroughly isolated. In one painful scene, Julie sits, her eyes closed, on a bench in the sun. A few feet away, an old woman, barely able to walk, attempts to dispose of an empty bottle. The woman tries again and again to reach the elevated opening of the trash container. At last she succeeds. This scene is reminiscent of one in Kieslowski's earlier film *The Double Life of Véronique* and is almost exactly duplicated in both *White* and *Red*. In *The Double Life*, Véronique sees an old woman struggling with a large package, but she immediately offers her help.

In *White*, the protagonist Karol watches an old man trying to reach the container opening and seems ready to help, but the man succeeds before he can offer his services. In *Red* as well, Valentine offers her assistance. But Julie is oblivious to what goes on around her.

Also revealing is a series of vignettes of an eerily empty pool in which Julie daily swims. We see the same scene—Julie swimming the length of the pool—repeated several times. Then, at the end of the film, the pool scene ends with her solitary swim being interrupted by a group of schoolchildren noisily running toward the pool. Kieslowski seems to be saying that the children have been there all along, but Julie has not allowed herself to notice them, since they would evoke memories of her daughter.[12] Given the extremity of Julie's isolation, her character begins to take on some of the attributes of her mother. She, too, fails to recognize others. Just as her mother sits passively watching television, Julie looks on passively as others go about their lives. She echoes her mother's inertia in her statement: "Now I have only one thing to do: nothing." Klein would argue that this cultivation of extreme solitude can only make creativity and morality impossible. For Klein, morality and creativity are essentially the same, and they involve active engagement in the attempt to restore some harmony and order to a conflict-ridden world.

We begin to see the signs of such active engagement in the second half of the film, when Julie begins the transition from a primarily paranoid-schizoid organization of experience to what Klein has described as "the depressive position." In Klein's work, the infant makes a transition to the depressive position in the latter half of the first six months of life. This transition is enabled first by the cognitive progress that allows the infant to perceive whole objects and, second, by the increasing strength of the good internal object that allows the infant to cope better with stresses such as ambivalence. The infant, through cognitive development and growing familiarity with the ways of the outside world, undergoes a process of integration (rather than its opposite, splitting). That is, she begins to perceive her mother not as a collection of parts (breast, eyes, hands) but as a whole person. Her perception of whole objects in the external world is part of the process that allows her to perceive her internal world in its entirety at once, including all its bad and good aspects. She is one and the same person; her mother, in both her good and bad aspects, is also one person. Thus, ambivalence comes to the fore, and the child can no longer resolve it by splitting. Now the baby needs ways to cope simultaneously with her good and bad self and her good and bad object. New kinds of defenses can achieve this because the infant has gained confidence in her ability to control her aggressive impulses and in the mother's resilience: after all, she continues to reappear in spite of the most vicious fantasized attacks on her.

In addition to a diminution of splitting, a decrease in projection characterizes this position, for the infant now begins to view the projection of aggression on the outside world as dangerous to her cherished relationships. There are corollary increases in introjection, to enrich the good internal object with positive experiences from the external world, and repression, to control the destructive potential of aggression. In addition, the infant begins to develop a capacity for a nondefensive mode of psychic functioning, reparation.[13]

In the depressive position, the impulse toward reparation accompanies the recognition of a whole self and whole objects. The self who loves is also the self who hates and wants to destroy; therefore, the baby feels guilt. The object who gratifies basic needs is also the object who often fails to meet the infant's desires: the infant must learn how to keep a relationship with the mother going even though she at times hates her mother. When she suffers the inevitable fantasies of destruction of the beloved object, she mourns the loss of the object, even though the object has only been destroyed in fantasy. The infant develops a sense of responsibility out of remorse for imagined matricide and feels compelled to accomplish acts of reparation that might, for example, repair what the infant experiences as a rupture in her relationship with her mother—perhaps the gift of a smile or a toy—or actually serve to repair the mother's destroyed body. This latter type of reparation might be accomplished by joining objects such as blocks together in the symbolic restoration of the mother's wholeness.

Klein asserts that no one ever outgrows the depressive position. A tragic reality of human life is that the moral responsibility of the adult springs from the soil of anxiety, ambivalence, guilt, and mourning. While our efforts to repair our broken world are indeed altruistic, the altruism is always a product of conscious or unconscious remorse. For example, in the latter part of *Blue,* when Julie begins to restore the past she has repudiated, a Kleinian analysis would insist that part of her motivation is guilt, even though she has not harmed her husband or child. Klein insists that the guilt that generates reparation in adulthood is almost always derived from early childhood fantasies rather than based on literal truth. Moreover, the fact that all important human relationships contain ambivalence means that the guilt and remorse of infancy, based on ambivalence toward the mother, easily reappear throughout life as the result of aggressive feelings in other significant relationships, including the most loving. Even when the aggression is never openly expressed, it generates guilt that calls for reparation.

Brilliantly, Kieslowski has underscored the inability of Julie to escape entirely from her past even as she attempts to do so. As we have already seen, as Julie vacates her house, a small piece of blue candy (her daughter's) had fallen onto the bed, and Julie impulsively ate this in an unconscious act of preservation of her past and her memories of her child. That is, while this action may be interpreted as purely destructive—as an attempt to destroy her memory of her daughter by destroying an object associated with her—a Kleinian analysis might also interpret this as an effort at incorporation or introjection, as a move to bolster the devastated internal world by incorporating a positive object, the object in this case ultimately being not the candy but the daughter herself. But Julie leaves her home with another blue object: a small chandelier with blue beads. This symbol also bears ambiguity, for at a few points, Julie grabs the beads aggressively, in a display of the anger. On the other hand, the chandelier appears to be the only thing that Julie allows herself to become attached to after her loss. She gives all her belongings away with the exception of this. As she hurries away from her home toward a new life in Paris, she carries only a satchel and a box containing the blue chandelier. Julie thus has failed in one small but hopeful way in her program to destroy her past. The chandelier implies that lying dormant in her devastated mind is the potential for regeneration.

Our past, Kieslowski appears to be suggesting, is not ours alone, not moments that we can choose to disregard or to deny in their entirety. And even when the very thought of our past is too painful to bear—as certainly it was for Julie, who lost not only her husband and daughter but her mother has well—we always bear part of it within ourselves. We are not as alone in the world as bourgeois ideology would imply. Moreover, even when we seek to be alone and seek to detach ourselves from those around us, circumstances compel us into relations with others that provide the framework for moral action. Kieslowski, that is, views liberty as something that we can find only through our connectedness to others, both to those whom we have loved in the past and those whom we might grow to love in the present. We are—as the film *Blue* demonstrates with immense narrative power—never entirely alone. And if *Blue* symbolizes liberty, liberty is not to be understood as purely individual freedom but as freedom within society, the freedom that enables us to become moral beings.

Once in Paris, Julie is pulled back into social relationships by refusing to enter into relationships with her co-tenants. A tenant in her apartment building approaches her with a petition to evict another tenant, a prostitute named Lucille. Julie refuses to sign the petition, saying that she doesn't want to get involved. But this effort to preserve her isolation leads to a new relationship. Lucille stops by Julie's apartment to express her appreciation to her for not having signed the petition. Julie learns that even though everyone else in the building had signed the petition, her refusal was enough to prevent the eviction.

Not surprisingly Julie is reluctant to have anything to do with Lucille. And Kieslowski portrays this refusal as leading to a horrifying moment of despair and anxiety—an existential moment in which Julie faces the world entirely on her own. Shortly after Lucille's visit, Julie is putting up her groceries when she discovers a nest of mice in her pantry. Julie, who until this point had been entirely without emotion, is overcome with anxiety. As Klein observes, "The feeling of being disintegrated, *of being unable to experience emotions*, of losing one's objects, is in fact the equivalent of anxiety."[14] But now when Julie sees the mice, she is transfixed, horrified at what she has found and yet unable to walk away. The power of her response invites the interpretation that the anxiety lurking underneath her severed emotions is the anxiety of her own death: "anxiety originates in the fear of annihilation."[15] One might wonder why Kieslowski has chosen the mice as the precipitating cause of his character's anxiety attack. Klein would see this choice as reasonable, for creatures such as mice would make logical symbolic substitutes for the fantasized multiple persecutors, created by projected aggression, who threaten to destroy the subject. In other words, the mice represent Julie's anger. In the following scene, we see Julie in bed, still so preoccupied with the mice that she is unable to sleep. The next day, she desperately attempts to find a new apartment; she learns that there is a shortage of such apartments in her district and that she will need to wait. At last, she resorts to a more violent solution: she borrows a neighbor's cat, pushes it into her apartment, shuts the door, and goes away. Later in the day, she is too distraught to return home and encounters Lucille at the pool. Lucille offers to go to her apartment and clean the mess up. Thus Julie, who has expended all her energy in cutting herself off from relationships that will invoke her past, enters a relationship of mutual loyalty and obligation.

When Julie returns Lucille's favor, the narrative takes its most important turn. One night Lucille calls Julie and asks her to meet her at the live sex show where she works. It is late; Julie has already gone to bed. Nonetheless, she says she will come. This is the first attempt Julie has made during the course of the film actively to maintain a relationship. When she arrives, she finds Lucille upset because she has seen her (Lucille's) father in the audience. In explaining why she has called Julie, she says, "I didn't know who I could count on. You saved my life." Julie replies, "I did nothing." And Lucille insists, "I asked you to come and you came." These simple words echo the Gospel. Lucille had asked nothing more of her; and Julie's response—her willingness to enter again into a social relationship—is a turning point.

On the one hand, two performers on stage engage in intercourse with total detachment from each other—a form of radical alienation. At the same time, through pure coincidence, the large television screen in the club broadcasts images with which Julie is familiar: Julie first catches a glimpse of herself on the screen, then of her husband with another woman, and then of Olivier. The piece is an interview with Olivier, who praises Patrice's unfinished composition—the concerto—and states that he will complete it. Through this juxtaposition of the mechanical, dehumanizing sex show and the power of the televised interview to engage a particular individual's fantasies, Kieslowski underscores Homan's point that the screen is in fact that ubiquitous intermediate space through which each of us might find a new series of connections. In this case, Julie's connection with Olivier begins with anger. She seeks out Olivier and confronts him:

> "I heard you're finishing Patrice's concerto. You can't. You have no right. It will never be the same."
> "I may never finish. I'll tell you why. It was a way to make you cry, make you run. The only way of making you say, 'I want' or 'I don't want.'"
> "It's not fair."
> "You left me no choice."
> "You don't have the right to . . ."
> "You want to see what I've done?"

Next we see Olivier seated at the piano and Julie helping him. It is at this moment that the film progresses from one of denial to one of mourning; and it does so, significantly, through the power of the screen (the screen that Julie sees with clips of Olivier's interview is an epitome of the film *Blue*, as both are designed to force us into the recognition of the reality of community). In the film, Julie begins to accept the deaths and work through them by reviving the past. Initially, her turn to the past consists of focusing on the concerto. Olivier doesn't know the words form the chorus of the concerto, and she tells him the text is from I Corinthians 13. Then, abruptly, she asks who the other woman in the photographs is. Olivier initially appears surprised that she doesn't know; he reveals that she was Patrice's mistress and that they had been together many years. Julie asks where she can find this woman; Olivier says she is a lawyer and that she can probably find her in court.

Julie sees the woman, Sandrine, at court and follows Sandrine to the restaurant where she joins a group for lunch. Eventually, the two encounter each other in the cloakroom. When Julie asks, Sandrine admits that she was Patrice's mistress. Sandrine then reveals that she is carrying Patrice's child. She says, with a tone of sadness and resignation, "Now you'll hate him [Patrice]. You'll hate me, too." Julie says only, "I don't know."

If this were a more predictable film, the rest of the story might be dominated by themes of bitterness and revenge. But this is no *Fatal Attraction*. While it might be understandable for Julie to retreat again into her diminished existence, this time blaming her husband for his years of deception, her reaction is the opposite: the new personal connection that she has forged with Lucille and the possibility she has of forging a new connection with Olivier enables her to begin the process of repairing her broken world, of reincorporating her past, albeit with ambiguity, into her own sense of identity and thereby to resurrect her husband and her daughter. For Klein, all morality has its origins in the attempt to repair symbolically the attacked body of the mother characteristic of the depressive position. The course that Julie follows marks her retrieval of the depressive mode of relating to the world and recapitulates the early activity of repairing the mother, attacked and murdered in fantasy.

The process of symbolically re-creating the dead husband and daughter begins when Julie shows Sandrine kindness instead of contempt. There is a homecoming. Julie takes her house, which had not yet sold, off the market and invites Sandrine and her son (who is also Julie's deceased husband's son) to share this home with her. Julie, who until this point had only a fragmented existence, has now found the means to piece these fragments together. She has returned home; she has recovered Patrice through his son; she has forged a friendship with a woman who, like her, had loved Patrice. Sandrine, who might have expected nothing but hatred from Julie, is overcome by Julie's kindness and love, and remarks: "I knew it. Patrice told me a lot about you. That you are good and generous. People can always count on you. Even me."

Julie's renewed generosity is a sign that she has been able to summon up the basic gratitude that comes from early experiences of satisfaction and warmth and that her gradual renunciation of her isolation has strengthened her internal "good object." As Klein expresses it: "Gratitude is closely bound up with generosity. Inner wealth derives from having assimilated the good object so that the individual becomes able to share its gifts with others. This makes it possible to introject a more friendly outer world, and a feeling of enrichment ensues."[16]

Julie also begins with the reparative act of finishing Patrice's concerto. Her greater knowledge of her husband's intentions (and perhaps greater talent) allow her to work out the problems Olivier has been having. When she calls Olivier to tell him that she is done, he says that he will not claim credit for completing the work; credit will go to her alone. Julie at last seems to realize that Olivier has been engaged in a reparative activity of his own: he has filled the void of the loss of his collaborator and friend with work on the concerto. The completed concerto itself represents not only the restoration of Patrice's gifts but the restoration of freedom to Europe. Kieslowski ties political and personal themes together at this point. The parallels between Kieslowski's concerns and those of Klein imply that there are political implications in the latter's work as well. And indeed this is the case: the paranoid-schizoid and depressive positions are characteristic of groups as well as individuals, and hopes for rational and constructive solutions to political turmoil do depend on the ability of groups to overcome paranoia directed toward outsiders and adopt a reparative stance toward the world.[17]

In the end, Kieslowski and Klein appear to have the same interpretation of liberty: false liberty is the freedom of having no serious ties: the freedom of atomistic individualism now dominant in the West. True liberty involves the use of one's creative capacities to fashion a better society in cooperation with others.

Mourning makes reparation, morality, and love possible, and it seems fitting that the film ends with the words of St. Paul: "So faith, hope, love abide, these three; but the greatest of these is love"—the very words that Olivier had not recognized in his friend's concerto. In a post-Christian world, Kieslowski allows us to recognize that we still bear fragments of the Christian past with us, even in our most ostensibly secular moments. In a post-Christian world, film has the potential to serve as a ritual form that gathers up various fragments that, pieced together, can point to something new, both in the lives of individuals and in the life of political society.

Notes

The author would like to thank Diane Jonte-Pace for her example and encouragement and Mary Jacobus whose NEH seminar "Literature, Aesthetics, and Psycholanalysis: The Legacy of British Object Relations" at Cornell University (1999) inspired a renewed interest in Melanie Klein.

1. Peter Homans, *The Ability to Mourn: Disillusionment and the Social Origins of Psychoanalysis* (Chicago: University of Chicago Press, 1989), 310–11.
2. Eric L. Santner, *Stranded Objects: Mourning, Memory, and Film in Postwar Germany* (Ithaca, NY: Cornell University Press, 1990), 151.
3. Stuart Klawans, "Three Colors: Blue," *Nation* 257 (December 20, 1993): 788; Geoffrey Macnab, "Three Colors: Blue," *Sight and Sound* (November 1993): 54–56; and James M. Wall, "Blue," *Christian Century* 111 (March 16, 1994): 267.
4. Anthony Lane, "Blue," *New Yorker* 69 (December 13, 1993): 122–26.
5. Krzysztof Kieslowski, *Three Colors: Blue* (1993); *Three Colors: White* (1994); *Three Colors: Red* (1994). The titles *White* and *Red* are ironic as well. The film *White* depicts contemporary Poland, in which equality seems less attainable than it was during the cold war, and *Red* focuses on a retired judge whose only connection with his neighbors consists of the act of tapping their phones and listening to their desperate conversations.
6. Unless otherwise noted, references to the work of Sigmund Freud are from the *Standard Edition of the Complete Psychological Works of Sigmund Freud*, trans. and ed. James Strachey (London: Hogarth Press, 24 vols., 1966–1974). Sigmund Freud, "Mourning and Melancholia," *Standard Edition*, 14: 243–60 (first published 1917).
7. For a helpful discussion of Klein as "a psychoanalyst of the passions," concerned primarily with love and hate, see C. Fred Alford, *Melanie Klein and Critical Social Theory: An Account of Politics, Art, and Reason Based on Her Psychoanalytic Theory* (New Haven, CT: Yale University Press, 1989), esp. ch. 1 and ch. 2.
8. Melanie Klein, "Love, Guilt and Reparation" (1937) in *The Writings of Melanie Klein*, vol. 3: *Envy and Gratitude and Other Works* (New York: Free Press, 1984), 306–7. Unless otherwise noted, all references to Klein's work are to this volume.
9. Melanie Klein, "Notes on Some Schizoid Mechanisms" (1946), *Writings*, 6.
10. Some of the most notable of these successors have been Wilford Bion, Joan Rivière, and Hanna Segal.
11. A version of the scene also appears in *The Double Life of Véronique* (1991). In both cases Kieslowski uses the contents of the handbag to reveal aspects of character.
12. Klawans, "Three Colors: Blue," 780.
13. For excellent discussions of Kleinian theory, see Hanna Segal, *Introduction to the Work of Melanie Klein* (New York: Basic Books, 1974) and Jay Greenberg and Stephen Mitchell, *Object Relations in Psychoanalytic Theory* (Cambridge, MA: Harvard University Press, 2003), chap. 5.
14. Klein, "Notes on Some Schizoid Mechanisms", 21.
15. Melanie Klein, "The Theory of Anxiety and Guilt" (1948), *Writings*, 29.
16. Melanie Klein, "Envy and Gratitude" (1957), *Writings*, 189.
17. Alford, *Melanie Klein*, 57–103.

SUSAN E. HENKING

If SILENCE = DEATH, Then What Is Life?

RENEWING THE POLITICS OF MOURNING

IN 1981, several newspapers in the United States reported unusual pneumonias and cancers among a small group of gay men. These stories heralded the onset of what has been called the worst epidemic in seven hundred years. At first labeled "gay cancer," Gay-Related Immune Deficiency, or even Wrath of God Syndrome, the epidemic has come to be called HIV/AIDS.[1] Ignored by many and initially misdiagnosed as the correlate of specific marginalized identities (the four H's: homosexuals, heroin users, Haitians, and hemophiliacs), it was years into the epidemic before a U.S. president used the term "AIDS."

In response to government inaction and the oppressive socio-politics that exacerbate(d) the epidemic, men and women, both in the United States and internationally, created new identities, institutions, and social formations, often built upon prior feminist and lesbian/gay or other social justice movements, health activism, and social support networks. AIDS raised challenges to science, to academic discourse, and to formulations of activist and identity politics. It brought with it volunteerism and political activism, reformist and transgressive approaches. The "reverse discourses" of the age of AIDS created against phobic subjectivities of AIDS, homosexuality, race, and gender were subjectivities of resistance and solidarity. They offered, as well, a renewed politics of mourning.[2]

The history of "reverse discourses" and the politics of mourning responding to AIDS includes one of the most well-known images of U.S. activist art of the 1980s and thereafter, SILENCE = DEATH. This emblem, its text "printed in white Gill sanserif type underneath a pink triangle on a black background," as Douglas Crimp explains, "has come to signify AIDS activism to an entire community of people confronting the epidemic." Crimp writes:

> Our emblem's significance depends on foreknowledge of the use of the pink triangle as the marker of gay men in Nazi concentration camps, its appropriation by the gay movement to remember a suppressed history of our oppression, and, now, an inversion of its positioning (men in the death camps wore triangles that pointed down; SILENCE = DEATH's points up). SILENCE = DEATH declares that silence about the oppression and annihilation of gay people, *then and now*, must be broken as a matter of our survival. As historically problematic as an analogy to AIDS and the death camp is, it is also deeply resonant for gay men and lesbians, especially insofar as the analogy is already mediated by the gay movement's adoption of the pink triangle.[3]

Through condensation, the SILENCE = DEATH image brings together repeated metaphors that informed and inform AIDS activism, including genocide, Nazis, and the Holocaust, as well as the closet.[4] As a product of political analysis, Crimp notes, the graphic and the phrase served as an organizing and fund-raising tool, as a way to articulate and create political positions.[5]

Twenty-five years after the initial newspaper accounts and two decades after the creation of the graphic, AIDS/HIV affects many millions of people. Both the United Nations and the U.S. government have recognized its seriousness: in January 2000, "the United Nations Security Council held a precedent-setting special session, in which for the first time it identified a disease—AIDS—as a global security threat"; in May 2000, the U.S. federal government concurred that "AIDS is a threat to our national security."[6]

As a global pandemic, patterns of prevalence vary dramatically. So, too, do patterns of speech and silence, loss and mourning. The problems of which silences and which speech have long been exemplified in representations of the impact of HIV/AIDS on women.[7] And in the 2004 U.S. national election, ongoing racial and geographic politics became newly visible in the inability of either vice presidential nominee to address questions about African American communities and AIDS.[8] Both candidates responded by speaking of AIDS in Africa. Such examples reveal the ongoing paradoxes of silence as speech about something else.

Given such responses, the linking of U.S. AIDS-related foreign aid to abstinence education and the politicization of erotic life, connections of anti-gay activism with specific forms of illiberal religion, and contradictions inherent to a widely commodified queer/gay/ lesbian life burgeoning alongside hate crimes and hostile legislation, the iconoclastic phrase SILENCE = DEATH continues to carry significant meaning. In its multivalent referencing of silence, death, and equivalence, the graphic and, more often these days, the decontextualized phrase direct viewers, readers, and listeners toward both unspeakability and the requirement of speech.[9] As Tim Dean has written: "on the one hand, it implies that if silence = death, then speech (or discourse or symbolization) equals life, in the sense of lives saved by a discourse of AIDS education and the official mandate for AIDS research; while on the other hand, it implies that symbolization equals death, in the sense of conferring proper dignity on the dead."[10]

In its breadth of reference, SILENCE = DEATH is paradoxically vital testimony, noisy mourning, newly critical in the twenty-first century. SILENCE = DEATH indexes the voices of the epidemic, the simultaneous singularity and multiplicity of AIDS/HIV and of mourning. As there are many kinds of silence,[11] there are many kinds of mourning.[12] Many deaths; only one death. In the challenge of SILENCE = DEATH lies the question of life—and of mourning in our time. The challenge is Freudian: "To tolerate life remains, after all, the first duty of all living beings."[13] In the age of AIDS, as in Freud's era, we must ask, as Deborah Britzman has: "But what is it to tolerate life? It is to tolerate not just the myriad disappointments, failures, broken meanings and missed opportunities, but also the vicissitudes of its chances, the detours of suffering—indeed, life and death. Freud's last impossible sentence says as much: 'If you want to ensure life, prepare for death.'"[14]

The Age of AIDS

SILENCE = DEATH was created to speak against the specificities of AIDS/HIV in mid-1980s America—against homologies connecting homosexuality with death, against death itself—and thus against a particular silence. By 1986, the year that the image was created and President Reagan first uttered "AIDS," 16,301 people were known to have died in the United States alone.[15] Over against silence, its creators and longtime users offered "[t]ransgressive discourse . . . contemptuous of controlling heterosexist values and homophobic practices . . . the refusal to remain silent or to follow proper protocol . . . interrupting institutional discourse with angry expletives, shrill noises, a chorus of boos and hisses, chants, whistles, and shouts."[16]

For some, the equivalence of SILENCE = DEATH refers to the liberation of or the liberatory power of voice. For others, SILENCE = DEATH rejects death's invisibility (conjoining metaphors of audibility and visibility). The phrase and graphic resists stigma and contests the use of symbols to stigmatize.[17] As Espin writes: "For whatever reason, my intuition told me that when experiences are reported repeatedly, they become legitimized, 'normal'; when silence is given voice, it becomes reality; when life is witnessed, it becomes presence."[18]

In the graphic and the phrase SILENCE = DEATH, a certain un-answerability (and unspeakability) meets the requirement of speech—and the search for listeners to hear, remember, act. As an event (or set of events) that occurs in what Felman and Laub label both our "post-traumatic" era and "the age of testimony," the American (and global) experiences of HIV/AIDS are, undoubtedly, shaped by a crisis of witnessing associated with unrepresentability.[19] As Thomas Yingling has written: "Inscribed since its appearance as profoundly unimaginable, as beyond the bounds of sense, the AIDS epidemic is almost literally unthinkable in its mathematical defeat of cognitive desire."

And yet, the epidemic is characterized as well by the overwhelming "totality of discourse" about AIDS.[20] What has come to be called HIV/AIDS carries along with it, as Treichler has said, "an epidemic of signification."[21] This proliferation was, perhaps, an (un)expected reversal of the silence that has appeared and reappeared throughout the twenty-five years of AIDS/HIV, a silence accompanied by cacophony, proliferation, multiplicity, misdirection—an increasingly open secret that has, some claim, changed the world.[22]

How might we comprehend SILENCE = DEATH, this rem(a)inder of the time of AIDS, now substantially less present than the red ribbon? How might we comprehend its paradoxes? Doing so requires exploring its paradoxical silences, testimony, and mourning.

Paradoxical Silence

Rather than raising questions, those who created the image of SILENCE = DEATH—and those who wore it on T-shirts, carried it on placards, put it on book covers or in window installations, plastered it on walls—followed a different path. They offered something else. That "something else" is, in large measure, the multivalence of a particular, situated silence. In some such contexts, "silence is the language of . . . strong passions: love, anger, surprise, fear."[23] Linked to shunning and to hesitation, silence is not univocal. Silences are neither simple nor simplistic. Some suffer in silence, and some revel in it. Some silences allow—or, indeed, require—complicity. Others refuse the voice of complicity. Silence is not always quiet. For some, "silence is to speech as the white of this paper is to this print."[24] Yet, as Bruneau notes, "Repetition which is undifferentiated may approach and eventually equal ambiguous forms of silence. Both silence and repetition, to a certain point, seem to elicit a questioning uncertainty."[25]

SILENCE = DEATH elicits just such uncertainty, carrying with it complex equivalences, opposites, contradictions. The phrase resonates with silence and powerlessness, the absence of agency and listeners, the quiet of tombs and the noise of protest or testimony, the politics of mourning, lamentation, and elegy.[26] Poet Rachel Hadas pushes us: silence as friend, as enemy, as style, stubbornness, stoic courage, expedience, patience, fear does not mean that speech is "always heroic," "interesting or necessary." "Death," she writes, "doesn't release us from the snare of language."[27]

Nor, perhaps, does silence. Silence of certain sorts may, as Nelle Morton has put it, "hear others to speech."[28] To do so, it must be an active silence, analogous, perhaps, to the "passive agency" advocated by Lee Edelman.[29]

These many meanings are revealed in discussions of similarities and differences between the Holocaust and the AIDS pandemic. In a discussion of the pink triangle and the survival value of silence, for example, Stuart Marshall directs attention to the testimony of Herr Weymann, an active gay man who survived the period of the Holocaust. According to Weymann's testimony: "the only way to avoid the concentration camps and death was to remain silent. Those lesbians and gay men who lived to tell their tales survived by subterfuge, self-concealment, and secrecy. Both [Weymann's] testimony and the testimony of another gay man, who was tortured by the Gestapo in its attempt to gain a confession of homosexual activities and the names of homosexual partners, demonstrated that at that time the equation would have been SILENCE = SURVIVAL."[30]

The many meanings of silence appear, as well, in Peter M. Bowen's concluding remarks in "AIDS: 101" where he describes a student whose uncle died from AIDS and who could talk about it only in class. He writes:

> Her silence, inherited from family and neighbors, however was less . . .
> the absence of words than the overwhelming white noise of cultural
> misconceptions about AIDS and the people it has affected. While it

would be overly optimistic to believe that this class could completely silence for her and others these public silences, could completely clear away the dense verbiage around AIDS so she could hear herself think, the critical undercutting of such language nonetheless opened a space in which discourse about AIDS became not only a topic but a topos—albeit perhaps no bigger than the classroom—in which students could begin to locate their bodies as well as their fears and prejudice.[31]

SILENCE = DEATH; SILENCE = SURVIVAL; SILENCE = TESTIMONY. "Silence equals" proliferated its associations over decades, just as the network of activism drew on tactics of action, agency, silence, loving, mourning, and testimony as multivocal and paradoxical as the emblem itself. As SILENCE = DEATH opens out in these ways, what, then, is life? By implication, it is those who mourn, rather than those who die. It is what we all do before we die. It is what we build—or fail to build—from the recognition that we will die and that those we love have died—or will die.[32] And, it is the silent testimony of SILENCE = DEATH.

Paradoxical Testimony

For a religious studies scholar, particularly one with a personal history rooted in some experience of evangelical youth groups, testimony is not simply a legal or a literary phenomenon but a religious one. Witnessing, for me, conjures up now the embarrassingly guilty secret of the hours spent in King of Prussia shopping mall distributing the "Four Spiritual Laws" to unsuspecting shoppers in the 1970s. Its synonym (symptom) was testimony.

Given the historical and cultural centrality of Protestantism to American culture, it is, perhaps, not surprising that religion appears, disappears, and reappears within the context of AIDS in America. Nor that it does so in several guises.[33] Indeed, SILENCE = DEATH is peculiarly religious in its secular testimony.[34] The paradoxical testimony of SILENCE = DEATH serves its role in the public theater of moral transformation sometimes called civil or cultural religion.

Tied to a politics of data, of articulate grief, of building community, SILENCE = DEATH offers information, witness, and judgment. And it utters more. It resonates with my guilty secret. It offers testimony. Yet, what is testimony?

Paul Ricoeur argues testimony is both quasi-empirical and quasi-juridical. It is quasi-empirical because it presumes factual description from the viewpoint of the witness but requires belief on the part of the audience. It is quasi-juridical because the witness's words weigh on the scales of justice, tipping society's judgment to one side or the other.[35] Also, according to Ricouer, ordinary language usage of the category of testimony understands it as taking place within the situation of a trial. This "quasi-juridical" meaning of testimony qualifies its ordinary language meaning by focusing upon "a dispute between parties." As such, it also focuses upon "the very notion of the decision of justice" and testimony as "an element in a treatise of argumentation."[36] The third "dimension" of the ordinary language meaning of testimony emphasizes an understanding of the person who offers testimony. As Ricouer puts it: "The witness, in fact, is not only the one who utters testimony; the problem of the witness constitutes a distinct problem which arises in certain aspects of testimony of which we have said nothing. Thus *false testimony* cannot at all be reduced to an error in the account of things seen: false testimony is a lie in the heart of the witness. . . . The meaning of testimony seems then inverted; the word no longer designates an action of speech, the oral report of an eyewitness about a fact to which he was witness. Testimony is the action itself as it attests outside of himself, to the interior man, to his conviction, to his faith."[37] Testimony is, thus, multivocal.

Though paradoxical and multivalent, the paradoxical testimony of SILENCE = DEATH does not point to religion, beyond the chain of signification linking it to the anti-Judaism of Nazism. Yet, the notion of testimony does. As Ricouer argues, within historical Christianity, the category of testimony has its roots in biblical texts.[38] In contemporary Christian thought and practice, testimony refers to a specific type of verbal action performed within particular contexts. In Pentecostalism, for example: "*Testifying* is one verbal activity that all members are expected to perform within any given church service; a member is expected [to] rise at the pew and give an extemporaneous testimony of faith in God or in God's particular goodness to him or her. Testifying is part of the duty of a good saint. Personal experience stories serve to witness for the Lord; the act of testifying is a witness of the saint's effort to be a good model for others."[39]

Testimony as autobiography has a "singularly important" place in religions where membership requires a conversion narrative.[40] Such speech acts are "illocutions," performances that both map territory and are themselves acts. As Titon puts it: "To say what God has done in one's life is performance, to be sure; God requires public witnessing. But to testify is also to describe and interpret experience."[41]

A form of religious practice and religious language, testimony enacts and constructs identity, community, and morality.[42] As such, it "literally forms and presents the self, to the teller as much (more, surely) as the audience." More particularly, testimony, in Titon's words, "enables the believer to traverse the boundary between the ordinary social structures of their daily life outside the church and the extraordinary social utopian community embodied in the idea of the heavenly homecoming reunion."[43] Here, testimony, as Dell Hymes notes, is grounded in a life narrated in a distinct form: "Not that the difference is in the topics. The difference is in the silences. There is a certain focusing, a certain weighting."[44]

Such strategies of self-assertion and self-articulation, of community mending and making at the boundary of public and private, are not unfamiliar to gay, lesbian, and queer people. As Michael Warner has put it: "One way fundamentalists have contributed to the culture of minority identities is by developing the performative genres of identity-talk." He notes that witnessing is "explained to the budding Pentecostalist in much the same language of necessity, shame and pride, stigma and cultural change" as is the act of coming out.[45] This notion of testimony, too, is about identity and exemplification, for the sake of self and others, of lives ordered through language, and "a certain focusing, a certain weighting."

Like those offered within Pentecostal services, the testimony of SILENCE = DEATH requires (or enables) the listener (reader) to discern the possibilities (and liabilities) of identity and community. Just as the crisis of witnessing may, as well, be a crisis of readership,[46] the crisis of AIDS is one of audibility and of listening. SILENCE = DEATH is testimony for life. As Rebecca Chopp has written: "The telling of these stories is for life, for the mending of life, the healing of life, the ability to live and survive and thus conquer this extremity. If, traditionally, we may have made testimony say 'this is the truth, I tell it even if I have to die,' testimony now becomes 'I will live to tell this story, I will survive for an hour, a day, however long I can.' If one is not authorized to live, then surviving is both resistance and hope."[47]

"No one," Erika Apfelbaum has written, "can live in silence forever."[48] A renewed politics of mourning is thus about silence *and* its opposites, life *and* death, mourning *and* melancholia, religion *and* religious studies. It requires taking our ambivalence seriously. Indeed, it requires living with and within our ambivalences.

The Equivalence of Death: Paradoxical Mourning

The ambivalences and equivalences of SILENCE = DEATH resonate with and resist the quiet of the tomb, the newly quiet mourning of (Western) modernity. SILENCE = DEATH calls for noisy mourning, refusing the many euphemisms and avoidances accompanying death in American culture of our era.[49] Calling us to recognize the reach of our mourning—the scope of HIV/AIDS (not to mention continuing genocidal violence and wars across the globe)—SILENCE = DEATH makes evident that Felman and Laub's "post-traumatic age" remains illusory, a dream. Like analysis and education, trauma and loss may be interminable.[50] While Freud understood melancholia as pathological failure to move beyond mourning, later thinkers challenge this view. Perhaps later events do as well.

What if "the grief stricken are intensely alive", as Holtz-Warhaft expresses it?[51] What if the grief is, in fact, disenfranchised grief?[52] Or catastrophic mourning?[53] Perhaps grief is ongoing because death is. What if disengaging is not the point?[54] What, then, of our agency through and beyond grief, through and beyond mourning? What of the paradoxical mourning of SILENCE = DEATH as grief ritualized?[55]

Twenty-five years into the AIDS/HIV pandemic, SILENCE = DEATH requires us to consider the volatility of grief and the possibility of "political outrage."[56] SILENCE = DEATH drives from testimony toward political action. It requires recognition of the peculiar cultural and historical specificity of living our mourning as disengagement. Thus, SILENCE = DEATH challenges the particular Freudian passivity that is only one of the meanings of silence and of grief: "Memorializing, remembering, knowing the person who has died, and allowing them to influence the present are active processes that seem to continue the survivor's entire life. . . . We are not talking about living in the past, but rather recognizing how bonds formed in the past can inform our present and our future. . . . We propose that rather than emphasizing letting go, the emphasis should be on negotiating and renegotiating the meaning of loss over time. While death is permanent and unchanging, the process is not."[57]

In this way, SILENCE = DEATH moves us from, as Crimp posits, mourning to militancy.[58] More than a rhetoric of hope, a rhetoric of "living with AIDS" or "AIDS is not a death sentence," Crimp's model of mourning calls for action and values that change(d) the world. As he puts it: "mourning troubles us; by 'us' I mean gay men confronting AIDS." He is correct; but the troubling reaches much wider, the ambivalence much deeper. In "The Spectacle of Mourning," Crimp renders both mourning and ambivalence specific: "In an epidemic that didn't have to happen, and whose continuing to this day to spread unabated is the result of political neglect or outright mendacity, every death is unacceptable. And yet death itself can never finally not be accepted. We have to accept death to continue to live. But the difference, and the resulting ambivalence, is precisely this: the difference between those of us who must learn to accept these deaths and those who still find these deaths acceptable."[59]

Crimp argues against Freud's analysis of mourning as normalizing —at least for those who mourn and whose normalcy remains in question. In doing so, Crimp draws on Freud's own warning against interference with mourning. Homophobic responses to AIDS deaths, in his view, interfere: "Freud does not say what might happen if mourning is interfered with, but insofar as our conscious defenses direct us toward social action, they already show the deference for reality that Freud attributes to mourning's accomplishment."[60]

Many have seen mourning and its products, religion and testimony, as unrealistic and potentially quietist substitutes for life, distraction at best and complicity at worst. And yet, from mourning and melancholia we build culture. We become, according to Crimp, militant. We build theory.[61] In our losses lie the possibilities of hope. Much of their educational force occurs later—in what Britzman labels (following Freud) "after-education."[62] These moments reveal education as, according to Freud, an "impossible profession," like life, contradictory at its very heart.[63] Here there is an echo of comments on the unspeakability of education[64] and a call to remember, with Crimp, that "to accept my humanity is to accept my frailty. Or to put it differently, it is to accept that I have an unconscious."[65]

In wrestling with HIV/AIDS, Crimp's ambivalence, like the iconic SILENCE = DEATH, becomes more than psychological, more than political. It becomes pedagogical. Mourning is both what we share and what differentiates us from one another. What remains as our shared troubling is the question of what to do with *this* mourning in *our* time. In SILENCE = DEATH, the accomplishment of mourning returns, interminably, to the question of living. A renewed politics of mourning sees its products as a realistic refusal of the normal.

Tolerating Life: "After-Education" and the Products of Mourning

Looking back, I recognize that these concerns came together in "AIDS: Scientific Investigation and the Human Experience," a course

I co-taught more than a decade ago and to which I return often in my mind's eye. Here, teaching became a third space in the ambivalence of grief displaced. Teaching about HIV/AIDS crystallized, for me, the ambivalence and equivalence of mourning, of teaching and learning, of religion and religious studies, of SILENCE = DEATH, and more.[66]

I first co-taught "AIDS: Scientific Investigation and the Human Experience" in 1990. Designed to meet institutional general education goals focusing on critical inquiry and writing as well as interdisciplinary concerns, the course was created and taught by a chemist (David Craig) and me, a religious studies professor at Hobart and William Smith colleges. We taught the course six times, modifying it and elaborating it in response to changes in our students and in ourselves, in the features of the trauma, the "epidemic of signification," and viral infection that is HIV/AIDS. Each time, the class had its own shape and character; in each case, mistakes were made and topics elided. And in each class, "something happened."[67]

As an endeavor in AIDS education, the course operated on multiple levels. By conjoining common readings with individualized research, it recognized the need for a shared discourse about HIV/AIDS as well as the many localized concerns that collide and come together around the pandemic. And, we created a structure addressing issues generally relevant to inquiry about HIV/AIDS, which could also respond flexibly to the then rapidly changing face of the epidemic.[68] By weaving together considerations of power and ethics, science and the making of knowledges, difference and discourse, by working as individual writers/researchers as well as in small groups, participants engaged with the complexities of cooperation, competition, and alliance characteristic of contemporary life, scholarship, and, not incidentally, politics.

Like many cultural products, this course was a product of silences and death. For me, it was produced in the third space some call the closet and others deem transitional, as "practices of negotiating between what is and what can be."[69] I was then an untenured faculty member struggling to maintain both a discreet privacy about my sexual orientation and a sense of personal integrity. Whatever (other) silences were being enacted by students and my co-teacher, the course allowed me to address issues of sexuality, speaking quite directly about gay men and lesbians, while eliding my own involvements in identity politics. The course permitted me to obscure the potential immorality of the closet by emphasizing the morality of addressing the trauma of HIV/AIDS. That is, I could engage in anti-homophobic education under the cover (sign) of AIDS with its complex historical and cultural links to homosexuality. I was able to engage in liberal education—indeed, to fit squarely under the rubrics of general education, as it was understood at my institution—while engaging in the highly politicized activity of AIDS education. (This was made easier, in some respects, by the participation of my colleagues and students in the "open secret" of the closet and by the simultaneous visibility and invisibility of lesbians under the signs gay, homosexual, and AIDS.)[70]

Aspects of the course both underplayed and enacted features of the American experience(s) of AIDS. Science as expert and betrayer, the omnipresence and invisibility of religion, and the emotional toll of the course for both faculty and students resonated with our sociocultural surround. My own rage, turning on occasion to maudlin sentimentality, is telling, as was the difficulty of assessing students in this situation. That the course was both a wonder and a quagmire enacting the very oppositions and resistances characterizing the cultural landscape of AIDS is indicated, perhaps, by two questions raised during the final class session in the first term we taught the course: "What about sex? What about the *people* with AIDS?" I was shocked by what I had assumed as known—about safer sex, for example—and what I found difficult to voice in the context of our course. We'd depersonalized AIDS/HIV and inadvertently obscured central features of what AIDS education must be.[71] Although the course seemed successful, it was shaped by paradoxical elisions and silences as well as the proliferation of discourses and voices endemic to the American (and global) experience(s) of HIV/AIDS.[72] It was shaped by our own (politics of) mourning. Like SILENCE = DEATH, the course was paradoxical testimony, paradoxical pedagogy.[73] Closeted, ambivalent mourning. Looking back, I wonder if I thought then: "If SILENCE = DEATH, might teaching be life?"

Two works that the course examined were particularly troubling, symptomatic, and powerful: the video *Common Threads: Stories from the Quilt* and Larry Kramer's book *Reports from the Holocaust*.[74] Examined together, as I subsequently came to understand they frequently have been, these works were and are critical for making sense of SILENCE = DEATH, mourning and testimony, as emblematic of the age of AIDS.

Every year we taught the course, we began with *Common Threads*, a 1989 television documentary, subsequently available as a video. The documentary weaves together lives of individuals with HIV/ AIDS and their caretakers with clips from news broadcasts about

the pandemic. Narrated by Dustin Hoffman, the production is organized both as a history moving from 1981 through 1989 and as a
visual quilting together of particular lives. Thus, the narrative thrust
of Common Threads is dual. The death toll mounts. The people
involved vary (a hemophiliac boy, several white gay men, an apparently African American HIV+ woman whose recovered IVDU (in-
travenous drug-use) husband died from AIDS).[75] Responses to the
disease differ. Like the Quilt that is its principal trope, *Common
Threads* memorializes, renders visible, brings together, and juxta-
poses particular individuals with anonymous numbers.[76] The quilt
and the video argue: *e pluribus unum.*

Each time we showed this film, I cried—as did many of the students. At first, I worried about needless trauma. This, perhaps, is
the film's aim: in the age of AIDS, tears may be an essential part
of education.[77] But might they immobilize? Numb? As Crimp has
noted, the quilt itself elicited ambivalent responses, in part because
it served and serves multiple functions: "The first is that it provides
a ritual of mourning and in two respects: the private mourning ritual
of a person or group involved in making a panel and the collective
mourning ritual of visiting the quilt to share that experience with
others. The second function is what we might call the spectacle of
mourning, the vast public-relations effort to humanize and dignify
our losses for those who have not shared them."

Crimp interrogates his own ambivalence about the quilt, asking:
"Does a visit to the quilt, or the media's approving attention to it, as-
suage the guilt of those who otherwise have been so callous, whether
that callousness takes the form of denial or of outright disgust? Does
it provide a form of catharsis, an easing of conscience, for those who
have cared and done so little about this great tragedy? . . . Does the
quilt sanitize or sentimentalize gay life? Does it render invisible what
makes people hate us? Does it make their continuing disapproval
possible?"[78] Was teaching *Common Threads* doubly voyeuristic?

As teachers, we learned to explore student responses, seeking to
acknowledge sadness and mourning *and* move from these emotions
to identify the range of attitudes and actions portrayed in the film:
artistic creation, education, political action (ACT UP), and others.
We used the film's "testimony" and its call to mourning and to life
in many ways.

In the context of the course, the spectacle of *Common Threads*
opened up to the anger and activism contained in Larry Kramer's
Reports from the Holocaust. (Indeed, Kramer appears in *Common
Threads.*) Like the video, Kramer's book offers a complex chronology.

The book, in its two editions, brings together Kramer's writings for gay and other media from 1978 through 1993. Appended to each piece are his subsequent reflections and efforts at contextualization. In addition, the book includes several reflective essays written especially for the two editions of the book. Here, too, the years are punctuated by numerical death tolls and, more occasionally, a roll call of the dead. Here, too, emotions run high, as reflected in Kramer's own rage and sadness and, indeed, student and faculty response to that rage.[79]

The dominant metaphor in Kramer's book, evidenced in part by its cover art (the inverted pink triangle of SILENCE = DEATH), evokes a profoundly different range of associations from those aroused by the quilt.[80] AIDS is construed as intentional (and later unintentional) genocide. Contemporary politicians are likened to Hitler while others are analogized to the Nazi medical establishment. A Jewish gay man, Kramer draws extensive parallels between Jewishness and gayness as well, worrying about similarities to Jewish collaboration with the death machinery of Nazism. In elaborating his views, Kramer draws on the work of Holocaust survivors as well as scholars of Holocaust studies (e.g., Primo Levi, Hannah Arendt, and Zygmunt Bauman) to authorize and elaborate his understanding of the AIDS epidemic as genocidal.[81]

Kramer's strategy is controversial.[82] For some readers (including some in the course), the metaphor smacks of anti-Semitism (or anti-Judaism), despite Kramer's caveats, and leads to blaming victims or diminishing the historical trauma of *the* Holocaust. In such views, Kramer, like other gay writers, draws upon a cultural framework that is both useful and profoundly problematic.

For some, though, Kramer's rage is their rage, invigorating them, mobilizing them. Even today, Simon Watney's words resonate: "the AIDS crisis continues, and the question of why so little has been done becomes more pressing than ever; hence the significance of Kramer's emphasis on the most murderous; and even genocidal, aspects of the social policies that have determined the course of the epidemic in both Britain and the United States. For it would be invidious indeed if we were to abandon any attempt to learn, in the midst of one catastrophe, from another and earlier tragedy." Watney enumerates two lessons from the Holocaust relevant to the AIDS epidemic:

> The lesson of the Holocaust is the facility with which most people, put into a situation that does not contain a good choice . . . argue themselves away from . . . moral duty . . . adopting instead the precepts of

rational interest and self-preservation. *In a system where rationality and ethics point in opposite directions, humanity is the main loser....* The second lesson tells us that putting self-preservation above moral duty is in no way predetermined, inevitable and inescapable. One can be pressed to do it, but one cannot be forced to do it, and thus one cannot really shift the responsibility for doing it on to those who exerted the pressure. *It does not matter how many people choose moral duty over the rationality of self preservation—what does matter is that some did.*[83]

Still, rage, however warranted, worries. For some, Kramer's metaphor is so overblown as to lead to numbness or so inaccurate as to encourage passivity. The demand for action shouted by SILENCE = DEATH risks, paradoxically, inaction. Like tears, anger can immobilize. Death can stop us in our tracks.

Such themes remain critical in the twenty-first century. As Tim Dean presciently wrote in the early 1990s, "War and AIDS occasion a confrontation not only with death but with its place in the unconscious and hence its relation to desire." And, death, he argues, "opens a hole in the real that symbolization must supply if mourning is to succeed."[84] It continues to do so. Memory, identity, community converge and collide. Many deaths; one death; death. The conundrum, as Jeff Nunokawa writes, is "the paradoxical individuality of the exemplum."[85] After-education reveals the ambivalent (and ambiguous) conjunction of the particular with that which we all must face—eventually. As Timothy Murphy writes: "Testimony about the dead is not driven by a desire to overcome death but to prevent it from eroding the meaningfulness of life itself. Testimony, not death, is the last word."[86]

In what Lee Edelman has called the "cultural fantasmatics of agency," neither mourning nor identity is static.[87] Nor are they simply accomplished. Edelman warns against activist participation in a rhetoric which characterizes gay men as narcissistic in an effort to mobilize collective action. Similarly, Jeff Nunokawa warns of a complex interaction between homophobic association of gay males and death in the act of memorialization.[88] Thomas Yingling brings these points together when he writes:

> Because AIDS has been read so persistently within a paradigm of group and/or individual identity, one of the continuing tasks facing those who respond to it has been to insist on it as a collective calamity. But one of those tasks has also been—because the "person with AIDS" would

otherwise signify non-being in a culture founded in and devoted to myths of being—the validation of any individual or collective identity threatened by the illness with erasure. We must think AIDS not only as a public issue of ideology, apparatus, and representation but also *as it is internalized and expressed* by those infected and effected, and we must do this not because disease is a matter of privacy nor because individual experience provides unmediated authority and knowledge but because "AIDS" as a signifier lodges in the deep subliminal zones of memory, loss, and (im)possibility, zones that in the end are among the most crucial sites on which disciplinarity is inscribed and therefore potentially disrupted.[89]

Like tears and anger, mourning and melancholia, SILENCE = DEATH moves across culture, politics, and classrooms, building connections through its equivalences and paradoxes. Risky. Ambivalent. Alive.

The age of AIDS has many other labels—the post-traumatic age, the age of witnessing, the age of uprooting, the age of uncertainty. With AIDS/HIV (as with war), Jeffrey Weeks writes: "A sense of the contingency and uncertainty of life has been brought to many people, many of whom are very young, by the threat of premature illness and death. But it has also produced something else: a sense of the meaning that can be brought to life by the threat of death. . . . That sense of our humanity being reaffirmed through the experience of death is I believe a profoundly transforming experience, a democratizing experience, also, which gives new meaning to our experience of, and need for, human relationships in all their diversity."[90]

In this era when certainties combat uncertainty, memory and forgetfulness embrace in what Deborah Britzman has called "difficult knowledge"[91]—knowledge that challenges the framing of education as progress or development; knowledge that is more than merely cognitive, more than merely experiential or conscious; knowledge that "interferes." In this after-education, the classroom opens out to make analyzable what we (as teachers and students schooled in how to act and, indeed, be within the settings of higher education) suppress, ignore, even repress. The tears required by *Common Threads*, the rage called out by Kramer, the awkward balance of silence and speech, like the iconic SILENCE = DEATH, are polyvalent, revealing the effort to be (gay and lesbian) positive amid the miseries of everyday life as well as the clash between desires for knowledge to move us and the puzzle of what to do when it does so in unexpected ways.

Loss and mourning are keywords in the age of AIDS.[92] Now, as always, as Paul Rosenblatt has noted, "a loss is often a series of losses" and "with the first significant loss in one's life . . . comes a realization of one's own mortality and of the human incapacity to stop death or reverse it."[93] Teaching, like life, builds on, and resists, this learning. Parker J. Palmer is, perhaps, more literally than figuratively accurate when he writes that successful teaching means that some of us join: "a powerful community marked by the ability to talk with the dead. This is not a mark of madness but of an educated person. Learning to speak and listen in that invisible community of history and thought makes one's world immeasurably larger and forever changes one's life."[94] For Palmer, this is the mark of education. It is also the mark of mourning.

SILENCE = DEATH invites us to speak with the dead, to listen, and to take up their call for change. Even as I/we emerge from the silences and closets that shape our lives and our deaths, we are reminded that "teaching . . . must in turn *testify*, make something happen."[95] So, too, must mourning. It must make life—in the third space between silence and death, in the awful equivalence and ambivalence of mourning.

Notes

1. Early accounts relied upon the 5 June 1981, *Morbidity and Mortality Weekly*. To situate AIDS within a broader history, see Gerald J. Stine, *AIDS Update 2004: An Annual Overview of Acquired Immune Deficiency Syndrome* (San Francisco: Pearson/Benjamin Cummings, 2004), 1–12. On the presence of AIDS/HIV prior to 1981, see, for example, Douglas Crimp, *Melancholia and Moralism: Essays on AIDS and Queer Politics* (Cambridge, MA: MIT Press, 2002), 59 n. 11.
2. On the politics of mourning, see Gail Holst-Warhaft, *The Cue for Passion: Grief and Its Political Uses* (Cambridge, MA: Harvard University Press, 2000). On Foucault's terminology of reverse discourses, see Robert Goss, *Jesus Acted Up: A Gay and Lesbian Manifesto* (New York: Harper Collins, 1993), 8. The tension between reformist and transgressive is sometimes articulated as that between the Gay Men's Health Crisis (an AIDS service organization) and the AIDS Coalition to Unleash Power (ACT UP). See Philip M. Kayal, *Bearing Witness: Gay Men's Health Crisis and the Politics of AIDS* (Boulder, CO: Westview Press, 1993).
3. Douglas Crimp with Adam Rolston, *AIDS Demographics* (Seattle: Bay Press, 1990), 34. For the original version of the graphic, see 30–31; the image also appears throughout the book. For analysis of SILENCE = DEATH in relation to social movement theory, see Joshua Gannon, "Silence, Death, and the Invisible Enemy: AIDS Activism and Social Movement 'Newness,'" in *Ethnography Unbound: Power and Resistance in the Modern Metropolis*, ed. Michael Burawoy et al., 35–57 (Berkeley: University of California Press, 1991). Crimp also discusses the image in *Melancholia and Moralism.*
4. Parallels between AIDS/HIV and the Holocaust and connections between homophobic heterosexism and Nazism are rooted in the historical treatment of homosexuality in Nazi Germany. Goss is one of many who use such analogies:

see *Jesus Acted Up*, 20, 78, 103, 111, 119, and 222–23, n. 11 and n. 12. Conjoining the SILENCE = DEATH image with photographs of Nuremberg trials makes this connection more explicit; see Crimp, *Melancholia and Moralism*, 33–35, 38. For related discussions, see Stuart Marshall, "The Contemporary Political Use of Gay History: The Third Reich," in *How Do I Look? Queer Film and Video*, ed. Bad Object-Choices [organization], 65–89 (Seattle: Bay Press, 1991) and the discussion on 90–102; also Sander L. Gilman, "Plague in Germany 1939/1989: Cultural Images of Race, Space and Disease," in *Writing AIDS: Gay Literature, Language, and Analysis*, ed. Timothy F. Murphy and Suzanne Poirier, 54–82 (New York: Columbia University Press, 1993). On the equation of queers and Jews, see Daniel Boyarin, Daniel Itzkovitz, and Ann Pellgrini, *Queer Theory and the Jewish Question* (New York: Columbia University Press, 2003). On parallels between Holocaust and illness narratives, see Lucy Bregman and Sara Thiermann, *First Person Mortal: Personal Narratives of Illness, Dying and Grief* (New York: Paragon House, 1995), 62–67; and Arthur W. Frank, *The Wounded Storyteller: Body, Illness, and Ethics* (Chicago: University of Chicago Press, 1995). On the closet, see Eve Kosofsky Sedgwick, *The Epistemology of the Closet* (Berkeley: University of California Press, 1990).

5. Crimp, *AIDS Demographics*, 20.
6. Stine, *AIDS Update 2004*, 495.
7. Nancy L. Roth and Katie Hogan, eds. *Gendered Epidemic: Representations of Women in the Age of AIDS* (New York: Routledge, 1998).
8. Both popular and scholarly literature emphasize the disproportionate impact of HIV/AIDS on African Americans and other communities of color. See, for example, "AIDS at 25: Special Report," *Newsweek*, 15 May 2006. For scholarly perspectives, see Kelly Brown Douglas, *Sexuality and the Black Church: A Womanist Perspective* (Maryknoll, NY: Orbis Books, 1999), and Patricia Hill Collins, *Black Sexual Politics: African Americans, Gender, and the New Racism* (New York: Routledge, 2004). That the politics of the phrase has shifted in the twenty-first century is illustrated by Stephen Lewis, "Silence = Death: AIDS, Africa, and Pharmaceuticals," *Toronto Globe and Mail*, 26 January 2001, http://www.corpwatch.org/article.php?id=491 (accessed 23 Dec. 2007).
9. See Rebecca S. Chopp, "Theology and the Poetics of Testimony," *Criterion* 37, 1 (Winter 1998): 2–12.
10. Tim Dean, "The Psychoanalysis of AIDS," *October* 63 (Winter 1993), 100–101. On paradox, see also Jeffrey Weeks, *Invented Moralities: Sexual Values in an Age of Uncertainty* (New York: Columbia University Press, 1995), 88–101. I am grateful to Betty Bayer for recommending this book.
11. On silence, see Thomas J. Bruneau, "Communicative Silences: Forms and Functions," *Journal of Communication* 23 (March 1973): 17–46; Bernard P. Dauenhauer, *Silence: The Phenomenon and Its Ontological Significance* (Bloomington: Indiana University Press, 1980); Deborah Tannen and Muriel Saville-Troike, eds. *Perspectives on Silence* (Norwood, NJ: Ablex, 1985); and Kipling D. Williams, *Ostracism: The Power of Silence* (New York: Guilford Press, 2001). On ontological issues, see Gaston Bachelard, *The Poetics of Space*, trans. Maria Jolas (Boston: Beacon Press, 1969), 180. Only at the end of the writing process did I discover Foucault: "There is not one, but many silences, and they are an integral part of the strategies that underlie and permeate discourse." From Foucault's *The History of Sexuality*, quoted by Paula Treichler and Catherine Warren, "Maybe Next Year: Feminist Silence and the AIDS Epidemic," in Roth and Hogan, *Gendered Epidemic*, 109–52.
12. On the historical and cultural variability of grief and mourning, see Gary Laderman, *Rest in Peace: A Cultural History of Death and the Funeral Home in Twentieth-Century America* (New York: Oxford University Press, 2003); Karla F. C. Holloway, *Passed On: African American Mourning Stories* (Durham, NC:

Duke University Press, 2003); and Robert E. Goss and Dennis Klass, *Dead but Not Lost: Grief Narratives in Religious Traditions* (Walnut Creek, CA: Alta Mira Press, 2005). On the historic specificity of theories of grief and mourning, see Margaret Stroebe, Mary Gergen, Kenneth Gergen, and Wolfgang Stroebe, "Broken Hearts or Broken Bonds?" In *Continuing Bonds: New Understandings of Grief*, ed. Dennis Klass, Phyllis R. Silverman, and Steven L. Nickman, 31–44 (Washington, DC: Taylor and Francis, 1996).

13. From Sigmund Freud, "Thoughts for the Times on War and Death" as cited in Deborah P. Britzman, *Lost Subjects, Contested Objects: Toward a Psychoanalytic Inquiry of Learning* (Albany: State University of New York Press, 1998), 130.

14. Britzman, *Lost Subjects*, 130–31.

15. "So Little Time . . . An AIDS History," http://www.aegis.com/topics/timeline/ (accessed 23 Dec. 2007).

16. Goss, *Jesus Acted Up*, 28–39.

17. For an example linking aural and auditory metaphors (voice, silence, being heard, listening, speaking) with visual metaphors (seeing, being invisible, becoming visible), see Oliva Espin, "Giving Voice to Silence: The Psychologist as Witness," *American Psychologist* 48, no. 4 (April 1993): 411. For examples related to HIV/AIDS, see Nancy Roth and Katie Hogan, part 3: "Gendered Silence: Representations—Exclusions and Inclusions," in Roth and Hogan, *Gendered Epidemic*. On stigma, see Stine, *AIDS Update 2004*, 15 and ch. 13. See also Gannon, "Silence, Death."

18. Espin, "Giving Voice to Silence." 413.

19. Shoshana Felman and Dori Laub, *Testimony: Crises of Witnessing in Literature, Psychoanalysis and History* (New York: Routledge, 1992), 1, 5. Elie Wiesel labeled the post-Holocaust era the age of testimony, and many subsequent scholars then affirmed this view. Thus, Rebecca Chopp ("Theology and the Poetics of Testimony," 2) cites Wiesel's comment: "If the Greeks invented tragedy, the Romans the epistle, and the Renaissance the sonnet, our generation invented a new literature, that of testimony." Original in Elie Wiesel, "The Holocaust as a Literary Inspiration," *Dimensions of the Holocaust* (Evanston, IL: Northwestern University Press, 1977), 9. In discussing her own experience of the disappearance and gassing of her father as well as much of the post–World War II era Erika Apfelbaum has used the phrase "age of uprooting." See, in this regard, Apfelbaum, "Against the Tide: Making Waves and Breaking Silences," in *Alternative History of Psychology in Autobiography*, ed. Leo Moss (n.p.: Kluwer Academic/Plenum, n.d.) as well as her related works: "Restoring Lives Shattered by Collective Violence: The Role of Official Public Narratives in the Process of Memorializing," invited address for the conference on "Narrative, Trauma and Memory—Working through the Southern African Armed Conflicts of the 20th Century," 3–5 July, 2001, Cape Town, South Africa; also "The Dread: An Essay on Communication across Cultural Boundaries," in "Under the Covers: Theorising the Politics of Counter Stories," special issue, *International Journal of Critical Psychology* 4 (2001): 19–35. I am grateful to Betty Bayer for introducing me to Erika and to Erika for sharing her work.

20. Thomas E. Yingling, "AIDS in America: Postmodern Governance, Identity, and Experience," in *Inside/Out: Lesbian Theories, Gay Theories*, ed. Diana Fuss, 291–310 (New York: Routledge, 1991), 291–92. See also Yingling, "AIDS, Confession, and Theory: The Pedagogical Dilemma," in *AIDS and the National Body*, ed. Robyn Weigman (Durham, NC: Duke University Press, 1997). On the literatures of HIV/AIDS, see Susan E. Henking, "The Legacies of AIDS: Religion and Mourning in AIDS-Related Memoirs," in *Spirituality and Community: Diversity in Lesbian and Gay Experience*," ed. J. Michael Clark and Michael L. Stemmeler, 3–28, Gay Men's Issues in Religious Studies Series, vol. 5 (Los Colinas, TX: Monument Press, 1994); Marilyn Chandler, "Voices from

the Front: AIDS in Autobiography," *A-B: Autobiography Studies* 6, no. 1 (Spring 1991): 65–75; Robert G. Franke, "Beyond Good Doctor, Bad Doctor: AIDS Fiction and Biography as a Developing Genre," *Journal of Popular Culture* 27 (Winter 1993): 93–101; and David Jarraway, "From Spectacular to Speculative: The Shifting Rhetoric in Recent Gay AIDS Memoirs," *Mosaic: A Journal for the Interdisciplinary Study of Literature* 33, no. 4 (December 2000).

21. Originally published in 1987, Paula Treichler's essay "AIDS, Homophobia, and Biomedical Discourse: An Epidemic of Signification," *October* 43: 31–70, reappeared in her book *How to Have Theory in an Epidemic: Cultural Chronicles of AIDS* (Durham, NC: Duke University Press, 1999). On the "crisis" of language circulating around HIV/AIDS, see Dean, "Psychoanalysis of AIDS," 83–116.

22. On mystifications that construct patriarchy, see Mary Daly, *Gyn/Ecology: The Metaethics of Radical Feminism* (Boston: Beacon Press, 1978). On ways the emergence of AIDS has changed the world, see the many magazine and newspaper pieces in June 2006 responding to the 25th "anniversary" of the syndrome's initial recognition. Examples include: "AIDS at 25: A Special Report," *Newsweek*, 15 May 2006, as well as the following articles from the *New York Times*, Sunday, 4 June 2006, p. 15: Abraham Verghese, "AIDS at 25: An Epidemic of Caring"; Jonathan Rauch, "Families Forged by Illness"; John Moore and Nicoli Nattrass, "Deadly Quackery"; and Nicholas Kristof, "Race against Death." For more scholarly assessments, Gary Laderman, in *Rest in Peace*, 140–41, lists changing burial practices, new perspectives on how communities care for the dying, new understandings of scapegoating in crisis, and reminders of the limitations of health care in the United States; Jeffrey Weeks, in *Invented Moralities*, 42, writes: "The AIDS crisis, in all of its frightening impact, bearing the burden of fear of disease and death in the wake of pleasure and desire, seems to many to embody the downside of the transformations of sexuality in recent years, a warning of the dangers of 'going too far.' Yet in many of the responses to it we can see something else: a quickening of humanity, the engagement of solidarity, and the broadening of the meanings of love, love in the face of death." The effort to avoid simple-minded metaphoric redemption of the suffering associated with HIV/AIDS demands caution in considering these changes.

23. Bruneau, "Communicative Silences," 34.

24. Ibid., 18. Tannen and Saville-Troike, in *Perspectives on Silence*, seek to reverse the polarity.

25. Bruneau, "Communicative Silences," 19.

26. On lamentation and elegy, see Robert Pogue-Harrison, *The Dominion of the Dead* (Chicago: University of Chicago Press, 2003), 65ff., and Holst-Warhaft, *Cue for Passion*, passim. On the many contradictions and equivalences resonate within SILENCE = DEATH, see Crimp, *Melancholia and Moralism*, 129. Crimp, citing the work of Lee Edelman, mentions literal/figurative, proper/improper, inside/out, and self/not self. In *Jesus Acted Up*, Goss mentions action = life, ignorance = fear, and silence = apathy (55, 56).

27. Rachel Hadas, *The Empty Bed* (Hanover, NH: Wesleyan University Press by the University Press of New England, 1995). See especially, "Peculiar Sanctity," 62–63, and "Arguments of Silence," 74–76. The main points here are rendered most explicitly in the latter poem.

28. Nelle Morton, *The Journey Is Home* (Boston: Beacon Press, 1986).

29. See Lee Edelman, "The Mirror and the Tank: 'AIDS,' Subjectivity and the Rhetoric of Activism," in Murphy and Poirier, *Writing AIDS*, 9–38 (New York: Columbia University Press, 1993), 30.

30. Marshall, "Political Use of Gay History," 69–70. Erika Apfelbaum makes a similar point in "The Dread."

31. Peter M. Bowen, "AIDS 101," in Murphy and Poirier, *Writing AIDS*, 158.

32. Robert Pogue-Harrison, *The Dominion of Death* (Chicago: University of Chicago Press, 2003). On the democratizing impact of human vulnerability to death, see Weeks, *Invented Moralities*, 43. On courageous listening, see Apfelbaum, "Restoring Lives" and "The Dread."

33. Whether construed as a force of discrimination or a resource for survival, traces of religion or spirituality (defined variously) are intertwined with testimony regarding the ravages faced by persons with AIDS and those who care for them, with testimony about the strengths and passions that make up lives in this "traumatic" era. (Here, I resist Felman and Laub's characterization of our time as "post-traumatic.") See Henking, "Legacies of AIDS." On defining religion and spirituality, see, for example, C. Daniel Batson, Patricia Schoenrade, and W. Larry Ventis, *Religion and the Individual: A Social-Psychological Perspective* (New York: Oxford University Press, 1993), ch. 1; also Jonathan Z. Smith, *Relating Religion: Essays in the Study of Religion* (Chicago: University of Chicago Press, 2004), especially ch. 7 and ch. 8.

34. Martin Marty has described America as "peculiarly secular and peculiarly religious": Martin E. Marty, *Modern American Religion*, vol. 1: *The Irony of It All* (Chicago: University of Chicago Press, 1986), 90.

35. Paul Ricouer, "The Hermeneutics of Testimony," in *Essays on Biblical Interpretation*, ed. Lewis S. Mudge, 119–54 (Philadelphia: Fortress Press, 1980), 123–24, 125, 126.

36. Ibid., 125, 126.

37. Ibid., 129, 130.

38. In discussing the relation of testimony to biblical matters, Ricouer turns to the root *martus*, citing Isaiah 43:8–13 as relevant to a prophetic understanding of testimony and witness. He then moves to New Testament depictions, emphasizing the "'confessional' kernel of testimony" (131, 134). Here, too, lie the origins of what Ricouer calls the hermeneutics of testimony.

39. Elaine J. Lawless, *God's Peculiar People: Women's Voices and Folk Tradition in a Pentecostal Church* (Lexington, KY: University Press of Kentucky, 1988), 53.

40. Jeff Todd Titon, *Powerhouse of God: Speech, Chant, and Song in an Appalachian Baptist Church* (Austin: University of Texas Press, 1988), 354. On testimony within the context of conversion, see also Lewis R. Rambo, *Understanding Religious Conversion* (New Haven, CT: Yale University Press, 1993), 137–39.

41. Titon, *Powerhouse of God*, 354.

42. On community and identity, see Titon, *Powerhouse of God*, 369–72. On morality, see Chopp, "Theology and the Poetics of Testimony," 7ff., whose use of morality is *not* the moralism Crimp criticizes in *Melancholia and Moralism*. See also Weeks, *Invented Moralities*, on the effort to recover the notion of values from conservatives and on the particular values emergent in what he labels the "age of uncertainty."

43. Titon, *Powerhouse of God*, 403, 407.

44. Lawless, *God's Peculiar People*, 138. See Dell Hymes, "The Grounding of Performance and Text in a Narrative View of Life," *Alcheringa*, n.s. 4, no. 1 (1978): 137–40.

45. Michael Warner, "Tongues Untied," in *Que(e)rying Religion: A Critical Anthology*, ed. Gary David Comstock and Susan E. Henking, 223–31 (New York: Continuum, 1997), 230.

46. Horowitz, "Rethinking Holocaust Testimony."

47. Chopp, "Theology and the Poetics of Testimony," 7. While written regarding Holocaust testimony, Chopp's point is broader. For an interesting contrast emphasizing statements around mourning, see Pogue-Harrison, *Dominion of Death*, 69–70.

48. Apfelbaum, "Restoring Lives."
49. See Laderman, *Rest in Peace;* Holst-Warhaft, *Cue for Passion.*
50. The term "interminable" alludes to Freud. On the interminability of education, see Deborah P. Britzman, *After-Education: Anna Freud, Melanie Klein, and Psychoanalytic Histories of Learning* (Albany: State University of New York Press, 2003), as well as Britzman, *Lost Subjects;* and Susan E. Henking, "Difficult Knowledges: Gender, Sexuality, Religion," *Spotlight on Teaching,* October 2006. Dean's comment that there is "something fundamentally incurable about being human" ("Psychoanalysis of AIDS," 116) is also relevant, as is Weeks's notion that transgression may be interminable (*Invented Moralities,* 108).
51. Holst-Warhaft, *Cue for Passion,* 200.
52. Kenneth J. Doka, ed. *Disenfranchised Grief: Recognizing Hidden Sorrow* (Lexington, MA: Lexington Books, 1989).
53. Marc Nichanian, "Catastrophic Mourning," in *Loss: The Politics of Mourning,* ed. David L. Eng and David Kazanjian, 99–124 (Berkeley: University of California Press, 2003); David Kazanjian and Mark Nichanian, "Between Genocide and Catastrophe," in Eng and Kazanjian, *Loss,* 125–47 (Berkeley: University of California Press, 2003).
54. Dennis Klass, Phyllis R. Silverman, and Steven L. Nickman, eds., *Continuing Bonds: New Understandings of Grief* (Washington, DC: Taylor and Francis, 1996).
55. On ritual, see Catherine Bell, *Ritual Theory/Ritual Practice* (New York: Oxford University Press, 1992), and *Ritual: Perspectives and Dimensions* (New York: Oxford University Press, 1997). For links to mourning and grief, see, for example, Holst-Warhaft, *Cue for Passion;* Klass, Silverman, and Nickman, *Continuing Bonds,* 19–20; Pogue-Harrison, *Dominion of Death,* 57.
56. Holst-Warhaft, *Cue for Passion,* 2.
57. Klass, Silverman, and Nickman, *Continuing Bonds,* 17, 19.
58. Crimp, "Mourning and Militancy," in *Melancholia and Moralism.*
59. Crimp, *Melancholia and Moralism,* 173, 202.
60. Ibid., 131, 135, 137.
61. Pogue-Harrison, in *Dominion of the Dead,* xi, for example, has written: "human culture, unlike nature, institutes a living memory, not just a mineral retention, of the dead. Culture is the condensed residue of such perpetuation, unless we prefer to think of it as the nonorganic residue-forming process itself." On theory, Chopp, in "Theology and the Poetics of Testimony," 7–8, has written: "The poetics of testimony places all theory, even contemporary theories of culture, on trial for their moral responsibility to engage this 'reverence for life.'. . . Theory is neither objective judge nor subjective experience; rather, it is now summoned to help, to aid, to serve." Chopp's "reverence for life" is not the contradictory "pro-life" of the right wing in the United States.
62. Britzman, *After-Education.*
63. Britzman, *Lost Subjects.*
64. Gail B. Griffin, *Calling: Essays on Teaching in the Mother Tongue* (Pasadena, CA: Trilogy Books, 1992).
65. Crimp, *Melancholia and Moralism,* 300.
66. As Weeks, *Invented Moralities,* 139, and others have noted, HIV/AIDS acts as a "symbolic crystallization of wider cultural shifts." Dean, "Psychoanalysis of AIDS," 84, comments: "AIDS is structured, radically and precisely, as the unconscious real of the social field of contemporary America."
67. Felman and Laub, *Testimony,* 53, write: "teaching . . . must in turn testify, make something happen."
68. Some have argued that in the classroom "faces matter." See Richard B. Miller, Laurie L. Patton, and Stephen H. Webb, "Rhetoric, Pedagogy and the Study of Religion," *Journal of the American Academy of Religion* 62, no. 3: 819–50,

especially 821. This emphasis on "face" is also problematic. See Douglas Crimp, "Portraits of People with AIDS," in *Cultural Studies*, ed. Lawrence Grossberg, Cary Nelson, and Paula Treichler, 117–33 (New York: Routledge, 1992). On flexibility, see Emily Martin, *Flexible Bodies: Tracking Immunity in American Culture from the Days of Polio to the Age of AIDS* (Boston: Beacon Press, 1994). I am grateful to Betty Bayer for introducing me to Martin's work.

69. On the closet, see Sedgwick, *Epistemology of the Closet*. On the third space/transitional space, see Peter Homans, *The Ability to Mourn: Disillusionment and the Social Origins of Psychoanalysis* (Chicago: University of Chicago Press, 1989). Britzman in *Lost Subjects* and *After-Education* discusses the third space of the classroom, connecting psychoanalysis and education. On the closet and the teacher/scholar, see Bowen, "AIDS 101," 141–54; and Ed Cohen, "Are We (Not) What We Are Becoming? 'Gay' 'Identity,' 'Gay Studies,' and the Disciplining of Knowledge," in *Engendering Men: The Question of Male Feminist Criticism*, ed. Joseph A. Boone and Michael Cadden, 161–75 (New York: Routledge, 1990). For the final quotation, see Chopp, "Theology and the Poetics of Testimony," 11.

70. On the problematic character of the "open secret," see Richard D. Mohr, "The Outing Controversy: Privacy and Dignity in Gay Ethics," a chapter in his book *Gay Ideas: Outing and Other Controversies* (Boston: Beacon Press, 1992), 11–48.

71. On the contradictions, both conscious and unconscious, see Britzman in *Lost Subjects* and *After-Education*; see also Henking, "Difficult Knowledges."

72. Here a central concern is identifying criteria for a "successful" AIDS education course. See Bowen, "AIDS 101."

73. On the paradoxes of pedagogy, see Britzman, *Lost Subjects* and *After-Education*. Also see Yingling, "AIDS, Confession, and Theory," 105–7. Yingling considers the material conditions of pedagogy raised by "coming out with AIDS" as a professor, thereby also raising issues relevant to feminist pedagogy and material conditions of women's professorial lives.

74. Robert Epstein and Jeffrey Friedman, dirs., *Common Threads: Stories from the Quilt* (San Francisco: Telling Pictures/The Coutune Company, 1989). There are two editions of Larry Kramer's book, which vary in contents: *Reports from the Holocaust: The Making of an AIDS Activist*, 1st ed. (New York: St. Martin's Press, 1989); and *Reports from the Holocaust: The Story of an AIDS Activist*, expanded 2nd ed. (New York: St. Martin's Press, 1994).

75. The variety is obscured by the summary on the video that nowhere uses the word "gay."

76. See John M. Clum, "'And Once I Had It All': AIDS Narrative and Memories of an American Dream," in Murphy and Poirier, *Writing AIDS*, 200–224; Jeff Nunokawa, "'All the Sad Young Men': AIDS and the Work of Mourning," in Fuss, *Inside/Out*, 311–23, especially 319 ff.; Yingling, "AIDS in America," 307; and Holst-Warhaft, *Cue for Passion*, ch. 5.

77. See Henking, "Difficult Knowledges."

78. Crimp, *Melancholia and Moralism*, 198, 200. On the quilt, see also Dean, "Psychoanalysis of AIDS," 98ff.

79. That emotion runs high is illustrated in an exchange that took place one class session. The class was divided in half and asked to make the strongest arguments possible for and against militant activism, based on their reading of Kramer's book *Reports from the Holocaust* and Campbell's "Ethics and Militant Activism." By the end of the class, those assigned to favor militant activism (including me) were yelling "Fuck you! Fuck you!" at those assigned to argue against militant activism. See Courtney S. Campbell, "Ethics and Militant Activism," in *AIDS and Ethics*, ed. Frederic G. Reamer, 155–87 (New York: Columbia University Press).

80. On metaphor, see Susan Sontag, *AIDS and Its Metaphors* (New York: Farrar, Straus and Giroux, 1988) and "Culture, Metaphor and AIDS," pp. 24–54 in *AIDS: Readings on a Global Crisis*, ed. Elizabeth Rauh Bethel (Boston: Allyn and Bacon, 1995), including Christopher C. Taylor, "AIDS and the Pathogenesis of Metaphor," in Bethel, *AIDS*, 36–44. After writing this, I came across a thoughtful analysis of war metaphors in relation to AIDS: Michael S. Sherry, "The Language of War in AIDS Discourse," in Murphy and Poirier, *Writing AIDS*, 39–53. See especially page 45, where Sherry notes the divergence between associations to the Holocaust and to the quilt. For a critique of Sontag, see Dean, "Psychoanalysis of AIDS," 93–94.

81. Kramer, *Reports from the Holocaust: The Making of an AIDS Activist*, 1st ed., 227, 263.

82. See note 4 above.

83. Simon Watney, foreword to Kramer, *Reports from the Holocaust: The Story of an AIDS Activist*, expanded 2nd ed., xxv–xxvii. On Bauman, see also 342ff.

84. Dean, "Psychoanalysis of AIDS," 109, 89.

85. Nunokawa, "'All the Sad Young Men,'" 313. See also Chopp, "Theology and the Poetics of Testimony," 8–9; Weeks, *Invented Moralities*, 18–19.

86. Murphy and Poirier, *Writing AIDS*, 316.

87. Edelman, "Mirror and the Tank," esp. 12–13.

88. Nunokawa, "'All the Sad Young Men,'" 319. See also Ellis Hanson, "Undead," in Fuss, *Inside/Out*, 324–40.

89. Yingling, "AIDS in America," 303.

90. Weeks, *Invented Moralities*, 43.

91. Britzman, *Lost Subjects* and *After-Education*.

92. Jan Zita Grover, "AIDS: Keywords," in *AIDS: Cultural Analysis/Cultural Activism*, ed. Douglas Crimp, 17–31 (Cambridge, MA: MIT Press, 1989).

93. Klass, Silverman, and Nickman, *Continuing Bonds*, 50–51.

94. Parker J. Palmer, *The Courage to Teach: Exploring the Inner Landscape of a Teacher's Life* (San Francisco: Jossey Bass, 1998), 137.

95. Felman and Laub, *Testimony*, 53.

BERTRAM J. COHLER

Nostalgia and the Disenchantment with Modernity

MEMORY BOOKS AS ADAPTIVE RESPONSE TO SHOAH

NOSTALGIA HAS often been viewed as an expression of the inability to resolve loss, an attempt to take recourse in an imagined past as a means of avoiding present realities and escaping from a painful present. This critique of nostalgia is implicit in Freud's discussion of religion as an illusion that humankind should have long since outgrown: Freud expressed bewilderment about why we continue to dwell on images and ideas that do not solve problems in the real world.[1] Other psychoanalytic thinkers in later decades continued to view both nostalgia and religion with suspicion. We argue that nostalgia is in fact an adaptive solution to the sense of fragmentation produced by significant loss. It is our view that the ability to construct a past that provides a sense of personal coherence fosters enhanced integration and makes it possible for people to deal more effectively with present problems. We bring this understanding of nostalgia to two interrelated phenomena: the broad sense of fragmentation pervading contemporary social life in modernity; and the more specific fragmentation and disorientation produced by Shoah. We argue in particular that memory books produced during and after the Holocaust represent adaptive forms of nostalgia. The study of the function of nostalgia in the memory books provides us with a window into the understanding of nostalgia in a broader sense, as a response to the disillusionment produced by modernity.

The appeal of narratives of the Holocaust, some written by survivors and others by those who perished in the ghettos and death camps of the Third Reich, is imbedded in the testimony of a time before the Holocaust. For those telling or writing these narratives, and those hearing or reading them, the very activities of narrating and hearing the narration is adaptive in fostering a sense of a life story rendered coherent even as confronted by deliberate actions designed to destroy personal coherence.[2] Memory books created by survivors re-create continuity with the past, reflect and reestablish a sense of coherence, and function in ways that are psychologically soothing.

How are the memory books of Shoah related to broader dimensions of modernity? Although modernity seemed to promise a means of resolving personal and social ills through reliance upon rationality, it actually spawned an industrial revolution that threatened the sense of continuity of communities and social institutions.[3] Unable to mourn the impact of this social and technological change whose dimensions have grown ever more frightening, our culture has been confronted with an increasing sense of disenchantment with the world and a continuing collective melancholia. The crisis of modernity brought about by rational science reached catastrophic proportions in the two world wars fought in the first half of the twentieth century, which were founded on the application of rationality to destruction in what Omer Bartov has described as "industrial killing."[4]

While this industrial killing was evident in the very manner in which these wars were conducted, perhaps the "ideal type" of rationality systematically applied to destruction of a way of life was the emergence of the genocide of the Jewish people of the European continent between 1933 and 1945. The Holocaust thus represents paradigmatically an extreme form of modernity: it is modernity at its worst. The psychological response to the Holocaust as a particular phenomenon, and to modernity as a broad cultural experience, is the same: disillusionment and fragmentation—melancholia, in Freud's vocabulary. Although it may be premature to offer diagnoses of this cultural melancholia produced by modernity, the function of the memory books in relation to Shoah is instructive: the nostalgia of the memory books does not lead to the healing that we would see in experiences of mourning, but it does lead to a sense of coherence and soothing with resonance for individuals and for the culture more broadly. Nostalgia, in other words, functions as an adaptive response to the melancholia produced by modernity.

Loss and Disillusionment in Modernity

In 1916 in a brief essay on transience Freud first presented the argument that would later appear in his essay on mourning.[5] All that we cherish, he said, is necessarily transient. This makes it difficult for us to enjoy fleeting moments of beauty soon to be lost: we mourn in anticipation of future loss. Later Freud observed that, recognizing the necessary disappointment and loss that are a part of all relationships, it is remarkable that we have the courage to let ourselves love another person or to feel an attachment to an experience or place.[6] Freud extended his discussion of loss and mourning not only to the process we use to come to terms with this kind of loss, but also to symbolic losses.[7] Freud described a process in which we come to terms with the reality of loss in a world that now feels depleted: "Mourning is regularly the reaction to the loss of a loved person, or to the loss of some abstraction which has taken the place of one, such as one's country, liberty, an ideal and so on."[8] Freud notes that mourning leads to withdrawal from the world, to internal preoccupation, and to self-absorption.

Ideally, Freud argued, mourning comes to an end with the activity of re-creating through memory the experience of being with the person we have lost. Just as with the death of a person, failure to mourn and resolve symbolic losses inevitably leads to that profound sadness and loss of interest in the world that Freud termed "melancholia." Freud describes the melancholic as a person who lacks the ability to mourn or to resolve a sense of profound disappointment following a loss. Feelings of worthlessness, denigration of self and others, and the experience of personal depletion are the consequence of the failure to work through and resolve this experience of disappointment and loss. Thus as mourning shades into melancholia, there is a sense of disillusionment and confusion.

Social psychologist Peter Marris suggests that melancholia calls into question issues of meaning and purpose, that loss through death of a loved one is personally disruptive and causes a crisis of meaning.[9] Social and historical change may be viewed in a similar manner. Social change leads to disruption of a sense of personal and social continuity and requires a period of working through, leading to the capacity to make peace with the loss. However, just as in mourning a death, the losses invoked by social change may not be successfully mourned, and as Freud has portrayed, mourning may succumb to melancholia and a sense of profound disenchantment, disappointment, and feeling of fragmentation.[10] Quoting E. M. Forster's famous frontispiece epigraph "Only connect . . ." in his 1910 novel *Howards End*, Marris observes that bereavement can lead to the experience of incoherence.[11]

As Freud suggested, mourning becomes melancholia when loss cannot be resolved. Melancholia is most often accompanied by a sense of disenchantment or disappointment. Although Roy Schafer has observed that the experience of disappointment is an inevitable aspect of life, pointing out that people feel disappointed when experiences fail to confirm hopes and wishes, he also suggests that this experience of being disappointed in life stems from childhood memories of disappointment and loss or avoidance of the good things of life out of the fear of impending loss and change.[12] This sense of disappointment, in turn, is linked to a belief that one does not deserve enjoyment because of guilty feelings. Since disappointment is inevitable, present enjoyment presumes disappointment in its wake. Schafer also notes, however, that feelings of disappointment may provide an adaptive element since they offer a "protective wall of resignation or despair" against having hopes dashed in difficult circumstances.[13] In the case of imprisonment in the death camps of the Third Reich, for example, where it was not reasonable to hope that things might get better, disappointment may have functioned adaptively.

This experience of disappointment and loss may be observed both in a person experiencing a loss and also within a social group sharing in common a "symbolic loss."[14] As Peter Homans observes:

> in the case of symbolic loss the object that is lost is, ordinarily, sociohistorical, cognitive and collective. The lost object is a symbol or rather a system of symbols and not a person. And the inner work of coming to terms with the loss of such symbols is by no means always followed by generative or creative repair or recovery, but as often by disillusionment, or disappointment, or despair. Some sort of combination of "resignation," along with some mourning, is the best way to describe the most common form of this kind of "coming to terms" with the past.[15]

Nostalgia and the Crisis of Modernity

I believe that we have failed to complete the task of mourning in our era. We are witnessing a pervasive and widespread cultural melancholia linked to the failure to resolve the problems of technological social change and associated with emergence of modernity and the problems of meaning associated with the Holocaust. Yet, it is important to ask whether this pervasive melancholia is in some way adaptive. Through invocation of nostalgia, melancholia offers a sense of personal and collective coherence permitting us to preserve some meaning and order in a world otherwise experienced as beyond understanding.[16] I see this, in other words, not as an inability to mourn the loss of faith in reason: rather, I see nostalgia, and even melancholia, as adaptive.

Reviewing Freud's contributions to the study of grief and mourning, psychoanalyst George Pollock has suggested that mourning reflects a process of adaptation to a new reality, seeking to establish again the equilibrium that existed prior to the loss.[17] Melancholia, however, is typically seen as pathological. Yet I believe that melancholia and nostalgia can function very differently from what psychoanalytic theorists have called "the inability to mourn."

How can melancholia be adaptive? Leo Spitzer reports on his discovery of photographs of an early postwar gathering of his parents and other refugees from the Third Reich who had escaped to Bolivia.[18] Gathered in a restaurant, the group in the photograph was dressed in the Austrian peasant costumes of their childhood. Reflecting the emotional hurt following exile from their homeland, these photographs express nostalgia enacted in apparent denial both of the Andean culture surrounding the refugees, and the willing Austrian participation in the destruction of European Jewry. Spitzer views these photographs as reflections of a pervasive sense of loss and rejection, an attempt to maintain solidarity with the Austria of their youth. Yet he sees it as adaptive: "when the future seemed darkest to them . . . and Nazi atrocities against Jews enveloped them, and their own life chances seemed more precarious, they turned to the past as a way to gain some sustenance and stability in their present."[19]

Nostalgia and Melancholy

Preoccupation with a presently construed positive recollection of the past provides the experience of solace and enhanced coherence even when confronted by wrenching social change or collective adversity. Malcolm Chase and Christopher Shaw suggest that modernity itself has uprooted us from a past where there seemed to be answers for every dilemma including that of mortality.[20] We live now in a time in which social and personal life have become fragmented.[21] If the future is viewed as inevitably disappointing or a source of danger, there is little room left for hope. In this context it is understandable that we seek comfort, imagining a simpler time of greater connection between people and place. Chase and Shaw observe that nostalgia is experienced in the context of a present that is believed to be empty: "There is no space which we authentically occupy, and so popular culture fills the gap by manufacturing images of home and rootedness."[22] Similarly, the Russian historian Svetlana

Boym has observed: "Modern nostalgia is a mourning for the impossibility of mythical return, for the loss of an enchanted world with clear border and values; it could be secular expression of a spiritual longing, a nostalgia for an absolute, a home that is both physical and spiritual. . . . The nostalgic is looking for a spiritual addressee. Encountering silence, he looks for memorable signs, desperately misreading them."[23]

As sociologist Fred Davis has written in one of the few comprehensive discussions of nostalgia, "it is *always* the adoration of the past that triumphs over the present . . . for to permit present woes to douse the warm glow from the past is to succumb to melancholy."[24] Kathleen Stewart has suggested that nostalgia has become ever more significant in the present time when traditions appear to be ever more diffuse and when alternative lifeways are now possible in ways that were less evident in the past. The task of nostalgia is to provide a means for evoking memories of a time when there was greater certainty through a story designed to "reassemble a broken history into a new whole."[25] Christopher Lasch, inquiring about a *preoccupation* with the activity of nostalgia in contemporary criticism, suggests that concern with the present phenomenon of nostalgia has accompanied the postwar experience of political upheaval and social change.[26]

Social and Psychological Perspectives on Nostalgia

In spite of the importance of this means of protecting ourselves from the painful experience of loss accompanying melancholy, little has been written about nostalgia. Although some historians critically refer to nostalgia in the popular (mis)use of national history, little systematic study has explored this strategy for making meaning within threatened lives.[27]

Let us examine a few recent efforts to theorize nostalgia. Contemporary theorists have pointed out that the term "nostalgia" may be traced to the seventeenth-century Swiss physician Johannes Hofer, who observed that mercenaries fighting in foreign lands often felt homesick for their own country.[28] These soldiers reported overwhelming melancholy with absence from home and family. Davis suggests that almost from the outset, nostalgia was observed in response to a sudden discontinuity in lived experience.[29] In particular, loss of home and, symbolically, loss of traditional lifestyles, such as experienced by the weavers of the midlands of England prior to the industrial revolution, fostered nostalgia accompanying the rapid social changes and dramatic social dislocation across the nineteenth century.[30]

Psychoanalyst David Werman develops a psychoanalytic critique of nostalgia.[31] He argues that while the work of mourning is never complete, nostalgia functions as a substitute for the work of mourning. In his view, nostalgia leads to a preoccupation with, and idealization of, the past loss, accompanied by depreciation of the present time and a sense of continuing bittersweet disappointment. He states emphatically, that "maintenance of the lost object in nostalgic memory . . . impedes an effective renunciation which would permit a new object to be libidinally invested." In his view, "the failure of mourning leads to a continuing search for the idealized lost object, an inability to love new objects, a depreciation of objects in one's current life, and an endless pursuit of nostalgic memories for themselves at the expense of an inhibition in many areas of existence. Noteworthy is the disappointment of these patients in new objects which are regularly found to fall short of their idealized representation."[32] Werman also observes that nostalgia is more often about places and times than about people. Indeed, people seem often to be absent in the expression of nostalgia.

Historian of Russia Svetlana Boym has differentiated reflective nostalgia and restorative nostalgia.[33] Reflective nostalgia dwells on themes of longing and loss and on efforts at remembering the past. It is visible in nationalistic discourse. Restorative nostalgia seeks to remake the past in the light of present historical change and social conflict. Restorative nostalgia uses evocative symbols to temper present distress and threatened sense of incoherence through enhanced connection with a presently remembered and exemplary past. Reflective nostalgia, evident in shared or collective memory, is more ironic than restorative nostalgia. Reflective nostalgia, as in Greek preoccupation with the "classical age," focuses on the discrepancy between a glorious past and an ignoble present, while restorative nostalgia attempts repair of a present crisis in the light of the presently remembered past. Boym's notion of restorative nostalgia may be particularly valuable in understanding not only the dislocations of modernity but also the remembering of the past in the aftermath of Shoah. We are concerned primarily with restorative nostalgia.

Geographer David Lowenthal has noted that restorative nostalgia is represented by a focus on "heritage"—the restoration of the estates of British aristocracy and the construction of living memorials such as Sturbridge Village in eastern Massachusetts or colonial Williamsburg in Virginia.[34] While evidence of nostalgia in the emphasis on "heritage" in both Europe and the United States was evident from the later years of the nineteenth century, this concept really became part of the popular lexicon following the Second World War. Michael Kammen traces the emergence of the heritage movement in the United States over this postwar period and reports on the development of both periodicals and museums designed to recollect a less troubled time when old-fashioned virtues and a less frenetic lifestyle were characteristic of family and community.[35] Anthony Brandt has suggested that the goal of the museum at the present time is less that of education than that of providing a sense of solace and of being touched by the past.[36] Relying upon shared or collective memories, we create this past as part of the construction of our own identities in the effort to maintain a sense of coherence in our lives. Feeling dislocated in the present, we buy tickets to the past as if attending theater.

Nostalgia and Self-Soothing

Sociologist Fred Davis questions the relevance of memorialized times and places outside our own experience as the content of nostalgia, but it is common for immigrant groups to appropriate such aspects of the American past as the Thanksgiving of colonial America into their own family traditions.[37] Indeed, one of the major functions of restorative nostalgia is to resolve possible loss of coherence as confronted by social change. Davis notes that successful nostalgia provides reassurance that we are now as we were in past times, a soothing experience at times of social stress and change. Chase and Shaw, as well as Boym, have observed that nostalgia is made possible by our own culture, which views time as linear and irreversible, and in which the past disappears.[38]

As noted above, Werman is concerned that nostalgia is pathological because it replaces the effort to mourn and work through a loss.[39] This argument is resonant with Freud's own impatience with the reluctance in his own time to forsake illusion for realistic solutions made possible by the rational science of the Enlightenment to problems in social life. However, it is my view that nostalgia has an adaptive function that permits some relief and assistance when confronted with disappointment such as that engendered by the rapid social change and worldwide conflict marking the past century and into the present. If our age is an age of anxiety, then reliance on nostalgia may provide some respite while we search for resolution of these profound difficulties.[40]

Psychoanalysts Donald W. Winnicott and Heinz Kohut have written about the capacity for soothing and the conditions that promote or interfere with this important ability for calming oneself and fostering enhanced personal coherence. In his classic paper on the transitional object, Winnicott describes the manner in which, relying upon memory for a satisfactory care-giving experience, the baby is able to find a substitute for maternal soothing in the physical absence of the mother.[41] Both sucking the corner of the quilt or preoccupation with a special stuffed animal reflects this ability to find self-soothing. This illusory experience is essential for development and the management of tension states from the first momentary absence of the mother to the inevitable disappointments of adult life. What is at first a bridge between the experience of the mother's soothing care and the baby's sense of being soothed, hence "transitional," becomes, over time, an aspect of oneself adapted to other situations posing frustration or threat to personal safety. Transitional phenomena, both objects and recollected experience, symbolically "stand for" the soothing present in the initial "good-enough" care-giving situation.[42]

Tolpin expands Kohut's insights, arguing that the transitional object is a "better soother" than the mother in the sense that it can re-evoke the lost soothing of symbiotic fusion.[43] No matter how good her soothing capacity, the mother cannot re-create the earlier state that the infant provides for himself by his own creation.[44]

Over the course of psychological development from earliest childhood through oldest age, the transitional experience becomes the capacity to manage tension states and to realize self-soothing using language and memory. Nostalgia is clearly a transitional phenomenon. Nostalgia is adaptive in providing enhanced experience of coherence and personal integration and will yield to more reasonable means of dealing with the world when threats to personal and collective safety are resolved.[45] Indeed, as Gerald Adler shows, it is precisely the lack of capacity for self-soothing and inability to use this memory of past care that is found among more troubled adults who report feelings of panic, emptiness, aloneness, and sense of impending personal disintegration.[46] For whatever reason, perhaps because their caregivers were preoccupied and emotionally unavailable during early childhood, these people are unable to call upon the symbolic function of the transitional phenomenon. Under circumstances of enhanced tension these adults are unable to realize self-soothing.

The intermediate or transitional zone of experience, founded on illusion, is potentially available when, confronted by personal or shared adversity, there is no recourse for preserving coherence except reliance on an illusory experience. Freud, as we have seen, had struggled to understand why we continue to rely on illusory experiences as religion at the cost of facing reality.[47] What Freud had failed to recognize was the significance of religion as a form of illusory experience that provides for self-soothing, especially when challenged by impending disaster.

Horton and Sharp have observed that language, including story and song, can serve as an illusory experience, providing through symbolic expression the original soothing represented in the care-giving experience of early childhood.[48] For example, Greenson describes the plight of a Royal Air Force pilot whose plane was forced down over the English Channel during the Second World War.[49] Standing on the wing of the plane and awaiting rescue, the pilot recalled a Flemish song that his mother used to sing to him as a child as he was falling asleep. Even though he knew no Flemish and had never thought of the nursery song in the intervening years, he began to sing this song and was able to hold himself together while he awaited rescue. The song was an illusory experience based on the soothing he had enjoyed as a child, which he could call upon in the present in a situation of extreme danger facing the threat of attack from enemy aircraft. The use of story and song in the context of religion offers a psychological parallel to the transitional experience of the pilot.

Nostalgia is a transitional or illusory experience providing solace when confronted with such threats to existence such as that experienced by Jewish and other inmates of the death camps of the Third Reich. An experience of extreme and overwhelming stress, the illusory experience of nostalgia, expressed as remembrance of times past, helped to forestall personal fragmentation.[50] Women of the Thereisenstadt (Terezin) ghetto camp, a way station to almost certain death in the gas chambers of Auschwitz, Majdanek, and Treblinka, for example, recalled baking in their mothers' kitchens and collected recipes from this past time, assuaging their present distress, state of near starvation, and fear for the future.[51]

Mourning and efforts to work through a loss takes place on both an individual and collective level. We can speak of collective or public memory as the shared experience of a loss and efforts to come to terms with and work though this loss. The concept of collective memory was first discussed in detail by sociologist Maurice Halbwachs, himself a victim of the persecution of the Third Reich.[52] Halbwachs suggested that personal memory is itself constructed on the basis of shared experiences and understandings of self, others, and the larger world in which we live.

Linguist Charlotte Linde has observed that these shared experiences reflect a "narrative induction" of participants into a shared genre.[53] Participants in this ring of shared narrative need not even be present at the time an event later recounted had first taken place to become a part of this paradigmatic, dominant, or master narrative.[54] Induction into the master narrative leads to the formation of a new identity as this shared story becomes one's own story. Narrative induction may take place not only through speech and text but also through representation and action.[55]

As both Barry Schwartz and James Wertsch have noted, construction of the past is an active, continuing process, carried out by members of a culture sharing symbolic meanings in common and embodied in such aspects of culture as text and monument.[56]

These insights are particularly relevant to the question of narratives of the Holocaust. Geoffrey Hartman has observed that the vast collection of testimony from survivors of Shoah has changed over time.[57] Earlier testimony becomes shared understanding of the events of 1933 to 1945 and their antecedents as later testimony is influenced both by earlier testimony and continuing historical study of the Third Reich.

In the study of Holocaust survivor accounts, for example, it is clear that the telling of the life story is shaped by the genre of such stories told, written, and retold on numerous occasions, together with such media as films and television that portray the lives of Holocaust victims.[58] The act of retelling provides an effort to work through and mourn the catastrophe of Shoah. Evocative texts such as Elie Wiesel's account of his experiences in a Third Reich death camp (Night)[59] and iconic representations such as the freight car used to transport Jews to the death camps and the ill-fated refugee ship, the St. Louis (both portrayed in the Washington Holocaust museum) are all powerful means for narrative induction in subsequent generations. The paradox of this collective memory of Shoah is that while mourning is designed to work through and resolve loss, it is precisely this concern that underlies the effort to induct subsequent generations into this master narrative or collective memory of Shoah. Fearing that memory of this European catastrophe might fade from collective memory and be repeated, many American synagogues emphasize the slogan "lest we forget." The master narrative of Shoah necessarily leads to melancholia rather than mourning followed by working through in the collective memory of this event. This melancholia, rather than functioning as a personal or cultural pathology, has an adaptive or soothing function: it represents a form of restorative nostalgia recollecting a time before the disaster that disrupted European Jewish life.

Nostalgia and Shoah: Narrative and Meaning in Recollections of the Past

A coherent story of the past, including present recollection of past traditions, fosters an enhanced sense of integrity. Recollection of the time before this tragedy offers solace by presenting a coherent narrative that leads to otherwise incoherent, incomprehensible, and disconnected events, such as the "industrial killings" of Shoah and its aftermath. Chase and Shaw and Stewart have observed that when we are confronted with painful social problems for which rational science has failed to provide a solution, we feel that we have lost control of our destiny and our ability to change public life.[60] In such a context restorative nostalgia becomes an adaptive solution that in turn permits us to search for a better solution.

The genocide of the Third Reich is perhaps the paradigmatic Weberian "ideal type" of a loss presenting an ultimate challenge to mourning and working through. Indeed, the concern is often expressed that the death of the last survivors of this horrific experience over the coming years—those who were children at the time of incarceration —might finally work through and resolve this tragedy, leading to a forgetting that risks the repetition of this genocide in the future. The slogan "lest we forget" reflects this concern. Melancholy, exhibited in the continuing recollection of the perfidy of Shoah, reflects an adaptive response to the threat that this disaster might recur. Through the collection of survivors' accounts and through the construction of monuments to the Holocaust, we struggle to work through this loss, but at the same time we prevent the working through and completion of the process of mourning the tragedy of Shoah.[61] The apparent rise once again of anti-Semitism in parts of Europe legitimates this concern. Precisely because of its traumatic nature, the Holocaust provides a unique opportunity for the study of nostalgia as an adaptive capacity facilitating maintenance of personal and shared sense of continuity when confronted with the ultimate and deliberate evil of destroying a people and its traditions.

Nostalgia or the use of the past as an aid in realizing renewed sense of personal coherence or soothing, may be observed in monument and text alike. James Edward Young has provided a remarkable pictorial account of the significance of both local monuments and those of the former death camps as a kind of narrative of the Holocaust.[62] Visiting these shrines is presumed to foster the work of mourning. However, understood as one of many consequences of the failure of the Age of Reason, these monuments become monuments to the ultimate failure of rationality, the use of modernity in the service of destruction. These monuments may serve to enhance melancholia rather than to work through loss and grief in the process of mourning. The pilgrimage to the shrines and the observation of monuments and death camps may even function as acts of nostalgia, making possible a more integrated story than that represented by bleak experience of the Holocaust.

Perhaps the most significant texts of nostalgia are the testimonies provided by survivors of Shoah, together with the diaries left behind by those, primarily adolescents, who were forced into the urban ghettos after 1941 on the way to the death camps. Hartman has observed that providing testimony of the Holocaust provides comfort for teller and listener alike.[63] With more than 100,000 video and audio survivor accounts, half of which were collected in the project initiated by Steven Spielberg using the proceeds from his film *Schindler's List*, these records are more important as means of fostering personal integrity—the consequence of telling one's life story—than as traditional oral history. Compare, for example, the Fortunoff oral history collection at Yale in 1981, which included only 1,500 of these testimonies.[64]

Nostalgia and the Discourse of Survivor Accounts

Not only are these survivor accounts told "backwards" in the context of an ever-changing understanding of the Holocaust and its significance, but they are also told in the context of the paradigmatic accounts of other survivors.[65] These master narratives, recorded as testimony in libraries of survivor accounts, have been published as personal accounts of the experience of surviving the death camps of the Third Reich.[66] The unprecedented effort devoted to the collection of survivor accounts suggests that some other function beyond their value as historical documents is served by this extensive effort. I believe these narratives assume such value because they remind the listener or reader of a time before this disruption of a traditional way of life, thus soothing listener and teller alike.

Perhaps the ideal form of this narrative of disruption and loss is *The Diary of Anne Frank*, an account not of a survivor but of a gifted adolescent writer portraying her life in Germany as a young girl, her family's life and later escape to Amsterdam, and the years spent in hiding from the Gestapo—until the family was discovered and deported to the death camps in the waning months of the war.[67]

The version of the diary edited by Anne's father, together with Elie Wiesel's autobiographical novel *Night,* has become a staple in junior high school literature classes and is read and recommended by people otherwise having little connection with the Holocaust. These accounts provide a narrative induction into the master narrative or collective memory of the Holocaust.[68]

Daniel Schwarz observes that Wiesel tries to find coherence in the inexplicable events of the years between 1933 and 1945.[69] In the same manner, the Anne Frank diary attempts to tie present and past together, creating a sense of coherence out of the fragmentation and chaos that marked the years of the Third Reich. Each of these texts offers the reader solace, providing what is most often regarded as hope for the future in a nostalgic appeal to the essential goodness of humanity. In a famous passage in the Anne Frank diary, concluding a lengthy entry from July 15, 1944, only a few weeks before the family was discovered and deported to the death camps, the author writes that "in spite of everything I still believe that people are good at heart."[70] However, in a little quoted addendum she adds, "I simply can't build up my hopes on a foundation consisting of confusion, misery and death. I see the world being gradually turned into a wilderness, I hear the ever approaching thunder, which will destroy us too."[71]

Schwarz observes that Anne Frank's diary is in reality a statement of disappointment and disruption of a past fondly remembered in contrast to the terrifying present.[72]

Memory Books as Nostalgia

The traditional life way destroyed by the Nazis was unique in maintaining a distinctly premodern cast.[73] Villagers sought the wisdom of the rabbi as teacher and spiritual leader who fostered literacy, and learning and tradition were both highly prized.[74] Isolated from the social change and dislocation that swept across Europe in the late nineteenth and early twentieth centuries, residents of these small rural communities venerated the traditions passed on across generations. Indeed, one could say that these communities first confronted the problems of modernity when forced to by the Third Reich.

A traditional life way abruptly disrupted by the Third Reich is reflected in a unique set of narratives known as memory books. These narratives recollecting life in the shtetl prior to the Third Reich were collected primarily within the Polish and other Eastern European communities in the aftermath of the war, well before the systematic recording of survivor accounts, sharing with this later genre the structure of the narrative written backward. Excerpts from these memory books have been translated and published in English.[75] They are typically organized into sections. The first sections portray the villages before Shoah. They focus on the residents of the villages and their valued traditions, special occasions, and prized folklore. The second sections describe the impact of the Holocaust, the experience of returning to the villages following the war (the theme of continuing anti-Semitism greeting the survivors upon their return is common), and the experience of migrating to the United States or Canada.

In their introduction to the collection, Jack Kugelmass and Jonathan Boyarin note that the memory books reflect spontaneous efforts at documenting not only the cruelty of Nazi destruction but also of a way of life that disappeared with the events surrounding Shoah. As returnees sat around the table, trying to re-create the buildings and residents of the town, they were engaging in a nostalgic activity, sharing with each other memories of people, places, and stories of a world they had lost. It is the activity of recollection as much as the product of this labor that bespeaks the effort to find solace in remembering this lost world by maintaining a sense of coherence with their own youth. The editors also observe that these collective efforts to portray a world now lost has precedent in the tradition of the Jewish mourning literature: one finds this pattern in the Book of Lamentations. This ever-incomplete cycle of loss and mourning is perhaps best represented by the stories of Sholem Aleichem and the fictional town of Anatevke that became the basis for the ever-popular musical theater *Fiddler on the Roof.* Viewed in the context of Shoah, this musical recounting the destruction of a traditional way of life with the pogroms of the early twentieth century has had repeated revivals and itself represents the use of nostalgia to seek comfort when dealing with a cultural loss that can never be worked through and resolved.

The editors of the memory books observe that for the Jewish people, remembering the past has long provided a means for maintaining this sense of coherence with the past. From the time of the destruction of the first temple and exile, melancholia and the accompanying effort to seek solace in remembering have characterized much of Jewish culture. The melancholia surrounding the tragedy of Shoah reiterates the process by which Jewish culture has dealt with misfortune across the centuries. While the impact of Shoah was terrible, the means for adapting to the tragedy were those already well known within Jewish culture, focusing on inevitable disappointment following exile a thousand years in the past and the use of the past as a means of realizing solace in the present.[76]

Conclusion

The sense of disenchantment following the emergence of modernity, expressed anew through two world wars and their aftermath, remains with us today. A growing sense of disenchantment with modernity and the rational sciences has led to an increased focus on the internal world, to the emergence of the study of both personal and collective memory, and to the act of remembering a time prior to this sense of crisis and social dislocation, that is, to nostalgia. Nostalgia continues to offer a solution to a continuing sense of fragmentation through constructed memories of a past time presumed prior to our present distress. Religion can represent one form of nostalgia, as can the retelling of stories of past times and other cultures less threatened than the present. In the early twentieth century, Freud urged us to mourn religion, moving on into a post-religious future.

In the twenty-first century we can see that our cultural response to the losses associated with religion has been melancholic rather than mournful. Religion is in some sense both the lost object and the nostalgic re-creation of meaning in the face of that loss. We find ourselves creating nostalgic narratives of religious and spiritual meaning, nostalgic monuments and museums that provide sources of solace. Just as a bereaved kindred realize enhanced spiritual peace by visiting the gravesites of family members, so we realize solace by revisiting the sites of major battles such as Gettysburg and cemeteries such as Arlington. Even in the twenty-first century, we remain in the midst of our collective melancholia, unable to work through the crisis of modernity, yet finding solace in nostalgic narratives of a meaningful past. We may be unable to mourn, but our melancholia is not pathological: the Jewish memory books provide a paradigmatic model for an adaptive nostalgia with hopeful possibilities for our broader culture.

Notes

1. Unless otherwise noted, references to the work of Sigmund Freud are from *The Standard Edition of the Complete Psychological Works of Sigmund Freud*, trans. and ed. James Strachey (London: Hogarth Press, 24 vols., 1966–1974). Sigmund Freud, "The Future of an Illusion," *Standard Edition*, 21: 5–58 (first published 1927).

2. Bruno Bettelheim, "Mass Behavior in an Extreme Situation," *Journal of Abnormal and Social Psychology* 38 (1943): 417–52; also Bettelheim, *The Informed Heart: Autonomy in a Mass Age* (New York: Free Press/Macmillan, 1960).
3. E. P. Thompson, *The Making of the English Working Class* (New York: Random House, 1966).
4. Omer Bartov, *Murder in Our Midst: The Holocaust, Industrial Killing, and Representation* (New York: Oxford University Press, 1996).
5. Sigmund Freud, "On Transience," *Standard Edition,* 14: 305–7 (first published 1916).
6. Freud, "Future of an Illusion," 59–145.
7. Peter Homans, introduction to *Symbolic Loss: The Ambiguity of Mourning and Memory at Century's End,* ed. Homans, 1–42 (Charlottesville: University Press of Virginia, 2001).
8. Sigmund Freud, "Mourning and Melacholia," *Standard Edition,* 14: 237–58, quote on 243 (first published 1917).
9. Peter Marris, *Loss and Change,* rev. ed. (London: Routledge and Kegan Paul, 1974).
10. Freud, "Mourning and Melancholia," 237–58.
11. E. M. Forster, *Howards End* (New York: Modern Library, 1999; first published 1910).
12. Roy Schafer, *Bad Feelings* (New York: Other Press, 2003).
13. Schafer, *Bad Feelings,* 23.
14. Homans, introduction to *Symbolic Loss,* 1–42.
15. Ibid., 20.
16. Malcolm Chase and Christopher Shaw. "The Dimensions of Nostalgia," in *The Imagined Past: History and Nostalgia,* ed. Shaw and Chase, 1–17 (Manchester, UK: Manchester University Press, 1989).
17. George H. Pollock, "Mourning and Adaptation," *International Journal of Psychoanalysis* 42 (1961): 341–61.
18. Leo Spitzer, "Back through the Future: Nostalgic Memory and Critical Memory in a Refuge from Nazism." In *Acts of Memory: Cultural Recall in the Present,* ed. Mieke Bal, Jonathan Crewe, and Leo Spitzer, 87–104 (Hanover, NH: University Press of New England, 1999).
19. Ibid., 95.
20. Chase and Shaw, "Dimensions of Nostalgia."
21. Kenneth J. Gergen, *Realities and Relationships: Soundings in Social Construction* (Cambridge, MA: Harvard University Press, 1994).
22. Chase and Shaw, "Dimensions of Nostalgia," 15.
23. Svetlana Boym, *The Future of Nostalgia* (New York: Basic Books/Persus, 2001), 8.
24. Fred Davis, *Yearning for Yesteryear: A Sociology of Nostalgia* (New York: Free Press/Macmillan, 1979), 16.
25. Kathleen Stewart, "Nostalgia—A Polemic," *Cultural Anthropology* 3 (1988): 227–41.
26. Christopher Lasch, "The Politics of Nostalgia: Losing History in the Mists of Ideology," *Harper's Magazine,* Nov. 1984, 65–70.
27. Michael G. Kammen, *The Mystic Chords of Memory: The Transformation of Tradition in American Culture* (New York: Random House/Vintage Books, 1991); David Lowenthal, "Nostalgia Tells It Like It Wasn't," in Shaw and Chase, *The Imagined Past: History and Nostalgia,* 18–31; Suzanne Vromen, "The Ambiguity of Nostalgia," *YIVO Annual* 21 (1993): 69–86.
28. Jean Starobinski and William S. Kemp, "The Idea of Nostalgia," *Diogenes* 14, no. 54 (1996): 81–103.
29. Davis, *Yearning for Yesteryear.*
30. Thompson, *Making of the English Working Class.*

31. David S. Werman, "Normal and Pathological Nostalgia," *Journal of the American Psychoanalytic Association* 25 (1977): 387–98.
32. Ibid., 396.
33. Boym, *Future of Nostalgia.*
34. Lowenthal, "Nostalgia Tells It Like It Wasn't." See also Richard Handler and Eric Gable, *The New History in an Old Museum: Creating the Past at Colonial Williamsburg* (Durham, NC: Duke University Press, 1997).
35. Kammen, *Mystic Chords of Memory.*
36. Anthony Brandt, "A Short History of Nostalgia," *Atlantic*, no. 242 (1978): 58–63.
37. Davis, *Yearning for Yesteryear.*
38. Chase and Shaw, "Dimensions of Nostalgia"; Boym, *Future of Nostalgia.*
39. Werman, "Normal and Pathological Nostalgia." See also Leslie Sohn, "Nostalgia," *International Journal of Psychoanalysis* 64 (1983): 203–10.
40. Marris, *Loss and Change.*
41. Donald W. Winnicot, "Transitional Objects and Transitional Phenomena," *International Journal of Psychoanalysis* 34: 89–97.
42. Heinz Kohut, *The Restoration of the Self* (Madison, CT: International Universities Press, 1977); Kohut, "Idealization and Cultural Self Objects," in *Self Psychology and the Humanities: Reflections on a New Psychoanalytic Approach,* ed. Charles B. Strozier, 224–43 (New York: Norton, 1985).
43. M. Tolpin, "On the Beginnings of a Cohesive Self—An Application of the Concept of Transmuting Internalization to the Study of the Transitional Object and Signal Anxiety," *Psychoanalytic Study of the Child* 26 (1971): 316–52; see also E. Wolf, "Some Comments on the Self-object Concept," in *Self and Identity: Psychosocial Processes,* ed. Krysia Yardley and Terry Honess, 259–71 (New York: John Wiley and Sons, 1987); Howard Bacal, "Does an Object Relations Theory Exist in Self Psychology?" *Psychoanalytic Inquiry* 10 (1990): 197–220.
44. Tolpin, "On the Beginnings of a Cohesive Self," 326.
45. Stephen Toulmin, *Return to Reason* (Cambridge, MA: Harvard University Press, 2001); Bettelheim, "Mass Behavior in an Extreme Situation"; Bettelheim, *Informed Heart.*
46. Gerald Adler, "How Useful Is the Borderline Concept?" *Psychoanalytic Inquiry* 8 (1988): 353–72.
47. Freud, "Future of an Illusion."
48. P. Horton and S. Sharp, "Language, Solace, and Transitional Relatedness," *Psychoanalytic Study of the Child* 39 (1984): 167–94.
49. R. Greenson, "A Dream While Drowning," in *Separation-Individuation: Essays in Honor of Margaret S. Mahler,* ed. John B. McDevitt and Calvin F. Settlage, 377–84 (Madison, CT: International Universities Press, 1971).
50. Bettelheim, "Mass Behavior in an Extreme Situation."
51. Cara DeSilva, *In Memory's Kitchen: A Legacy from the Women of Terezin,* trans. B. S. Brown (New York: Jason Aronson, 1996).
52. Maurice Halbwachs, *On Collective Memory,* trans. and ed. Lewis A. Coser (Chicago: University of Chicago Press, 1992; first published 1941).
53. Charlotte Linde, "The Acquisition of a Speaker by a Story: How History Becomes Memory and Identity," *Ethos* 28, no. 4 (2000): 608–32.
54. Kenneth Plummer, *Telling Sexual Stories: Power, Change, and the Social Worlds* (New York: Routledge, 1995).
55. Emile Durkheim, *Elementary Forms of the Religious Life,* trans. Karen E. Fields (New York: Basic Books, 1995; first published 1912).
56. Barry Schwartz, "Memory as a Cultural System: Abraham Lincoln in World War II," *American Sociological Review* 61 (1996): 908–27; James V. Wertsch, *Voices of Collective Remembering* (New York: Cambridge University Press, 2002).

57. Geoffrey H. Hartman, *The Longest Shadow: In the Aftermath of the Holocaust* (New York: Palgrave/Macmillan, 1996).

58. B. Schiff, C. Noy, and B. Cohler, "Collected Stories in the Life Narratives of Holocaust Survivors," *Native Inquiry* 11 (2001): 159–94.

59. Eli Wiesel, *Night*, trans. S. Rodney (New York: Bantam Books, 1960).

60. Chase and Shaw, "Dimensions of Nostalgia"; Stewart, "Nostalgia—A Polemic."

61. James Edward Young, *The Texture of Memory: Holocaust Memorials and Meaning* (New Haven, CT: Yale University Press, 1993); also Young, "Against Redemption: The Arts of Countermemory in Germany Today," in Homans, *Symbolic Loss*, 126–46.

62. Young, *Texture of Memory*.

63. Hartman, *Longest Shadow*.

64. Robert Nathaniel Kraft, *Memory Perceived: Recalling the Holocaust* (Westport, CT: Praeger, 2002); Joan Miriam Ringelheim, *A Catalogue of Audio and Video Collections of Holocaust Testimony*, 2nd ed. (New York: Greenwood Press, 1992).

65. Peter Novick, *The Holocaust in American Life* (Boston: Houghton-Mifflin, 1999).

66. Linde, "Acquisition of a Speaker."

67. Anne Frank, *The Diary of Anne Frank: The Critical Edition*, prepared by the Netherlands State Institute for War Documentation, ed. David Barnouw and Gerrold Van der Stroom, trans. Arnold J. Pomerans and B. M. Mooyaart-Doubleday (New York: Doubleday, 1989).

68. Gary Weissman, *Fantasies of Witnessing: Postwar Efforts to Experience the Holocaust* (Ithaca, NY: Cornell University Press, 2004).

69. Daniel R. Schwarz, *Imagining the Holocaust* (New York: St. Martin's Press, 1999).

70. Frank, *Diary*, 694.

71. Ibid.

72. Schwartz, "Memory as a Cultural System"; Melissa Müller, *Anne Frank: The Biography*, trans. Rita Kimber and Robert Kimber (New York: Henry Holt and Metropolitan Books, 1998); Marris, *Loss and Change.*

73. Stephen Toulmin, *Cosmopolis: The Hidden Agenda of Modernity* (New York: Free Press, 1990).

74. Roman Vishniac, *To Give Them Light: The Legacy of Roman Vishniac*, ed. Marion Wiesel (New York: Simon and Schuster, 1993).

75. Jack Kugelmass and Jonathan Boyarin, *From a Ruined Garden: The Memorial Books of Polish Jewry*, 2nd ed. (Bloomington: Indiana University Press, 1998).

76. Yael Zerubavel, *Recovered Roots: Collective Memory and the Making of Israeli National Tradition* (Chicago: University of Chicago Press, 1995).

Afterword

CONVERSATIONS ON FREUD, MEMORY, AND LOSS

THE FOLLOWING conversations between Paul Ricoeur and Peter Homans took place in 2000, the first in a hotel in Paris, the second in Ricoeur's home. Ricoeur and Homans had been colleagues at the Divinity School of the University of Chicago during the 1970s and 1980s. Homans was interested in exploring with his colleague of many years the relation of loss to collective memory, cultural monuments, and illnesses such as melancholia.

HOMANS: When did you first become interested in Freud and why were you attracted to his work?

RICOEUR: My first interest was in the problem of guilt. In *The Symbolism of Evil* I studied the major myths concerning original evil, both the biblical myths and the Greek myths.[1] I tried to find a typology of the myths from the original myths of guilt. I began to wonder about the critique of religious myths in Freud. Then there was a kind of encounter—what I called the epistemology of suspicion—with Nietzsche, Freud, and Marx: the culture of suspicion. Then I turned to rereading Freud. I had read Freud when I was young because my first teacher in philosophy was himself a Thomist and Freudian.

HOMANS: Was that Roland Dalbiez?

RICOEUR: Yes, Dalbiez was the first Frenchman to write about Freud.[2] So my interest in Freud was really early, very early, but then I lost it. During the first years of teaching I taught Greek philosophy and German philosophy. But I returned, as I taught, to Freud and to the problem of guilt. I discovered, step by step, that it is impossible to separate the problem of guilt from the whole structure of the Freudian apparatus. Then I started a complete rereading of Freud. I read the works of Freud in German, in the English translation, and in the French translations. I began to develop, more and more, a very positive approach to Freud. In the beginning I had considered him a kind of enemy of Christian history. But I think that he wrote not only for physicians and M.D.'s, and not only for patients, but for the general public. And he developed a psychoanalysis of culture. I put him in correlation with the philosophy and theology of culture of Tillich. To me, this was a contribution to the anthropology of Tillich, the philosopher. The second step for me was the enlargement of his approach in terms of memory. I was more and more interested in the elaboration of memory.

HOMANS: Memory in Freud? Or in Tillich? Or in general?

RICOEUR: In general, as a personal problem. I came to the problem of memory over the period of several decades. I just published a book on memory, history, and forgetfulness. It is the last stage of a very long investigation concerning the structure of memory, the power of memory.

HOMANS: So you began with guilt and then memory. Do you mean that memory and guilt were related for you?

RICOEUR: The link was personal identity. It's a very old problem, coming from Augustine and *The Confessions*. In classical philosophy you have, I think, the most important approach in John Locke, in the famous chapter in *The Introduction to the Theory of Understanding*, chapter 22, a very important chapter on identity and diversity. Memory is the gate to personal identity. I was re-enforced in my interest in the problem of memory, for then the problem of guilt could be connected with a very radical problem, since it is, so to speak, a wound of identity in self-understanding, stemming from the past. So, you see, guilt is basically the sense of loss of integrity of personality. The next step was the connection I tried to make between the two wonderful essays of Freud, "Remembering, Repetition [Repeating], and Working Through" and "Mourning and Melancholia." I was interested in the correlation between the two essays and in the parallel structure of the essays. In the essay on remembering the opposing pair is remembering and repetition. And repetition comes from resistance.

HOMANS: Yes. I understand. The problems of guilt and memory led you to these two papers of Freud.

RICOEUR: And then there is the denial of the past, a kind of forgetfulness which is governed by the self, the defense. And this is, I could then say, that the relationship between remembering and repetition parallels the relation between mourning and melancholy.

In other words, melancholy is to mourning what repetition is to re-membering. So we could make a correlation also between repetition and melancholy. Because if melancholy is buried under the burden of the past, it's a permanent repetition of the same griefs and accu-sations. There is this famous sentence in the *Essays on Hysteria*, where Freud says "sometimes patients . . ."

HOMANS: "Suffer from reminiscences?"

RICOEUR: Yes, reminiscences, reminiscences. In German, it's very interesting, there is the same root when he speaks of grief and ac-cusation.

HOMANS: Does this include self-accusation?

RICOEUR: Self-accusation. In Freud, this is also loss of self-esteem. Not only the loss of something, loss of the loved object, but the loss of oneself in the loss of something and somebody. So it is this loss which I think has to be introduced into the theory of memory, be-cause a successful memory is also a memory which accepts that something is lost, that not everything can be recovered. The claim of a total recovery is a fantasy. We have to make of loss and therefore of mourning a component of memory. Not to put them together by this kind of correlation, but to say that a happy memory is a memory which has accepted the impossibility of a total recovery, and there-fore mourning is a component of memory. Is this understandable? I did that very quickly.

HOMANS: Yes. If I understand you correctly, by drawing upon sev-eral resources, you made a link between loss, mourning, and mem-ory on one hand, and guilt, self-accusation, and self-esteem on the other hand. Is that correct?

If that is so, what you have said is a good background for us to talk further about Freud and your work.

Please comment, if you will, on the distinction which historians often make between personal memory, that is, living memory, and historical memory, if you think that is important at this point.

RICOEUR: It is very important, for the simple reason that personal memory includes many fragments, because there is no memory with-out an account in linguistic terms. Therefore there is an element of a narrative component in what we may call declarative memory.

HOMANS: Declarative memory?

RICOEUR: Yes. We say what we have in memory; we speak about our memory. This is what Freud calls secondary elaboration. It is a secondary elaboration of memory which is at the birth of narrative, in memory, which we use to talk. Language is public language, there is no private language. Even when we speak about the most personal memories, we speak of them in public language. This is one reason we cannot separate personal memory from collective memory. The second reason is that, and this has to do with a narrative experience, we need to be helped to express our memory. Memory is not accessible. Again we are prevented from going deep in our memory. We need encouragement—we have to be authorized to remember. And I think that this has to do with the basic experience of psychoanalysis, which I know only by reading, the transference. There is a dialogical component in memory which may be silent but it's always more or less dialogue.

HOMANS: What do you mean by dialogue?

RICOEUR: In dialogue there is a relational alterity. I am not alone in front of myself. I am always within a certain community of language, but also a community of memories. I share memories with others. For example, many childhood memories are not lived memories. Some of them have been told to me by my parents or grandparents. I have interiorized them. An important part of my personal memory is the result of appropriation. I make my own something which was partly foreign.

My third argument is this: I not only use public language, and I not only need the support of others to remember, but, thirdly, many of my memories are public events. For example, if I speak to you about the beginning of the Second World War, which was a very important event of my life, it's also a public event. To speak of the outbreak of the war is to speak of an event that's both public and personal. They are so tightly linked that I cannot distinguish between them.

HOMANS: To help me understand still further the point you are making, would you please comment upon the following example? I am thinking of the situation of someone born after the Second World War, in contrast to someone born well before the war began and who lived through the war. The first person has no personal or living memory of the war, only historical or public memory. For this person, the war is accessible only through reading history books. But for the other person, living memory is much stronger. In the case of these two examples, would you still say that personal and collective memory are too intertwined to be distinguished?

RICOEUR: Oh, I have no doubt about that. Within this personal area of memory there are many borrowings from collective memory. I would say that the basic experiences of life have to do with relationships with others. We could not speak of the Oedipus complex without introducing a plurality of agents, for example. My personal memory is only the fragment of a system of relationships in which I am caught, a kind of intersubjective play. I would say that the patient who starts a psychoanalytic cure is not alone. He has to pay, he has to come at the right time, and so on. Even in the most personal experiences of that kind there are many social components.

HOMANS: Yes, I understand. Let us continue to discuss this topic. How do you treat loss and memory in your new book, *Memory, History, Forgetfulness*?

RICOEUR: It is a three-part book. I wanted to put the triadic structure into the title itself. Forgetfulness is a threat to both memory and history. Because memory and history rely on traces, I take the concept of trace as a central one, and not only in the neurological sense. There are traces, of course, in the brain, which is a "central tree" of the traces, but also, there are emotional traces. Freud's concept of the unconscious is not a biological concept, it's a psychological concept, and therefore we should speak of affective traces, emotional traces. This is what the scholastics and also the psychologies of the seventeenth and eighteenth centur[ies] called affections, that is to say, passive components of the psyche.

And then you have a third kind of trace, the documentary traces in our archives. Here we have a kind of public memory inscribed in a system traces. Monuments are traces, and so on. First, neurological, second, the affections, passive components of the psyche, and third, documentary traces in the archives, public monuments, and so on. This complex system of traces represents only one side, say, of forgetfulness, the effacing of traces.

But I don't think that this is the last word on forgetfulness. There is a positive function of forgetfulness which is not merely the destruction of traces. I would say, we put them "in reserve" as a treasure, as it were. We keep borrowing from this available reserve to remember, and remembering is not only fighting against memory, fighting against forgetfulness, but relying on forgetfulness. This is the reserve aspect of forgetfulness, which I call "forgetful reserve," *l'oublie de reserve.* I think that I have the support of Freud here because psychoanalysis relies on the possibility of rescuing from the past fragments which we thought were definitely forgotten. And this is a kind of confirmation of the positive function of forgetfulness. This conviction comes from way back, from Plato, the idea that to learn is to remember. Many of the Socratic dialogues say that when young, the child rediscovers the rules of the theory of geometry; to discover something new is to recover it in you. And my oldest son, who is a psychoanalyst, tells me that very often a patient says, "I have always known it, I always knew it."

HOMANS: Ah. When he finally understands something about himself, it seems as though he always knew it, because at one time he did know it.

RICOEUR: To discover is to rediscover. This is a great lesson of psychoanalysis concerning forgetfulness. I tried to make a connection between the anthropology of Freud and that of Bergson in *Matter and Memory*.[3] The most important chapter is about what he calls *la renaissance*, the renaissance of the past. The French is "a return to life," a kind of resurrection. I have studied historians, such as Collingwood and Michelet, who speak of the resurrection of the past.[4] This is the central theme in Michelet's book. It is a romantic book. The "Romantic" sometimes expresses the truth.

HOMANS: Yes. When you were speaking of traces, you mentioned that monuments are kinds of traces. What part do monuments, understood as traces, play in relation to forgetfulness and memory?

RICOEUR: Monuments are very interesting. The word comes from a Latin word which means "to remind."

HOMANS: Some say the Latin also means "to warn." Do you agree with that?

RICOEUR: Yes . . . a warning, to warn. Yes, a monument is a warning to someone. And then because this is the semiotic structure of the trace, we can assume that the trace is both present and absent. It's present in the sense that I see it, but it speaks about something that is not there. Let us start from one of the sources of the concept of the trace, coming from hunting a trace of an animal. We say, the animal passed there, it went there, or was there. And then, you have this wonderful word in English, a "reminder." It's a reminder because it helps to think about something that is not there. So the trace which is there brings back something which is no longer there but which was there. The deer passed there, was there. So, the most important part of a monument is the invisible part.

HOMANS: By "invisible" do you mean that which the trace signifies?

RICOEUR: Yes, the invisible, the nonvisible, the unvisible, the lost origin. Once more we hit upon the concept of loss. This fountain, for example, in the square outside this hotel, speaks of an anger during the Middle Ages which is now no longer there. So the lost past is rescued through this trace, which brings it back. This is why some would see nothing, only a heap of stones. But who sees it as a monument? Someone who has a culture and who is looking for a lost part of his memory, of collective memory.

HOMANS: I think that the life and thought of Max Weber illustrate many of the ideas you are advancing here, and so I would like to ask you whether you think that is so. As you know, Weber had what was then called "a nervous breakdown," but he also recovered.[5] Today, we would probably call his illness depression. When he became ill, his wife, Marianne Weber, took over and isolated him from everybody except herself and one or two visits from his mother. This went on for two or three years. Then, when he seemed ready, they traveled together. They went to Rome several times. After the last visit Weber began to recover. Later, looking back, Weber said his trip to Rome was the beginning of his recovery. He said, "an historical imagination is the key to understanding oneself." In other words, he went to Rome, a city filled with monuments and other beautiful things, he had a culture, as you have been saying, and he also got well.

RICOEUR: He recovered his own memory.

HOMANS: Yes, he recovered. Perhaps it was a form of self-healing.

RICOEUR: That confirms one of my arguments, that we need to be authorized to remember, we need to be authorized.

HOMANS: Would you say something more about that? Do you mean that monuments authorize us? If so, how does that happen?

RICOEUR: I am fascinated by this word, to be "authorized," because it's an encouragement. I become the author, I am authorized to become the author of my life.

HOMANS: Is it that one needs "permission"?

RICOEUR: Yes, but also, to be the author is to be the one who can say. It's a kind of allowed (aloud) signature.[6]

HOMANS: In the light of what you have just said about authorization and monuments, would you please speak about monuments that are widely known to many people, unlike the statue in the square outside this hotel? Are some monuments particularly powerful for you?

RICOEUR: No. I could not isolate any monument because a monument makes sense only within a system of memory, of monuments, the city, this city. A city is a progressive compilation of monuments of different ages. And the creator of each of these monuments would not have recognized the value of the previous monuments. For example, in the Gothic age they destroyed so many churches from the Romanesque age. And then in the Renaissance it was Gothic art, and so on. Romantic turns to classic, but the city is very tired because it makes memories. This is what happens with ourselves as well: memory is never isolated; it belongs to a series.

HOMANS: There is a network?

RICOEUR: A network. If you ask me for a memory, I give you back another memory. One monument is the work of the architect, but the city is not one architect but a series of them, and no one architect knows the whole city because the whole city is never finished. And its own roots are lost. When did Paris start?

HOMANS: It's the most layered monument imaginable.

RICOEUR: That is so. It is this layered structure which is its most interesting aspect. Not one monument but a network which is, at the same time, as you said, a layer. I think this is a power of the great city: it is a kind of summary of history.

HOMANS: Well, let's take a one-minute break. This is so important, so interesting.

HOMANS: Let us take up the topic of disease, especially mental disease, illness, and the ethics of respect.

RICOEUR: In disease there's something missing, a lack. There is a readjustment to a less dramatic surrounding, an adjustment to a restricted area. We must discover what values are implied in this adjustment to a restricted area. There is a constructive element, and this is the source of respect. It is not health minus something.

HOMANS: In America we have a phrase, "the medical model" or "the disease model" of mental illness. There is a terrible battle between scientific psychiatrists and the "neuroscientists," who think that neurosis and psychosis are diseases like cancer or heart failure, and those psychologists and psychiatrists who take a psychodynamic view. Is that what you are referring to now?

RICOEUR: Before having a disease model, we must have a health model, a model that makes an adjustment to an environment. It's not merely a response to the external forces of stimuli, but it's also a construction of the environment. The *Umwelt* of the surrounding world is always a projection of the living being which generates the compromises that pertain to the adjustment. These also have psychic implications in terms of self-esteem, self-evaluation. The individual has to elaborate new relations in terms of biological relationships and in terms of his own self-esteem. This is why he needs recognition, not only of his weaknesses but of his strength, and of the strength of his self-assertion. Do you see?

HOMANS: Yes, I do. But I am wondering, also, if this is a new theme in your work, in your writings?

RICOEUR: Yes, I've been influenced by Jacques Canguilhem, who wrote a book about life and the structure of life.[7] He was a biologist and taught on the epistemology of biology. I used to be his colleague at the Sorbonne. There is also a book called *The Logic of the Living Being* by Jacob.[8] I am sure that it has been translated. It's on the constructive role of the living organism in connection with

environment. The living organism keeps structuring its surroundings by adjusting its own evaluation in tacit evaluation of its own
capacity to live. It is not a mere response to stimuli but the construction of the stimuli themselves as, so to say, belonging to the world.
This is not only the summation of components taken one by one,
but as a whole as well. I taught about these topics in relation with
Jacques. We taught together several times focusing on this problem
of what we call the "hierarchy of values," which are always mixed.
Even in the most apparently biological setting there are always all
kinds of values which are already implied. To be a human being is
to live at the same time at several levels of self-structuring, of the
constitution of self-identity, which is layered. Therefore, disease and
illness hurt at each level. If I'm hurt at the biological level, I am hurt
at the psychic and the spiritual level. This is why to recognize the
values implied here in the disease of someone else I have to reconstruct the whole system of recovering meaning at all levels.

HOMANS: I would like to turn to a concrete example of what you
are saying about the problem of illness and respect. May we take
"melancholia"? The person suffering from melancholia is often said
to be ill. But let's back up for just a moment: we have talked about
mourning, memory, forgetfulness, and now about illness and disease.
Are there any connections here, between mourning, memory, and
forgetfulness on one hand, and melancholia, illness, and disease, on
the other?

RICOEUR: Yes, this element of loss. The lack, the loss. Something
not merely lacking, but lost. And then the adjustment to loss, the
need to cope with what I cannot do.

HOMANS: Yes. If that is so, then what is it that is lost in melancholia, in mental illness?

RICOEUR: I would not say that melancholy is only a mental disease. It's also a possibility of life. I am always threatened by melancholy. I would say that melancholy is complacency with sadness.

HOMANS: Complacency with sadness?

RICOEUR: Instead of considering sadness as a kind of threat to be
swallowed, sadness with complacency. In the history of monasticism
you have this notion of sadness as a sin, with the name of "acedia."
And you have this: the deepest sin is concupiscence, at the first level.
The second level is *la colère,* anger. The third one is greed, and the
last one is sadness, *tristitia.*

Speaking of monuments, I know a monument in Padua, in the
Scrovegni Chapel. It is a series in marble, not statues but engravings
in marble. The engravings are in pairs. You have *concupiscenza* and

then moderation. And then anger and peace. And then greed and then, what is the positive value? And then, *tristitia* and then *speranza*, hope.

HOMANS: Hope, yes.

RICOEUR: The contrary of hope is *tristitia*, which is Kierkegaard's despair, illness to death, disease to death.[9] How do you say it?

HOMANS: One English translation is *The Sickness unto Death*.

RICOEUR: At the Chapel of Scrovegni it's very interesting to see that the hierarchy of sins is not complete. *Tristitia* is elementary for a monk. It is a kind of despair. But sadness is not just sadness, it's a complacency, it's a yielding to sadness. I think Freud medicalized melancholy a bit too much. There's a long tradition around melancholy. With the famous painting by Durer, *Melancholia*, you see the posture of sadness in the disposition. The fist, you see the fist.

HOMANS: So many sculptors, and painters, have sought to represent melancholia.

RICOEUR: It is a long story, the story of melancholy. I have read a book, an excellent book, by several authors, *The History of Melancholy in the Arts*.[10]

HOMANS: There is an American book [on] the history of depression in Western thought by Stanley Jackson.[11]

RICOEUR: By the way, it's a common disease of our age.

HOMANS: Oh yes, yes.

RICOEUR: Mainly because the burden of responsibility placed on individuals. People rely less on communities.

HOMANS: Left to themselves, individuals break down.

RICOEUR: The burden is too heavy.

HOMANS: I understand why you characterize melancholia as sadness and complacency about sadness. That said, is there something specific which has been lost in the case of melancholia? Freud, for example, spoke of "the loss of the object" and of "object-loss."

RICOEUR: What you are asking about is not a disease. Melancholy is also the loss of the basic desire of being alive, the love of life, the pleasure in being alive. So, we can say, in melancholy there is the loss of self-esteem because of this loss.

HOMANS: Are you thinking of élan, or drive, or desire, or love of life?

RICOEUR: It is what Tillich is speaking of in *The Courage to Be*.[12] Courage is basically the desire as the main thrust. Melancholy is the loss of the courage to be. I keep returning to that because of my life and because of the awful experience of the suicide of one of my children.

230

HOMANS: Yes.

RICOEUR: It is very mysterious. [*Long pause*] Depression is not just a mental disease, but it is also a cultural disease, a societal disease. We talked earlier about the connection between personal memory and collective life, but it also involves the wounds supported by all my relationships and by the collective memories with different groups to which I belong. Sometimes it's a part of a new surrounding, but if I am compelled to stay in my room or in the hospital, it's as though I have lost the surrounding in my life. The fact that I am affected by that is not the mere quantitative diminution, but rather the loss of an intensity, of a sense of values. It is not just the loss of an extension but loss of an intensity.

HOMANS: Yes. Very much. I am thinking about what you said a moment ago about complacency and wondering whether Paul Tillich speaks, directly or indirectly, about melancholia and complacency. Tillich defines neurosis philosophically, in *The Courage to Be*, as the attempt to avoid nonbeing by avoiding being. This heavy ontological vocabulary is very impersonal. Does Tillich's formulation interest you?

RICOEUR: Yes, yes, it comes from the German tradition, post-Kantian. It provides some power and some hope.

HOMANS: When we spoke of melancholia, you used terms like "complacency" and "sadness." What thoughts do you have on the healing of melancholia?

RICOEUR: The community is very important. It cannot be cured simply by closed community. I need to be accepted, what we need to be is to be authorized to live, to love life, to help and be helped.

HOMANS: Authorization is so important, it seems to me, in everything that you have said.

RICOEUR: Yes, there's a lack of collective ties in modern culture. There are people who are left in front of television screens. They call it interaction because of the screen. [*Laughs*]

[End of First Conversation, Beginning of Second Conversation]

HOMANS: We have spoken of loss, desire, self-esteem, and melancholia, as well as of memory and monuments. But we have not spoken about mourning. Now I want to ask you, first, for your thoughts about the relationship between mourning and loss and memory.

Second, there is a tradition in modern Western thought, in Romantic medicine and literature, which claims that loss (and by implication mourning) gives rise to memory, that loss awakens the capacity to remember, and that remembering can, in turn, also heal. Perhaps you could say something about that. Can we begin with the place of mourning in personal life, and its possible relations to loss and memory?

RICOEUR: In Freud there is no explicit connection, to my mind, between the 1917 paper on mourning and the 1914 paper on remembering, repeating, and working through.[13] So it's by reading that I make a connection. But I make this connection to the extent that a healthy memory, and maybe a happy memory, implies the inclusion of an element of loss. First, this is because the past disappears: in a sense there is something lost by the very fact that it is past. In addition, memory is a kind of recovery of the past, beyond loss. This comes from the oldest definition of memory, in Greek philosophy, when Plato speaks of the presence of the absent thing in the image.

In my book, *Memory, History, Forgetting,* I start from this as the beginning of the problem of memory in Western thought, the connection between presence and absence.[14] But absence, the absence of the past is a very queer absence since it is the absence of something which has been present, an aporia constitutive of memory, a paradox. How is it possible to aim at the past as having been, through the presence of its absence? But this term expresses the paradox of memory itself, since memory is a way of bridging a gap between presence and absence. But it's a very great specific gap, because we must make a difference between two kinds of absences.

Let us speak of a character in literature, of Hamlet. Hamlet is not there, he is nowhere, and he was never anywhere. Therefore you have two kinds of absences—absence of something that was never part of reality and absence of events or persons or whatever which once existed, the loss of a previous existence. I would say all the paradoxes of memory are foreseen from this paradoxical structure of memory. First, the presence of an image, second the absence, and third an absence which was a presence. Therefore we could say that the place of mourning is implied in the place of loss, and loss is a place in the relationship itself of a presence to an absence which was the presence.

HOMANS: So, loss is implied in the "paradoxical structure of memory," and mourning is in turn implied in the reality of loss. Is that correct?

RICOEUR: Yes, in that sense. Did you mention that there are now some writings on this connection between mourning and memory? In Freud I haven't seen any explicit connection.

HOMANS: Yes. As you say, the paper on melancholia does not speak of any connection. But I think it is implicit in Freud, and much more explicit in some contemporary psychoanalytic writings. What Freud calls the work of mourning does not differ from what he also refers to as "reality testing," which is the gradual realization of the absence of the lost object. In this sense reality testing in the face of loss is also a kind of "work of mourning" and vice versa. One could say that the work of mourning is a kind of re-education of memory.

There is nothing "funerary" about mourning in Freud's paper. So, a link or connection between mourning and memory is implicit in the paper. The same can also be said of the paper on repetition and recollection. Recollection is a successful adaptive response to object-loss, just as repetition is the denial that the object has been lost. "Working through" is the transformation of repetition into recollection. I think this view is very similar to your own discussion just now of absence and presence. Would you agree with that?

RICOEUR: My discussion comes from Greek philosophy. With Plato and the following Socratics, it was about nonbeing. It is not by chance that the last dialogues are the *Philebus* and the *Sophist*. In these dialogues, which are called metaphysical dialogues, he struggles with the notion of nonbeing because it is a kind of objection to his own trend of philosophy, the philosophy of being. Now there is a gap here, because the Sophist himself was a man once discovered for Plato.[15] Then his problem was "How is the Sophist possible?" He had to deal with the problem of nonbeing. We have nonbeing occupying the place in our soul of mistakes, errors, forgetfulness. Memory itself is a witness of nonbeing.

HOMANS: Yes. I see. In this regard, I have often wondered whether mourning and time itself are related. It seems to me that the passing of time itself creates the realization that something is lost. Would you say that?

RICOEUR: The lost object, the loss is so strong. There is grief, and there is something beyond grief. Can you, do you, make a distinction between grief and mourning?

HOMANS: Yes.

RICOEUR: Grief is a separate thing from mourning. It is a negotiation with loss.

HOMANS: Yes. I find a distinction which some anthropologists make between grief and mourning very important. In this view, grief is present in some nonhuman primates, as well as in humans. In both cases, the physiology and psychology are virtually the same.

RICOEUR: Do primates shed tears?

HOMANS: Darwin initiated this kind of thinking about the emotions in animals and men. I don't know about the shedding of tears, but I think it's very important and will try to find an answer.

RICOEUR: Mourning is the expression of grief.

HOMANS: Yes. I would put it this way. Grief is an emotion common to humans and some nonhuman primates, whereas mourning is a social, symbolic, ritual activity found in humans but not in any nonhuman primates.

RICOEUR: They are capable of grief, but not of mourning?

HOMANS: Yes, exactly. Capable of grief, but not of mourning, and sometimes the nonhuman primates can actually die from grief.

RICOEUR: Capable of grief but not of mourning.

HOMANS: Yes, unless something very important and unusual happens. For example, they band together in order to avoid the grief. It is very hard to understand. They are so helpless. They don't have the symbolic registers necessary to create a ritual. So, mourning is a social, symbolic activity, and as such, it is a response to the emotion of grief. At least that is the theory.

RICOEUR: I suppose its principle is language. They are elaborating the notion of absence/presence.

HOMANS: Yes. I really think so. It seems to me that language is the crucial factor which makes it possible to distinguish between grief and mourning, and that this distinction is also present in your exposition of absence and memory. [*Pause*]

Since only a little time is left I would like to move on to several shorter questions. First, as you understand Freud's work as a whole, to what extent does the problem of loss occupy a central position in his thought? I myself find this view of Freud very convincing.

RICOEUR: To me, the real contribution of psychoanalysis is about the strategies for eluding it (loss) and covering it, more than the constitution of loss, and the particular experience of loss. It is in the notion of resistance too. I wonder whether the starting point would be the notion of screen memories, because the screening effect involves the confrontation with loss. And it would be in the notion of substitution, when Freud says that something substitutes for memory. And in the confrontation with loss, memory is confronted with the absent as an internalization.

HOMANS: Thank you. And so, another question. May I ask you to comment on a passage from your book *Critique and Conviction*? Some time ago, while I was reading your chapter on politics and totalitarianism, one remark in particular leapt off the page. You said, "and I mourn that," referring to the passing of the Middle Ages. I think I understand what you mean, but I want to be sure. Here is the passage in full: "It remains true that the classical, theologico-political regime is out-moded; the claim to found the political realm on a theology, or, to return to our framework, on the vertical axis of authority alone, itself dependent on a divine authority, this claim is at an end, and I mourn it. But it does not follow that everything belonging to the theologico-political domain has lost its meaning."[16]

RICOEUR: A wonderful age, the certitude of the Middle Ages. It is not grief, it is mourning: I have to reconcile myself with this loss. It is a political loss, par excellence, in our culture.

HOMANS: Yes. Do you have something more in mind?

RICOEUR: It is also about the fact that we are not left with this emptiness of which so many are now speaking, because behind us there were riches. We have lost it, but it is still there. I speak of heritage—we are the heirs. Heritage is always after death, but everything is not lost. We inherited it, by definition, from the dead.[17]

HOMANS: Another question. Previously we talked about melancholia and the healing of melancholia. Could we pick up on this and broaden it by talking about the healing of mental suffering in a more general sense? How do you understand psychotherapy in relation to the forms of illness and suffering which we have been discussing, such as melancholia, neurosis, and depression?

RICOEUR: Freud doesn't say a word about healing melancholy. And I wonder if it's not a basic skepticism, that finally we are hitting on something. Because the whole of psychoanalysis is directed elsewhere, towards neurosis. Melancholy is not a neurosis. It's on the line between neurosis and psychosis. Yesterday my son, who is a very successful psychoanalyst in Marseilles, told me that now the patients we have are quite different from Freud's patients. Their problem was quite different . . . *refoulement*?

HOMANS: Are you thinking of repression?

RICOEUR: Yes. That program was for repression, and now it's depression. In repression we have to fight with fantasies and try to replace them. They are sources of suffering. We can negotiate and deal with the fantasies. But there is a lack of symbolism in depression. A kind of emptiness in terms of major fantasy, a poverty. Psychoanalysis is possible only with people who are gifted with language, who are able to fight with words because even the oneiric life has to be put into words, into narrative. In depression there is no matter with which to [work]. I wonder whether this is the experience of American psychoanalysis too, this problem of the negative aspects of depression.

HOMANS: Oh, I think it is.

RICOEUR: My son told me that a new patient in psychoanalysis today is often the previous patient of Jung.

HOMANS: What did he mean?

RICOEUR: New patients are people who come with problems of "what is the meaning of my life?" On the other hand the problem of the young girls, the ladies, who came to Freud, was how to live. Melancholy is a dreadful enemy. Neurosis has not the place that it had at the beginning of the nineteenth century.

HOMANS: I think it is the same in American psychiatry. Many American psychoanalysts and psychotherapists now use such recent developments as self-psychology (Heinz Kohut) and object relations psychology (Melanie Klein and D. W. Winnicott). John Bowlby, who has contributed to the psychoanalytic theories of loss, was one of the leaders of the school of object relations. These workers did not use classical Freudian ideas and techniques very much.

RICOEUR: For the French, particularly with the emphasis on language, the main cure is talk. And they have to deal with people who have been poor, for whom the behavioral and affective dimensions are central. My son says [they struggle with] the capacity to speak, to elaborate in linguistic terms, and then to bring the disease to the center.

HOMANS: I have read cases like that, in which psychotherapy began with teaching the patient how to speak. Is your son representative of French psychiatry today, do you think?

RICOEUR: He was "raised" by Lacan. [Both laugh] The structures were so strong. They are moralists, content to do psychotherapies which don't require so much time. I think the cure is shorter and shorter. After half an hour there is nothing else to say. Have you had experiences like this?

HOMANS: Earlier in my career I did clinical training and then clinical work, and later left that for university teaching. But that work remains essential, because it helps me understand what psychoanalysis and the dynamic psychotherapists speak of and write about. It has become more and more common for American psychoanalysts and psychotherapists to see patients once or twice a week, instead of, say, four times a week, and also to see many different kinds of clinical disorders, not only the neuroses. I think the pathology in the

American situation today is simply historically and sociologically different from the neuroses of Freud's time.

I have two final questions. Do you still have time for that?

RICOEUR: Yes.

HOMANS: You have written extensively on metaphor, as well as on Freud's theory of dreams. How important is metaphor in Freud's work as a whole, in your estimate?

RICOEUR: I have wondered about the whole psychoanalytic situation, this arena between pure life and the situation of transference. Patients relive real situations in metaphorical terms. I have read some papers on the healing of mental diseases as a whole process of metaphorization of disease. Transference is a metaphorization of a whole relationship with the father and mother, and so on. It is not by chance that the word "metaphor" in Greek means transference, displacing, replacing.

HOMANS: Years ago, when you were teaching some of your ideas about Freud at the University of Chicago, I was an assistant professor auditing your classes. At one point you made a remark which I have always remembered. You said, as you finished some lectures on Freud, that you personally felt better, you felt you understood yourself better, as a result of your study of Freud. Would you comment on that?

RICOEUR: Yes, yes. Sure. As my son says to me, you try to make a self-analysis at a low price. [Laughs]

HOMANS: You mean "cheap?" A cheap self-analysis. It's less expensive. Could you say anything more about that?

RICOEUR: It's a joke, but it was a meaningful joke. [Laughs]

HOMANS: Oh. [Laughs] A meaningful joke. OK. I'm catching on.

RICOEUR: Why did Freud publish his lectures and even the five analyses? For whom? Not for his patients, and not for his colleagues, but for me, as a private reader. So therefore it helps us to address certain troubles in ourselves. Freud was very fond of his public relationship, not only because of his pride in psychoanalysis, but I think to help people, as if to say, "If you can't come to my couch . . ."

HOMANS: Yes, if you can't come, just read it, maybe you don't need to come. Perhaps that is another reason why Freud's writing style is so admired.

FINAL QUESTION: What is your critical sense of Henri Ellenberger's *The Discovery of the Unconscious*?[18] I especially wonder whether he should be situated more in the history of Romantic medicine, than in the history of psychiatry?

RICOEUR: I don't know. I don't like to critique without spending time reading. The Romantic period is one of the periods of European thought which I like very much, which is lost. But I mourn it. [*Smiles*]

HOMANS: [*Laughs*] OK. Now I'm really catching on. Thank you so much.

Notes

1. Paul Ricoeur, *The Symbolism of Evil*, trans. Emerson Buchanan (New York: Harper and Row, 1967).
2. Roland Dalbiez, *Psychoanalytical Method and the Doctrine of Freud*, trans. T. F. Lindsay (London: Longmans, Green, 1941).
3. Henri Bergson, *Matter and Memory*, trans. Margaret Paul and W. Scott Palmer (London: G. Allen; New York, Macmillan, 1911).
4. R. G. Collingwood, *Essays in the Philosophy of History*, ed. William Debbins (Austin: University of Texas Press, 1965); Jules Michelet, *History of the French Revolution*, trans. Keith Botsford (Wynnewood, PA: Livingston, 1972).
5. Peter Homans, "Loss and Mourning in the Life and Thought of Max Weber: Toward a Theory of Symbolic Loss," in *Symbolic Loss: The Ambiguity of Mourning and Memory at Century's End*, ed. Homans (Charlottesville: University Press of Virginia, 2000).
6. Editors' note: The recording of the conversation does not indicate whether Ricoeur intended to say "allowed" or "aloud."
7. Georges Canguilhem, *Ideology and Rationality in the History of the Life Sciences*, trans. Arthur Goldhammer (Cambridge, MA: MIT Press, 1988).
8. François Jacob, *The Logic of Life: A History of Heredity*, trans. Betty E. Spillmann (New York: Pantheon Books, 1973).
9. Søren Kierkegaard, *The Sickness unto Death*, trans. Walter Lowrie (Princeton, NJ: Princeton University Press, 1941).
10. Editors' note: The work being referred to as *The History of Melancholy in the Arts* is uncertain.
11. Stanley W. Jackson, *Melancholia and Depression: From Hippocratic Times to Modern Times* (New Haven, CT: Yale University Press, 1986).
12. Paul Tillich, *The Courage to Be* (New Haven, CT: Yale University Press, 1952).
13. Unless otherwise noted, references to the work of Sigmund Freud are from *The Standard Edition of the Complete Psychological Works of Sigmund Freud*, trans. and ed. James Strachey (London: Hogarth Press, 24 vols., 1966–1974). Sigmund Freud, "Mourning and Melancholia," *Standard Edition*, vol. 14 (first published 1917); Freud, "Remembering, Repeating, and Working Through," *Standard Edition*, vol. 12 (first published 1914).
14. Paul Ricoeur, *Memory, History, Forgetting*, trans. Kathleen Blamey and David Pellauer (Chicago: University of Chicago Press, 2004).
15. Editors' note: The meaning of Ricoeur's remarks in this paragraph remains obscure.
16. Paul Ricoeur, *Critique and Conviction: Conversations with François Azouvi and Marc de Launay*, trans. Kathleen Blamey (New York: Columbia University Press, 1998).
17. This may be relevant to Ricoeur's earlier remarks about forgetfulness and "reserve of memory."
18. Henri F. Ellenberger, *The Discovery of the Unconscious: The History and Evolution of Dynamic Psychiatry* (New York: Basic Books, 1970).

Bibliography

Abraham, Hilda C., and Ernst L. Freud, eds. *A Psycho-analytic Dialogue: The Letters of Sigmund Freud and Karl Abraham, 1907–1926.* New York: Basic Books, 1965.

Abraham, Karl. *Selected Papers of Karl Abraham, MD.* Trans. D. Bryan and A. Strachey. London: Maresfield Library, 1988 (first published 1927).

Ackerman, Robert. *J. G. Frazer: His Life and Work.* Cambridge: Cambridge University Press, 1987.

Adler, Gerald. "How Useful Is the Borderline Concept?" *Psychoanalytic Inquiry* 8 (1988): 353–72.

Agamben, Giorgio. *Homo Sacer: Sovereign Power and Bare Life.* Trans. Daniel Heller-Roazen. Stanford, CA: Stanford University Press, 1998.

"AIDS at 25: Special Report." *Newsweek,* 15 May 2006.

Albanese, Catherine. "The Magical Staff: Quantum Healing in the New Age." In *Perspectives on the New Age,* ed. James R. Lewis and J. Gordon Melton, 68–84. Albany: State University of New York Press, 1992.

———. "Religion and the American Experience: A Century After." *Church History* 57 (1988): 337–51.

———. "The Subtle Energies of Spirit: Explorations in Metaphysical and New Age Spirituality." *Journal of the American Academy of Religion* 67, no. 2 (1988): 305–26.

Alford, C. Fred. *Melanie Klein and Critical Social Theory: An Account of Politics, Art, and Reason Based on Her Psychoanalytic Theory.* New Haven, CT: Yale University Press, 1989.

Apfelbaum, Erika. "Against the Tide: Making Waves and Breaking Silences." In *Alternative History of Psychology in Autobiography,* ed. Leo Moss. N.p.: Kluwer Academic/Plenum, n.d.

———. "The Dread: An Essay on Communication across Cultural Boundaries." In "Under the Covers: Theorising the Politics of Counter Stories," special issue, *International Journal of Critical Psychology,* no. 4 (2001): 19–35.

———. "Restoring Lives Shattered by Collective Violence: The Role of Official Public Narratives in the Process of Memorializing." Invited address for the conference on "Narrative, Trauma and Memory—Working through the Southern African Armed Conflicts of the 20th Century," 3–5 July 2001, Cape Town, South Africa.

Arendt, Hannah. *The Origins of Totalitarianism.* San Diego, CA: Harcourt Brace, 1979 (first published 1948).

Augustine. *Confessions.* Trans. Henry Chadwick. New York: Oxford University Press, 1998.

Bacal, Howard. "Does an Object Relations Theory Exist in Self Psychology?" *Psychoanalytic Inquiry* 10 (1990): 197–220.

Bachelard, Gaston. *The Poetics of Space.* Trans. Maria Jolas. Boston: Beacon Press, 1969.

Baker, J. "Mourning and the Transformation of Object Relationships: Evidence for the Persistence of Internal Attachments." *Psychoanalytic Psychology* 18 (2001): 55–73.

Balint, Michael. *Primary Love and Psychoanalytic Technique.* New York: Liveright, 1965.

Bartov, Omer. *Murder in Our Midst: The Holocaust, Industrial Killing, and Representation.* New York: Oxford University Press, 1996.

Batson, C. Daniel, Patricia Schoenrade, and W. Larry Ventis. *Religion and the Individual: A Social-Psychological Perspective.* New York: Oxford University Press, 1993.

Beirnaert, Louis. "Romain Rolland, Les derniéres etapes du voyage intérieur." *Etudes* 44 (1945): 250–56.

Bell, Catherine. *Ritual: Perspectives and Dimensions.* New York: Oxford University Press, 1997.

———. *Ritual Theory/Ritual Practice.* New York: Oxford University Press, 1992.

Bellah, Robert N., et al. *Habits of the Heart.* Berkeley: University of California Press, 1985.

Benhabib, Seyla. *The Rights of Others: Aliens, Residents and Citizens.* Cambridge: Cambridge University Press, 2004.

Bergson, Henri. *Matter and Memory.* Trans. Margaret Paul and W. Scott Palmer. London: G. Allen; New York, Macmillan, 1911.

Bethel, Elizabeth R. *AIDS: Readings on a Global Crisis.* Needham Heights, MA: Allyn and Bacon, 1995.

Bettelheim, Bruno. *The Informed Heart: Autonomy in a Mass Age.* New York: Free Press/Macmillan, 1960.

———. "Mass Behavior in an Extreme Situation." *Journal of Abnormal and Social Psychology* 38 (1943): 417–52.

Blackburn, Robin. *The Making of New World Slavery: From the Baroque to the Modern, 1492–1800.* London: Verso, 1997.

Bouyer, Louis. "Mysticism: An Essay on the History of the Word." In *Understanding Mysticism,* ed. Richard Woods. Garden City, NY: Image Books, 1980.

Bowen, Peter M. "AIDS 101." In *Writing AIDS: Gay Literature, Language, and Analysis,* ed. Timothy F. Murphy and Suzanne Poirier, 141–54. New York: Columbia University Press, 1993.

Bowlby, John. *Attachment and Loss.* Vol. 3. London: Penguin, 1991 (first published 1980).

————. *Loss: Sadness and Depression.* New York: Basic Books, 1982.

————. "Pathological Mourning and Childhood Mourning." *Journal of the American Psychoanalytic Association* 11 (1963): 500–541.

Boyarin, Daniel, Daniel Itzkovitz, and Ann Pelligrini. *Queer Theory and the Jewish Question.* New York: Columbia University Press, 2003.

Boym, Svetlana. *The Future of Nostalgia.* New York: Basic Books, 2001.

Brandt, Anthony. "A Short History of Nostalgia." *Atlantic* 242, no. 6 (1978): 58–63.

Bregman, Lucy, and Sara Thiermann. *First Person Mortal: Personal Narratives of Illness, Dying and Grief.* New York: Paragon House, 1995.

Brickman, Celia. *Aboriginal Populations in the Mind: Race and Primitivity in Psychoanalysis.* New York: Columbia University Press, 2003.

Britzman, Deborah P. *After-Education: Anna Freud, Melanie Klein, and Psychoanalytic Histories of Learning.* Albany: State University of New York Press, 2003.

————. *Lost Subjects, Contested Objects: Toward a Psychoanalytic Inquiry of Learning.* Albany: State University of New York Press, 1998.

Bruneau, Thomas J. "Communicative Silences: Forms and Functions." *Journal of Communication* 23 (1973): 17–46.

Bucke, Richard Maurice. *Cosmic Consciousness.* New York: Citadel Press, 1993.

Burrow, J. W. *Evolution and Society: A Study in Victorian Social Theory.* London: Cambridge University Press, 1966.

Butler, Judith. *Precarious Life: The Powers of Mourning and Violence.* London: Verso, 2004.

Campbell, Courtney S. "Ethics and Militant Activism." In *AIDS and Ethics*, ed. Frederic G. Reamer, 155–87. New York: Columbia University Press, 1991.

Canguilhem, Georges. *Ideology and Rationality in the History of the Life Sciences.* Trans. Arthur Goldhammer. Cambridge, MA: MIT Press, 1988.

Certeau, Michel de. "Mysticism." *Diacritics* 22, no. 2 (1992): 11–25.

Chandler, Marilyn. "Voices from the Front: AIDS in Autobiography." *A-B: Autobiography Studies* 6, no. 1 (Spring 1991): 65–75.

Chase, Malcolm, and Christopher Shaw. "The Dimensions of Nostalgia." In *The Imagined Past: History and Nostalgia*, ed. Christopher Shaw and Malcolm Chase, 1–17. Manchester, UK: Manchester University Press, 1989.

Cheng, Anne Anlin. *The Melancholy of Race: Psychoanalysis, Assimilation and Hidden Grief.* Oxford: Oxford University Press, 2001.

Chopp, Rebecca S. "Theology and the Poetics of Testimony," *Criterion* 37, no. 1 (Winter 1998): 2–12.

Chow, Rey. *The Protestant Ethnic and the Spirit of Capitalism.* New York: Columbia University Press, 2002.

Cixous, Hélène, and Catherine Clément. *The Newly Born Woman.* Minneapolis: University of Minnesota Press, 1986.

Clément, Catherine, and Julia Kristeva. *The Feminine and the Sacred.* New York: Columbia University Press, 2001.

Clifford, James. "Of Other Peoples: Beyond the 'Salvage' Paradigm." In *Discussions in Contemporary Culture*, ed. Hal Foster. Seattle: Bay Press, 1987.

Clum, John M. "'And Once I Had It All': AIDS Narrative and Memories of an American Dream." In *Writing AIDS: Gay Literature, Language and Analysis*, ed. Timothy F. Murphy and Suzanne Poirier, 200–224. New York: Columbia University Press, 1993.

Cohen, Ed. "Are We (Not) What We Are Becoming? 'Gay' 'Identity,' 'Gay Studies,' and the Disciplining of Knowledge." In *Engendering Men: The Question of Male Feminist Criticism*, ed. Joseph A. Boone and Michael Cadden, 161–75. New York: Routledge, 1990.

Collingwood, R. G. *Essays in the Philosophy of History*. Ed. William Debbins. Austin: University of Texas Press, 1965.

Collins, Patricia Hill. *Black Sexual Politics: African Americans, Gender, and the New Racism*. New York: Routledge, 2004.

Crimp, Douglas. *Melancholia and Moralism: Essays on AIDS and Queer Politics*. Cambridge, MA: MIT Press, 2002.

———. "Portraits of People with AIDS." In *Cultural Studies*, ed. Lawrence Grossberg, Cary Nelson, and Paula Treichler, 117–33. New York: Routledge, 1992.

Crimp, Douglas, with Adam Rolston. *AIDS Demographics*. Seattle: Bay Press, 1990.

Crownfield, David, ed. *Body/Text in Julia Kristeva: Religion, Women, and Psychoanalysis*. Albany: State University of New York Press, 1992.

Dalbiez, Roland. *Psychoanalytical Method and the Doctrine of Freud*. Trans. T. F. Lindsay. London: Longmans, Green, 1941.

Daly, Mary. *Gyn/Ecology: The Metaethics of Radical Feminism*. Boston: Beacon Press, 1978.

Darwin, Charles. *The Expression of the Emotions in Man and Animals*. London: William Pickering, 1989 (first published 1872).

Dauenhauer, Bernard P. *Silence: The Phenomenon and Its Ontological Significance*. Bloomington: Indiana University Press, 1980.

Davis, David Brion. *Inhuman Bondage: The Rise and Fall of Slavery in the New World*. New York: Oxford University Press, 2006.

Davis, Fred. *Yearning for Yesteryear: A Sociology of Nostalgia*. New York: Free Press/Macmillan, 1979.

Dean, Tim. "The Psychoanalysis of AIDS." *October* 63 (Winter 1993): 83–116.

DeSilva, Cara. *In Memory's Kitchen: A Legacy from the Women of Terezin*. Trans. B. S. Brown. New York: Jason Aronson, 1996.

Dietrich, D. R., and P. C. Shabad, eds. *The Problem of Loss and Mourning: Psychoanalytic Perspectives*. Madison, CT: International Universities Press, 1989.

Doka, Kenneth J., ed. *Disenfranchised Grief: Recognizing Hidden Sorrow*. Lexington, MA: Lexington Books, 1989.

Douglas, Kelly Brown. *Sexuality and the Black Church: A Womanist Perspective*. Maryknoll, NY: Orbis Books, 1999.

Douglas, Mary. *Purity and Danger: An Analysis of the Concepts of Pollution and Taboo*. London: Ark, 1984 (first published 1966).

Durkheim, Emile. *The Elementary Forms of the Religious Life.* Trans. Joseph Ward Stain. New York: Free Press, 1965.

———. *Elementary Forms of the Religious Life.* Trans. Karen E. Fields. New York: Basic Books, 1995.

Edelman, Lee. "The Mirror and the Tank: 'AIDS,' Subjectivity and the Rhetoric of Activism." In *Writing AIDS: Gay Literature, Language and Activism,* ed. Timothy F. Murphy and Suzanne Poirier, 9–38. New York: Columbia University Press, 1993.

Eliade, Mircea. *Autobiography.* Vol. 1. New York: Harper and Row, 1981.

———. *Autobiography.* Vol. 2. Chicago: University of Chicago Press, 1998.

Ellenberger, Henri F. *The Discovery of the Unconscious: The History and Evolution of Dynamic Psychiatry.* New York: Basic Books, 1970.

Eng, David L. *Racial Castration: Managing Masculinity in Asian America.* Durham, NC: Duke University Press, 2001.

Eng, David L., and David Kazanjian, eds. *Loss: The Politics of Mourning.* Berkeley: University of California Press, 2003.

Epstein, Robert, and Jeffrey Friedman, directors. *Common Threads: Stories from the Quilt.* San Francisco: Telling Pictures/Coutune, 1989.

Erikson, Erik H. *Identity and the Life Cycle.* New York: Norton, 1980.

———. *Insight and Responsibility: Lectures on the Ethical Implications of Psychoanalysic Insight.* New York: Norton, 1964.

———. *Young Man Luther: A Study in Psychoanalysis and History.* New York: Norton, 1958.

Espin, Oliva. "Giving Voice to Silence: The Psychologist as Witness." *American Psychologist* 48, no. 4 (April 1993): 408–14.

Felman, Shoshana, and Dori Laub. *Testimony: Crises of Witnessing in Literature, Psychoanalysis and History.* New York: Routledge, 1992.

Fenichel, Otto. *The Psychoanalytic Theory of Neurosis.* New York: Norton, 1945.

Feuerbach, Ludwig. *The Essence of Christianity.* Trans. George Eliot. New York: Harper and Row, 1957.

Forman, Robert K. C., ed. *The Innate Capacity: Mysticism, Psychology, and Philosophy.* New York: Oxford University Press, 1997.

Forster, E. M. *Howards End.* New York: Modern Library, 1999.

Foucault, Michel. *The History of Sexuality.* Trans. Robert Hurley. New York: Pantheon Books, 1978.

———. "The Unities of Discourse." *The Archaeology of Knowledge and the Discourse on Language.* Trans. A. M. Sheridan Smith. New York: Barnes and Noble, 1993.

Frank, Anne. *The Diary of Anne Frank: The Critical Edition.* Prepared by the Netherlands State Institute for War Documentation. Ed. David Barnouw and Gerrold Van der Stroom. Trans. Arnold J. Pomerans and B. M. Mooyaart-Doubleday. New York: Doubleday, 1989.

Frank, Arthur W. *The Wounded Storyteller: Body, Illness, and Ethics.* Chicago: University of Chicago Press, 1995.

Franke, Robert G. "Beyond Good Doctor, Bad Doctor: AIDS Fiction and Biography as a Developing Genre." *Journal of Popular Culture* 27 (Winter 1993): 93–101.

Freud, Sigmund. "An Autobiographical Study." *Standard Edition*, vol. 20 (first published 1925).

———. "Creative Writers and Day-Dreaming. *Standard Edition*, vol. 9 (first published 1908).

———. "A Difficulty in the Path of Psychoanalysis." *Standard Edition*, vol. 17 (first published 1917).

———. "The Ego and the Id." *Standard Edition*, vol. 19 (first published 1923).

———. *The Freud-Jung Letters: The Correspondence between Sigmund Freud and C. G. Jung.* Ed. William McGuire. Trans. Ralph Manheim and R. F. C. Hull. Princeton, NJ: Princeton University Press, 1974.

———. "Group Psychology and the Analysis of the Ego." *Standard Edition*, vol. 18 (first published 1921).

———. "Inhibitions, Symptoms and Anxiety." *Standard Edition*, vol. 20 (first published 1926).

———. "Interpretation of Dreams." *Standard Edition*, vols. 4 and 5 (first published 1900).

———. "Moses and Monotheism." *Standard Edition*, vol. 23 (first published 1939).

———. "Mourning and Melancholia." *Standard Edition*, vol. 14 (first published 1917).

———. "New Introductory Lectures." *Standard Edition*, vol. 22 (first published 1933).

———. "Obsessive Acts and Religious Practices." *Standard Edition*, vol. 9 (first published 1907).

———. "On Narcissism." *Standard Edition*, vol. 14 (first published 1914).

———. "Three Essays on the Theory of Sexuality." *Standard Edition*, vol. 7 (first published 1905).

———. "On Transience." *Standard Edition*, vol. 14 (first published 1916).

———. "An Outline of Psychoanalysis." *Standard Edition*, vol. 23 (first published 1940).

———. "Remembering, Repeating, and Working Through." *Standard Edition*, vol. 12 (first published 1914).

———. *The Standard Edition of the Complete Psychological Works of Sigmund Freud.* Trans. and ed. James Strachey. 24 vols. London: Hogarth Press, 1966–1974.

———. "Thoughts for the Times on War and Death." *Standard Edition*, vol. 14 (first published 1915).

Freud, Sigmund, and Josef Breuer. "Studies on Hysteria." *Standard Edition*, vol. 2 (first published 1895).

Fuller, Robert. *Spiritual but not Religious.* New York: Oxford University Press, 2001.

Gaines, R. "Detachment and Continuity." *Contemporary Psychoanalysis* 33 (1997): 549–71.

Gannon, Joshua. "Silence, Death, and the Invisible Enemy: AIDS Activism and Social Movement 'Newness.'" In *Ethnography Unbound: Power and Resistance in the Modern Metropolis*, ed. Michael Burawoy et al., 35–57. Berkeley: University of California Press, 1991.

Gennep, Arnold van. *The Rites of Passage*. Trans. M. B. Vizedom and G. L. Caffee. Chicago: University of Chicago Press, 1960 (first published 1909).

Gergen, Kenneth J. *Realities and Relationships: Soundings in Social Construction*. Cambridge, MA: Harvard University Press, 1994.

Gilman, Sander L. *The Case of Sigmund Freud: Medicine and Identity at the Fin de Siècle*. Baltimore: Johns Hopkins University Press, 1993.

———. "Plague in Germany 1939/1989: Cultural Images of Race, Space and Disease." In *Writing AIDS: Gay Literature, Language, and Analysis*, ed. Timothy F. Murphy and Suzanne Poirier, 54–82. New York: Columbia University Press, 1993.

Goss, Robert. *Jesus Acted Up: A Gay and Lesbian Manifesto*. New York: Harper-Collins, 1993.

Goss, Robert, and Dennis Klass. *Dead but Not Lost: Grief Narratives in Religious Traditions*. Walnut Creek, CA: Alta Mira Press, 2005.

Greenberg, Jay, and Stephen Mitchell. *Object Relations in Psychoanalytic Theory*. Cambridge, MA: Harvard University Press, 2003.

Greenson, R. "A Dream While Drowning." In *Separation-Individuation: Essays in Honor of Margaret S. Mahler*, ed. John B. McDevitt and Calvin F. Settlage, 377–84. Madison, CT: International Universities Press, 1971.

Griffin, Gail B. *Calling: Essays on Teaching in the Mother Tongue*. Pasadena, CA: Trilogy Books, 1992.

Grover, Jan Zita. "AIDS: Keywords." In *AIDS: Cultural Analysis/Cultural Activism*, ed. Douglas Crimp, 17–31. Cambridge, MA: MIT Press, 1989.

Hadas, Rachel. *The Empty Bed*. Hanover, NH: Wesleyan University Press by the University Press of New England, 1995.

Hagman, George. "Mourning: A Review and Reconsideration." *International Journal of Psychoanalysis* 76 (1995): 909–25.

Halbwachs, Maurice. *On Collective Memory*. Trans. and ed. Lewis A. Coser. Chicago: University of Chicago Press, 1992.

Handler, Richard, and Eric Gable. *The New History in an Old Museum: Creating the Past at Colonial Williamsburg*. Durham, NC: Duke University Press, 1997.

Hanson, Ellis. "Undead." In *Inside/Out: Lesbian Theories, Gay Theories*, ed. Diana Fuss, 324–40. New York: Routledge, 1991.

Hartman, Geoffrey H. *The Longest Shadow: In the Aftermath of the Holocaust*. New York: Palgrave/Macmillan, 1996.

Hartmann, Heinz. *Ego Psychology and the Problem of Adaptation*. Trans. David Rapaport. New York: International Universities Press, 1958.

Henking, Susan E. "Difficult Knowledges: Gender, Sexuality, Religion." *Spotlight on Teaching* (forthcoming).

———. "The Legacies of AIDS: Religion and Mourning in AIDS-Related Memoirs." In *Spirituality and Community: Diversity in Lesbian and Gay Experience*, ed. J. Michael Clark and Michael L. Stemmeler, 3–28. Gay Men's Issues in Religious Studies Series, vol. 5. Los Colinas, TX: Monument Press, 1994.

Hertz, Robert. "A Contribution to the Study of the Collective Representation of Death." In *Death and the Right Hand*, trans. Rodney and Claudia Needham. Glencoe, IL: Free Press, 1960 (first published in *Année sociologique* 10 [1907]: 48–137).

Holloway, Karla F. C. *Passed On: African American Mourning Stories*. Durham, NC: Duke University Press, 2003.

Hollywood, Amy. "Mysticism, Death and Desire in the Work of Hélène Cixous and Catherine Clément." In *Religion in French Feminist Thought*, ed. Morny Joy, Kathleen O'Grady, and Judith Poxon, 145–61. London: Routledge, 2003.

Holst-Warhaft, Gail. *The Cue for Passion: Grief and Its Political Uses*. Cambridge, MA: Harvard University Press, 2000.

Homans, Peter. *The Ability to Mourn: Disillusionment and the Social Origins of Psychoanalysis*. Chicago: University of Chicago Press, 1989.

———. *Jung in Context: Modernity and the Making of a Psychology*. Chicago: University of Chicago Press, 1979.

———. "Loss and Mourning in the Life and Thought of Max Weber: Toward a Theory of Symbolic Loss." In *Symbolic Loss: The Ambiguity of Mourning and Memory at Century's End*, ed. Peter Homans. Charlottesville: University Press of Virginia, 2000.

———. "Once Again, Psychoanalysis East and West: A Psychoanalytic Essay on Religion, Mourning, and Healing." *History of Religions* 24, no. 2 (1984): 133–54.

———, ed. *Symbolic Loss: The Ambiguity of Mourning and Memory at Century's End*. Charlottesville: University Press of Virginia, 2000.

Horowitz, Mardi. "A Model of Mourning: Change in Schemas of Self and Other." *Journal of the American Psychoanalytic Association* 38 (1990): 297–324.

Horton, P. C., and S. L. Sharp. "Language, Solace, and Transitional Relatedness." *Psychoanalytic Study of the Child* 39 (1984): 167–94.

Hunt, Harry T. *Lives in Spirit: Precursors and Dilemmas of a Secular Western Mysticism*. Albany: State University of New York Press, 2003.

Hymes, Dell. "The Grounding of Performance and Text in a Narrative View of Life." *Alcheringa*, n.s. 4, no. 1 (1978): 137–40.

Jackson, Stanley W. *Melancholia and Depression: From Hippocratic Times to Modern Times*. New Haven, CT: Yale University Press, 1986.

Jacob, Francois. *The Logic of Life: A History of Heredity*. Trans. Betty E. Spillmann. New York: Pantheon Books, 1973.

James, William. *The Varieties of Religious Experience*. New York: Modern Library, 1929.

Jantzen, Grace. "'Death, Then, How Could I Yield to It?' Kristeva's Mortal Visions."

In *Religion in French Feminist Thought: Critical Perspectives,* ed. Morny Joy, Kathleen O'Grady, and Judith Poxon. New York: Routledge, 2003.

Jarraway, David. "From Spectacular to Speculative: The Shifting Rhetoric in Recent Gay AIDS Memoirs." *Mosaic: A Journal for the Interdisciplinary Study of Literature* 33, no. 4 (2000).

Joffe, W., and J. Sandler. "Notes on pain, depression, and individuation." *Psychoanalytic Study of the Child* 20 (1965): 394–424.

Jones, Ernest. *The Life and Work of Sigmund Freud.* New York: Perseus, 1981.

Jonte-Pace, Diane. "Situating Kristeva Differently: Psychoanalytic Readings of Woman and Religion." In *Body/Text in Julia Kristeva: Religion, Women, and Psychoanalysis,* ed. David Crownfield, 1–22. Albany: State University of New York Press, 1992.

———. "Julia Kristeva and the Psychoanalytic Study of Religion: Rethinking Freud's Cultural Texts." In *Religion, Society, and Psychoanalysis: Readings in Contemporary Theory,* ed. Janet Jacobs and Donald Capps. Boulder, CO: Westview Press, 1997.

———. *Speaking the Unspeakable: Religion, Misogyny, and the Uncanny Mother in Freud's Cultural Texts.* Berkeley: University of California Press, 2001.

Joy, Morny, Kathleen O'Grady, and Judith L. Poxon, eds. *French Feminists on Religion: A Reader.* New York: Routledge, 2002.

———. *Religion in French Feminist Thought: Critical Perspectives.* New York: Routledge, 2003.

Jung, Carl. *Memories, Dreams, Reflections.* New York: Vintage, 1961.

———. *Psychology and Religion.* New Haven, CT: Yale University Press, 1977.

Kakar, Sudhir. *The Analyst and the Mystic.* Chicago: University of Chicago Press, 1991.

———. "Clinical Work and Cultural Imagination." *Psychoanalytic Quarterly* 64, no. 2 (1995): 265–81.

———. *The Inner World.* Delhi: Oxford University Press, 1981.

———. "Reflections on Psychoanalysis, Indian Culture and Mysticism." *Journal of Indian Philosophy* 10 (1982): 295–96.

———. *Shamans, Mystics, Doctors.* New York: A. Knopf, 1982.

Kammen, Michael G. *The Mystic Chords of Memory: The Transformation of Tradition in American Culture.* New York: Random House and Vintage Books, 1991.

Kayal, Philip M. *Bearing Witness: Gay Men's Health Crisis and the Politics of AIDS.* Boulder, CO: Westview Press, 1993.

Kazanjian, David, and Mark Nichanian. "Between Genocide and Catastrophe." In *Loss: The Politics of Mourning,* ed. David L. Eng and David Kazanjian, 125–47. Berkeley: University of California Press, 2003.

Kierkegaard, Søren. *The Sickness unto Death.* Trans. Walter Lowrie. Princeton, NJ: Princeton University Press, 1941.

Kieslowski, Krzysztof. *The Double Life of Véronique.* Film. Sidéral Productions, 1991.

———. *Three Colors: Blue.* Film. CAB Productions, 1993.

————. *Three Colors: Red*. Film. CAB Productions, 1994.

————. *Three Colors: White*. Film. CAB Productions, 1994.

Kim, C. W. Maggie, Susan M. St. Ville, and Susan M. Simonaitis, eds. *Transfigurations: Theology and the French Feminists*. Minneapolis: Fortress Press, 1993.

Kimball, S. T. Introduction to *The Rites of Passage* by A. van Gennep. Chicago: University of Chicago Press, 1960.

Klass, Dennis, Phyllis R. Silverman, and Steven L. Nickman, eds. *Continuing Bonds: New Understandings of Grief*. Washington, DC: Taylor and Francis, 1996.

Klawans, Stuart. "*Three Colors: Blue*." *Nation*, 20 Dec. 1993.

Klein, Dennis. *Jewish Origins of the Psychoanalytic Movement*. New York: Praeger, 1981.

Klein, Melanie. "A Contribution to the Psychogenesis of Manic-Depressive States." In *The Writings of Melanie Klein*, vol. 1, *Love, Guilt and Reparation: And Other Works, 1921–1945*. London: Hogarth Press, 1935.

————. "Envy and Gratitude." In *The Writings of Melanie Klein*, vol. 3, *Envy and Gratitude and Other Works*. New York: Free Press, 1984 (first published 1957).

————. "Love, Guilt and Reparation." In *The Writings of Melanie Klein*, vol. 3, *Envy and Gratitude and Other Works*. New York: Free Press, 1984 (first published 1937).

————. "Mourning and Its Relation to Manic-Depressive States." In *The Writings of Melanie Klein*, vol. 1, *Love, Guilt and Reparation: And Other Works, 1921–1945*. Glencoe, IL: Free Press, 1975 (first published 1940).

————. "Notes on Some Schizoid Mechanisms." In *The Writings of Melanie Klein*, Vol. 3, *Envy and Gratitude and Other Works*. New York: Free Press, 1984 (first published 1946).

————. "Some Theoretical Conclusions Regarding the Emotional Life of the Infant." In *Developments in Psycho-Analysis*, ed. Melanie Klein, Paula Heimann, Susan Isaacs, and Joan Riviere, 198–236. London: Hogarth Press, 1952.

————. "The Theory of Anxiety and Guilt." In *The Writings of Melanie Klein*, vol. 3, *Envy and Gratitude and Other Works*. New York: Free Press, 1984 (first published 1948).

Kohut, Heinz. "Idealization and Cultural Self Objects." In *Self Psychology and the Humanities: Reflections on a New Psychoanalytic Approach*, ed. Charles B. Strozier, 224–43. New York: Norton, 1985.

————. "On Leadership." In *Self Psychology and the Humanities*, ed. Charles Strozier. New York: Norton, 1985.

————. *The Restoration of the Self*. Madison, CT: International Universities Press, 1977.

Kraft, Robert Nathaniel. *Memory Perceived: Recalling the Holocaust*. Westport, CT: Praeger, 2002.

Kramer, Larry. *Reports from the Holocaust: The Making of an AIDS Activist*. 1st ed. New York: St. Martin's Press, 1989.

———. *Reports from the Holocaust: The Story of an AIDS Activist.* Expanded 2nd ed. New York: St. Martin's Press, 1994.

Kripal, Jeffrey J. "A Garland of Talking Heads for the Goddess: Some Autobiographical and Psychoanalytic Reflections on the Western Kali." In *Is the Goddess a Feminist? The Politics of South Asian Goddesses,* ed. A. Hiltebeitel and K. M. Ernall. Sheffield, UK: Sheffield Academic Press, 2000.

———. *Kali's Child: The Mystical and the Erotic in the Life and Teachings of Ramakrishna.* Chicago: University of Chicago Press, 1995.

———. *Roads of Excess, Palaces of Wisdom: Eroticism and Reflexivity in the Study of Mysticism.* Chicago: University of Chicago Press, 2001.

Kristeva, Julia. *Black Sun: Depression and Melancholia.* New York: Columbia University Press, 1989.

———. *In the Beginning Was Love: Psychoanalysis and Faith.* New York: Columbia University Press, 1987.

———. *New Maladies of the Soul.* New York: Columbia University Press, 1995.

———. *Powers of Horror: An Essay on Abjection.* New York: Columbia University Press, 1982.

———. "Stabat Mater." In *The Kristeva Reader,* ed. Julia Kristeva and Toril Moi, 160–86. New York: Columbia University Press, 1986.

———. *Strangers to Ourselves.* New York: Columbia University Press, 1991.

Kristof, Nicholas. "Race against Death." *New York Times,* 4 June 2006, 15.

Kugelmass, Jack, and Jonathan Boyarin. *From a Ruined Garden: The Memorial Books of Polish Jewry.* 2nd ed. Bloomington: Indiana University Press, 1998.

Laderman, Gary. *Rest in Peace: A Cultural History of Death and the Funeral Home in Twentieth-Century America.* New York: Oxford University Press, 2003.

Lagache, Daniel. "Le travail du deuil." *Revue française de psychanalyse,* 10 (1938): 693–708.

Lane, Anthony. "*Blue.*" *New Yorker,* 13 Dec. 1993.

Langer, Suzanne. *Mind: An Essay on Human Feeling.* Vol. 1. Baltimore: Johns Hopkins University Press, 1967.

Lanzmann, C. *Shoah: A Film.* 1985.

Laplanche, J., and J.-B. Pontalis. *The Language of Psycho-analysis.* Trans. D. Nicholson-Smith. London: Hogarth Press, 1973 (first published 1967).

Lasch, Christopher. *The Culture of Narcissism.* New York: Norton, 1979.

———. "The Politics of Nostalgia: Losing History in the Mists of Ideology." *Harper's Magazine,* Nov. 1984, 65–70.

Lawless, Elaine J. *God's Peculiar People: Women's Voices and Folk Tradition in a Pentecostal Church.* Lexington: University Press of Kentucky, 1988.

Leach, Edmund R. "Magical Hair." In *Myth and Cosmos: Readings in Mythology and Symbolism,* ed. J. Middleton. Garden City, NY: Natural History Press, 1967.

Lechte, John. "Art, Love, and Melancholy in the Work of Julia Kristeva." In *Abjection, Melancholia, and Love: The Work of Julia Kristeva,* ed. John Fletcher and Andrew Benjamin. New York: Routledge, 1990.

Lévinas, Emmanuel. "Bad Conscience and the Inexorable." In *Face to Face with Lévinas*, ed. R. A. Cohen. Albany: State University of New York Press, 1986.

———. *God, Death and Time*. Trans. B. Bergo. Stanford, CA: Stanford University Press, 2000.

Lewis, James R., and J. Gordon Melton, eds. *Perspectives on the New Age*. Albany: State University of New York Press, 1992.

Lewis, Stephen. "SILENCE = DEATH: AIDS, Africa, and Pharmaceuticals." *Toronto Globe and Mail*, 26 Jan. 2001, http://www.corpwatch.org/article.php?id=491 (accessed 23 Dec. 2007).

Linde, Charlotte. "The Acquisition of a Speaker by a Story: How History Becomes Memory and Identity." *Ethos* 28, no. 4 (2000): 608–32.

Loewald, Hans W. "Internalization, Separation, Mourning, and the Superego." *Psychoanalytic Quarterly* 31 (1962): 483–504.

———. *Papers on Psychoanalysis*. New Haven, CT: Yale University Press, 1980.

Lowenthal, David. "Nostalgia Tells It Like It Wasn't." In *The Imagined Past: History and Nostalgia*, ed. Christopher Shaw and Malcolm Chase, 18–31. Manchester, UK: Manchester University Press, 1989.

Lutzky, Harriet. "Deity and the Social Bond: Robertson Smith and the Psychoanalytic Theory of Religion." In *William Robertson Smith: Essays in Reassessment*, ed. William Johnstone, 320–30. Sheffield, UK: Sheffield Academic Press, 1995.

———. "Desire as a Constitutive Element of the Sacred." *Archiv für Religionspsychologie* 25 (2003): 62–70.

———. "Reparation and Tikkun: A Comparison of the Kleinian and Kabbalistic Concepts." *International Review of Psychoanalysis* 16 (1989): 449–58.

———. "The Sacred and the Maternal Object: An Application of Fairbairn's Theory to Religion." In *Psychoanalytic Reflections on Current Issues*, ed. H. Siegel et al., 25–44. New York: New York University Press, 1991.

MacDonald, M. "Spirituality." In *The Encyclopedia of Religion*, ed. Lindsay Jones. 2nd ed. New York: Macmillan, 2005.

MacIntyre, Alasdair. *After Virtue: A Study in Moral Theory*. 2nd ed. Notre Dame, IN: University of Notre Dame Press, 1984.

Macnab, Geoffrey. "*Three Colors: Blue*." *Sight and Sound*, Nov. 1993.

Mahler, Margaret S. *On Human Symbiosis and the Vicissitudes of Individuation*. New York: International Universities Press, 1968.

Malcolm, Janet. *In the Freud Archives*. New York: New York Review of Books, 2002.

Marris, Peter. *Loss and Change*. Rev. ed. London: Routledge and Kegan Paul, 1974.

Marshall, Stuart. "The Contemporary Political Use of Gay History: The Third Reich." In *How Do I Look? Queer Film and Video*, ed. Bad Object-Choices [organization], 65–89. Seattle: Bay Press, 1991.

Martin, Emily. *Flexible Bodies: Tracking Immunity in American Culture from the Days of Polio to the Age of AIDS*. Boston: Beacon Press, 1994.

Marty, Martin E. *Modern American Religion*, vol. 1: *The Irony of It All*. Chicago: University of Chicago Press, 1986.

Maslow, Abraham. *Religions, Values and Peak-Experiences*. New York: Penguin Books, 1976.

Masson, Jeffrey, ed. *The Complete Letters of Sigmund Freud to Wilhelm Fliess, 1887–1904*. Cambridge, MA: Belknap Press of Harvard University Press, 1985.

———. "Indian Psychotherapy?" *Journal of Indian Philosophy* 7 (1979): 327–32.

———. *My Father's Guru: A Journey through Spirituality and Disillusion*. New York: Ballantine, 2003.

———. *The Oceanic Feeling: The Origin of the Religious Sentiment in Ancient India*. Dordrecht, Netherlands: D. Reidel, 1980.

———. "The Psychology of the Ascetic." *Journal of Asian Studies* 35 (1976): 611–25.

May, R. *Cosmic Consciousness Revisited*. Rockport, MA: Element, 1991.

Mbembé, Achille. *On the Postcolony*. Berkeley: University of California Press, 2001 (first published as *Notes provisoires sur la postcolonie*).

McCance, Dawne. "Kristeva's Melancholia: Not Knowing How to Lose." In *Religion in French Feminist Thought: Critical Perspectives*, ed. Morny Joy, Kathleen O'Grady, and Judith Poxon. London: Routledge, 2003.

McGrath, William. *Freud's Discovery of Psychoanalysis: The Politics of Hysteria*. Ithaca, NY: Cornell University Press, 1986.

McNeill, William H. "Eclipsed at Last?" *Times Literary Supplement*, 22 Oct. 1999.

Metcalf, Peter, and Richard Huntington. *Celebrations of Death: The Anthropology of Mortuary Ritual*. 2nd ed. New York: Cambridge University Press, 1991.

Michelet, Jules. *History of the French Revolution*. Trans. Keith Botsford. Wynnewood, PA: Livingston, 1972.

Miller, Richard B., Laurie L. Patton, and Stephen H. Webb. "Rhetoric, Pedagogy and the Study of Religion." *Journal of the American Academy of Religion* 62, no. 3 (1994): 819–50.

Mitscherlich, Alexander, and Margarete Mitscherlich. *The Inability to Mourn: Principles of Collective Behavior*. Trans. Beverley R. Placzek. New York: Grove Press, 1975 (first published 1967).

Mohr, Richard D. *Gay Ideas: Outing and Other Controversies*. Boston: Beacon Press, 1992.

Moore, Burness, and Bernard Fine, eds. *Psychoanalytic Terms and Concepts*. New Haven, CT: American Psychoanalytic Association and Yale University Press, 1990.

Moore, John, and Nicoli Nattrass. "Deadly Quackery." *New York Times*, 4 June 2006, 15.

Morton, Nelle. *The Journey Is Home*. Boston: Beacon Press, 1986.

Müller, Melissa. *Anne Frank: The Biography*. Trans. Rita and Robert Kimber. New York: Henry Holt and Metropolitan Books, 1998.

Needham, Rodney. "Robert Hertz." In *International Encyclopedia of the Social Sciences*, vol. 18, 295–97. New York: Macmillan, 1991.

Nichanian, Marc. "Catastrophic Mourning." In *Loss: The Politics of Mourning*, ed. David L. Eng and David Kazanjian, 99–124. Berkeley: University of California Press, 2003.

Noll, Richard. *The Jung Cult.* New York: Free Press, 1994.

Novick, Peter. *The Holocaust in American Life.* Boston: Houghton-Mifflin, 1999.

Nunokawa, Jeff. "'All the Sad Young Men': AIDS and the Work of Mourning." In *Inside/Out: Lesbian Theories, Gay Theories*, ed. Diana Fuss, 311–23. New York: Routledge, 1991.

Palmer, Parker J. *The Courage to Teach: Exploring the Inner Landscape of a Teacher's Life.* San Francisco: Jossey Bass, 1998.

Parker, Robert. *Miasma: Pollution and Purification in Early Greek Religion.* Oxford: Clarendon Press, 1983.

Parkes, C. M. "Separation Anxiety: An Aspect of the Search for a Lost Object." In *Loneliness: The Experience of Emotional and Social Isolation*, ed. R. S. Weiss. Cambridge, MA: MIT Press, 1973.

Parkin, Robert. *The Dark Side of Humanity: The Work of Robert Hertz and Its Legacy.* Amsterdam: Harwood Academic, 1996.

Parsons, William B. "The Ability to Mourn: Disillusionment and the Social Origins of Psychoanalysis: A Conversation with Peter Homans." *Criterion* 30, no. 1 (Winter 1999).

———. *The Enigma of the Oceanic Feeling.* New York: Oxford University Press, 1999.

Plummer, Kenneth. *Telling Sexual Stories: Power, Change, and Social Worlds.* New York: Routledge, 1995.

Pogue-Harrison, Robert. *The Dominion of the Dead.* Chicago: University of Chicago Press, 2003.

Pollard, Alton B. *Mysticism and Social Change: The Social Witness of Howard Thurman.* New York: P. Lang, 1992.

Pollock, George H. "Mourning and Adaptation." *International Journal of Psychoanalysis* 42 (1961): 341–61.

———. *The Mourning-Liberation Process.* Vols. 1 and 2. Madison, CT: International Universities Press, 1989.

———. "Process and Affect: Mourning and Grief." *International Journal of Psychoanalysis* 59 (1978): 255–76.

Principe, Walter. "Toward Defining Spirituality." *Studies in Religion* 12, no. 2 (1983): 127–41.

Rambo, Lewis R. *Understanding Religious Conversion.* New Haven, CT: Yale University Press, 1993.

Rauch, Jonathan. "Families Forged by Illness." *New York Times*, 4 June 2006, 15.

Reineke, Martha. *Sacrificed Lives: Kristeva on Women and Violence.* Bloomington: Indiana University Press, 1997.

Ricoeur, Paul. *Critique and Conviction: Conversations with Francois Azouvi and Marc de Launay.* Trans. Kathleen Blamey. New York: Columbia University Press, 1998.

———. "The Hermeneutics of Testimony." In *Essays on Biblical Interpretation,* ed. Lewis S. Mudge, 119–54. Philadelphia: Fortress Press, 1980.

———. *Memory, History, Forgetting.* Trans. Kathleen Blamey and David Pellauer. Chicago: University of Chicago Press, 2004.

———. *The Symbolism of Evil.* Trans. Emerson Buchanan. New York: Harper and Row, 1967.

Rieff, Philip. *Freud: The Mind of the Moralist.* Garden City, NY: Doubleday/ Anchor Books, 1961.

———. *The Triumph of the Therapeutic: Uses of Faith after Freud.* New York: Harper, 1968.

Ring, Kenneth. "Near-Death Experiences: Implications for Human Evolution and Planetary Transformation." In *The Near-Death Experience: A Reader,* ed. Lee Bailey and Jenny Yates. New York: Routledge, 1996.

Ringelheim, Joan Miriam. *A Catalogue of Audio and Video Collections of Holocaust Testimony.* 2nd ed. New York: Greenwood Press, 1992.

Roberts, J. M. *The History of Europe.* London: Penguin, 1996.

Robertson, Roland. *Meaning and Change: Explorations in the Cultural Sociology of Modern Societies.* New York: New York University Press, 1978.

Rolland, Romain. *Au Seuil de la dérniere porte.* Paris: Les Éditions de Cerf, 1989.

———. *Credo quia verum, Cahiers Romain Rolland.* Vol. 4. Paris: Éditions Albin Michel, 1949.

———. *Journey Within.* Trans. Elsie Pell. New York: Philosophical Library, 1947.

———. *The Life of Vivekananda and the Universal Gospel.* Trans. E. F. Malcolm-Smith. Calcutta: Advaita Ashrama, 1965.

———. *Mémoires et fragments du Journal.* Paris: Éditions Albin Michel, 1956.

———. *Le voyage intérieur.* Paris: Éditions Albin Michel, 1959.

Roth, Nancy L., and Katie Hogan, eds. *Gendered Epidemic: Representations of Women in the Age of AIDS.* New York: Routledge, 1998.

Roy, Dilip Kumar. *Among the Great: Conversations with Romain Rolland, Mahatma Gandhi, Bertrand Russell, Rabindranath Tagore, Sri Aurobindo.* Bombay; N. M. Tripathi, Nalanda Publications, 1945.

Santner, Eric. *Stranded Objects: Mourning, Memory, and Film in Postwar Germany.* Ithaca, NY: Cornell University Press, 1990.

———. *On the Psychotheology of Everyday Life: Reflections on Freud and Rosenzweig.* Chicago: University of Chicago Press, 2001.

Schafer, Roy. *Aspects of Internalization.* Madison, CT: International Universities Press, 1990 (first published 1968).

———. *Bad Feelings.* New York: Other Press, 2003.

Schiff, B., C. Noy, and B. Cohler. "Collected Stories in the Life Narratives of Holocaust Survivors." *Narrative Inquiry* 11 (2001): 159–94.

Schmidt, Leigh Eric. "The Making of Modern Mysticism." *Journal of the American Academy of Religion* 71 (June 2003): 273–302.

Schwartz, Barry. "Memory as a Cultural System: Abraham Lincoln in World War II." *American Sociological Review* 61 (1996): 908–27.

Schwarz, Daniel R. *Imagining the Holocaust.* New York: St. Martin's Press, 1999.

Sedgwick, Eve Kosofsky. *The Epistemology of the Closet.* Berkeley: University of California Press, 1990.

Segal, Hanna. *Introduction to the Work of Melanie Klein.* New York: Basic Books, 1974.

Sennett, Richard. *The Decline of Public Man.* New York: Norton, 1992.

Sherry, Michael S. "The Language of War in AIDS Discourse." In *Writing AIDS: Gay Literature, Language and Analysis,* ed. Timothy F. Murphy and Suzanne Poirier, 39–53 (New York: Columbia University Press, 1993).

Sil, Narasingha. *Ramakrishna Paramahamsa: A Psychological Profile.* New York: Brill, 1991.

Smith, Jonathan Z. *Relating Religion: Essays in the Study of Religion.* Chicago: University of Chicago Press, 2004.

Smith, William Robertson. *Lectures on the Religion of the Semites.* 2nd ed. London: Adam and Charles Black, 1914.

Sohn, Leslie. "Nostalgia." *International Journal of Psychoanalysis* 64 (1983): 203–10.

"So Little Time . . . An AIDs History," http://www.aegis.com/topics/timeline/ (accessed 23 Dec. 2007).

Sontag, Susan. *AIDS and Its Metaphors.* New York: Farrar, Straus and Giroux, 1988.

Spitzer, Leo. "Back through the Future: Nostalgic Memory and Critical Memory in a Refuge from Nazism." In *Acts of Memory: Cultural Recall in the Present,* ed. Mieke Bal, Jonathan Crewe, and Leo Spitzer, 87–104. Hanover, NH: University Press of New England, 1999.

Starobinski, Jean, and William S. Kemp. "The Idea of Nostalgia." *Diogenes* 14, no. 54 (1966): 81–103.

Starr, William Thomas. *Romain Rolland and a World at War.* Evanston, IL: Northwestern University Press, 1956.

Stewart, Kathleen. "Nostalgia—A Polemic." *Cultural Anthropology* 3 (1988): 227–41.

Stine, Gerald J. *AIDS Update 2004: An Annual Overview of Acquired Immune Deficiency Syndrome.* San Francisco: Pearson/Benjamin Cummings, 2004.

Stocking, George W., Jr. "The Dark-Skinned Savage: The Image of Primitive Man in Evolutionary Anthropology (1968)." Reprinted in *Race, Culture and Evolution: Essays in the History of Anthropology.* Chicago: University of Chicago Press, 1982.

———. *Victorian Anthropology.* New York: Free Press, 1987.

Stout, Jeffrey. *Ethics after Babel: The Languages of Morals and Their Discontents.* Boston: Beacon Press, 1988.

Stroebe, Margaret, et al. "Broken Hearts or Broken Bonds?" In *Continuing Bonds: New Understandings of Grief*, ed. Dennis Klass, Phyllis R. Silverman, and Steven L. Nickman, 31–44. Washington, DC: Taylor and Francis, 1996.

Sutich, Anthony J. "Transpersonal Psychology: An Emerging Force," *Journal of Humanistic Psychology* 8 (Spring 1968): 77–94.

Tambiah, S. J. "From Varna through Mixed Union." In *The Character of Kinship*, ed. J. Goody. Cambridge: Cambridge University Press, 1973.

Tannen, Deborah, and Muriel Saville-Troike, eds. *Perspectives on Silence*. Norwood, NJ: Ablex, 1985.

Taylor, Christopher C. "AIDS and the Pathogenesis of Metaphor." In *AIDS: Readings on a Global Crisis*, ed. Elizabeth Rauh Bethel, 36–44. Boston: Allyn and Bacon, 1995.

Thompson, E. P. *The Making of the English Working Class*. New York: Random House, 1966.

Tillich, Paul. *The Courage to Be*. New Haven, CT: Yale University Press, 1952.

———. *Systematic Theology*. Vol. 3. Chicago: University of Chicago Press, 1963.

Titon, Jeff Todd. *Powerhouse of God: Speech, Chant, and Song in an Appalachian Baptist Church*. Austin: University of Texas Press, 1988.

Tolpin, M. "On the Beginnings of a Cohesive Self—An Application of the Concept of Transmuting Internalization to the Study of the Transitional Object and Signal Anxiety." *Psychoanalytic Study of the Child* 26 (1971): 316–52.

Toulmin, Stephen. *Cosmopolis: The Hidden Agenda of Modernity*. New York: Free Press, 1990.

———. *Return to Reason*. Cambridge, MA: Harvard University Press, 2001.

Treichler, Paula. *How to Have Theory in an Epidemic: Cultural Chronicles of AIDS*. Durham, NC: Duke University Press, 1999.

Treichler, Paula, and Catherine Warren. "Maybe Next Year: Feminist Silence and the AIDS Epidemic." In *Gendered Epidemic: Representations of Women in the Age of AIDS*, ed. Nancy L. Roth and Katie Hogan, 109–52. New York: Routledge, 1998.

Turner, Victor. "Betwixt and Between: The Liminal Period in *Rites de passage*." In *Reader in Comparative Religion: An Anthropological Approach*, ed. William A. Lessa and Evon Z. Vogt. New York: Harper and Row, 1972 (first published 1964).

———. "Liminality, Kabbalah, and the Media." *Religion* 15 (1985): 205–17.

Tylor, E. B. *Primitive Culture: Researches into the Development of Mythology, Philosophy, Religion, Art, and Custom*. 2 vols. London: J. Murray, 1871.

Verghese, Abraham. "AIDS at 25: An Epidemic of Caring." *New York Times*, 4 June 2006, 15.

Vishniac, Roman. *To Give Them Light: The Legacy of Roman Vishniac*. Ed. Marion Wisel. New York: Simon and Schuster, 1993.

Vitebsky, Piers. *Dialogues with the Dead: The Discussion of Mortality among the Sora of Eastern Indian*. Cambridge: Cambridge University Press, 1993.

Vries, Hent de. *Philosophy and the Turn to Religion*. Baltimore: Johns Hopkins University Press, 1999.

Vromen, Suzanne. "The Ambiguity of Nostalgia." *YIVO Annual*, no. 21 (1993): 69–86.

Wall, James M. "Blue." *Christian Century*, 16 March 1994.

Wallwork, Ernest. "A Constructive Freudian Alternative to Psychotherapeutic Egoism." *Soundings* 69 (1986): 145–64.

———. "Ethics in Psychoanalysis." In *The American Psychiatric Publishing Textbook of Psychoanalysis*, ed. Ethel Spector Person, Arnold M. Cooper, and Glen O. Gabbard, 281–97. New York: International Universities Press, 2005.

———. *Psychoanalysis and Ethics*. New Haven, CT: Yale University Press, 1991.

———. "Psychodynamic Contributions to Religious Ethics: Toward Reconfiguring Askesis." *Annual of the Society of Christian Ethics* 19 (1999): 167–89.

Warner, Michael. "Tongues Untied." In *Que(e)rying Religion: A Critical Anthology*, ed. Gary David Comstock and Susan E. Henking, 223–31. New York: Continuum, 1997.

Wasserstrom, Steven M. *Religion after Religion: Gershom Scholem, Mircea Eliade, and Henry Corbin at Eranos*. Princeton, NJ: Princeton University Press, 1999.

Weber, Max. *The Protestant Ethic and the Spirit of Capitalism*. Trans. Talcott Parsons. New York: Charles Scribner's Sons, 1958.

———. *The Sociology of Religion*. Trans. Ephraim Fischoff. Boston: Beacon, 1963 (first published 1922).

Weeks, Jeffrey. *Invented Moralities: Sexual Values in an Age of Uncertainty*. New York: Columbia University Press, 1995.

Weinstein, Fred. *Freud, Psychoanalysis, Social Theory: The Unfulfilled Promise*. Albany: State University of New York Press, 2001.

———. *History and Theory after the Fall: An Essay on Interpretation*. Chicago: University of Chicago Press, 1990.

Weissman, Gary. *Fantasies of Witnessing: Postwar Efforts to Experience the Holocaust*. Ithaca, NY: Cornell University Press, 2004.

Werman, David S. "Normal and Pathological Nostalgia." *Journal of the American Psychoanalytic Association* 25 (1977): 387–98.

Wertsch, James V. *Voices of Collective Remembering*. New York: Cambridge University Press, 2002.

Wexler, Philip. *The Mystical Society: An Emerging Social Vision*. Boulder, CO: Westview Press, 2000.

Wiesel, Elie. *Dimensions of the Holocaust*. Evanston, IL: Northwestern University Press, 1977.

———. *Night*. Trans. S. Rodney. New York: Bantam Books, 1960.

Wilber, Ken. "Psychologia Perennis: The Spectrum of Consciousness." *Journal of Transpersonal Psychology* 7, no. 2 (1975): 105–32.

Williams, Kipling D. *Ostracism: The Power of Silence*. New York: Guilford Press, 2001.

Williams, Raymond. *The Country and the City*. New York: Oxford University Press, 1973.

Winnicott, Donald W. "The Location of Cultural Experience." In *Playing and Reality*. Harmondsworth, UK: Pelican, 1974 (first published 1967).

———. "The Mentally Ill in Your Caseload." In *Maturational Processes and the Facilitating Environment: Studies in the Theory of Emotional Development*, 217–29. New York: International Universities Press, 1965 (first published 1963).

———. "The Place Where We Live." In *Playing and Reality*. Harmondsworth, UK: Pelican, 1974 (first published 1971).

———. "Transitional Objects and Transitional Phenomena." *International Journal of Psychoanalysis* 34 (1953): 89–97.

Wolf, E. "Some Comments on the Self-object Concept." In *Self and Identity: Psychosocial Processes*, ed. Krysia Yardley and Terry Honess, 259–71. New York: John Wiley and Sons, 1987.

Wulff, David M. *Psychology of Religion: Classic and Contemporary*. 2nd ed. New York: John Wiley and Sons, 2000.

Yingling, Thomas E. "AIDS, Confession, and Theory: The Pedagogical Dilemma." In *AIDS and the National Body*, ed. Robyn Weigman. Durham, NC: Duke University Press, 1997.

———. "AIDS in America: Postmodern Governance, Identity, and Experience." In *Inside/Out: Lesbian Theories, Gay Theories*, edited by Diana Fuss, 291–310. New York: Routledge, 1991.

Young, James Edward. "Against Redemption: The Arts of Countermemory in Germany Today." In *Symbolic Loss: The Ambiguity of Mourning and Memory at Century's End*, ed. Peter Homans, 126–46. Charlottesville: University Press of Virginia, 2000.

———. *The Texture of Memory: Holocaust Memorials and Meaning*. New Haven, CT: Yale University Press, 1993.

Zaehner, R. C. *Mysticism Sacred and Profane*. New York: Oxford University Press, 1980.

Zerubavel, Yael. *Recovered Roots: Collective Memory and the Making of Israeli National Tradition*. Chicago: University of Chicago Press, 1995.

Contributors

CELIA BRICKMAN is a psychotherapist and faculty member at the Center for Religion and Psychotherapy of Chicago, where she is also co-director of the graduate Education Program. She is the author of *Aboriginal Populations in the Mind: Race and Primitivity in Psychoanalysis* (2003), among other articles and reviews. At the time of writing this essay, she was a senior fellow at the Martin Marty Center of the Divinity School of the University of Chicago.

BERTRAM J. COHLER is the William Rainey Harper Professor in the College, Committee on Human Development, and the Departments of Psychiatry and Psychology of the University of Chicago. He is also a faculty member at the Institute for Psychoanalysis (Chicago). He is the author of *Psychoanalysis: A Contemporary Introduction* (2003); *The Psychoanalytic Study of Lives over Time: Clinical and Research Perspectives on Children Who Return to Treatment in Adulthood* (2000); *Mothers, Grandmothers, and Daughters: Personality and Child Care in Three-Generation Families* (1981); and *The Essential Other: A Developmental Psychology of the Self* (1993).

SUSAN E. HENKING is Professor of Religious Studies at Hobart and William Smith Colleges. She has written on the history of American sociology, on AIDS-related memoirs, and on teaching as the work of public intellectuals. She is coeditor, with Gary David Comstock, of *Que(e)rying Religion: A Critical Anthology* (1997) and founding editor of the "Teaching Religious Studies" series of the American Academy of Religion.

PETER HOMANS is Professor Emeritus of Psychology and Religious Studies in the Divinity School, the Social Science Collegiate Division, and the Committees on Human Development and the History of Culture at the University of Chicago. His publications include *Jung in Context: Modernity and the Making of a Psychology*

(1979, 1995); *The Ability to Mourn: Disillusionment and the Social Origins of Psychoanalysis* (1989); and *Symbolic Loss: The Ambiguity of Mourning and Memory at Century's End* (2000).

DIANE JONTE-PACE is Professor of Religious Studies and Vice Provost for Undergraduate Studies at Santa Clara University. She is the author of *Speaking the Unspeakable: Religion, Misogyny, and the Uncanny Mother in Freud's Cultural Texts* (2001), and the editor of *Teaching Freud* (2003) and (with William B. Parsons) *Religion and Psychology: Mapping the Terrain* (2001).

HARRIET LUTZKY is Adjunct Assistant Professor of Psychology at John Jay College, City University of New York, and a psychoanalyst in private practice. Her articles include "Reparation and Tikkun: A Comparison of the Kleinian and Kabbalistic Concepts" (1989); "The Sacred and the Maternal Object: An Application of Fairbairn's Theory to Religion" (1991); and "Desire as a Constitutive Element of the Sacred" (2003).

WILLIAM B. PARSONS is Associate Professor of Religious Studies at Rice University. He is author of *The Enigma of the Oceanic Feeling* (1999) and coeditor with Diane Jonte-Pace of *Religion and Psychology: Mapping the Terrain* (2001). His articles have appeared in numerous journals and edited books, including the *Journal of Religion*, and *Vishnu on Freud's Desk: A Reader in Psychoanalysis and Hinduism* (1998).

MARY ELLEN ROSS is Associate Professor of Religious Studies at Trinity University. She has published in the fields of ethics, the psychoanalytic study of religion, and feminist theory. She is coeditor with Paula Cooey and Sharon Farmer of *Embodied Love: Sensuality and Relationship in Feminist Values* (1987). Her essay "The Humanities of the Gods: The Future and Past of Freud's Psychoanalytic Interpretation of Religion," appeared in *Sigmund Freud and His Impact on the Modern World* (2001).

ERNEST WALLWORK is Professor of Religion in the Department of Religion at Syracuse University and a psychoanalyst in private practice in Syracuse, New York, and Washington, D.C. He is the author of *Durkheim: Morality and Milieu* (1971); coauthor of *Critical Issues in Modern Religion* (1973, 1991); *Psychoanalysis and Ethics* (1991), and numerous articles on psychoanalysis, religion, and ethics.

Index

STUDIES IN RELIGION AND CULTURE